THE
DARK LORD

THE
DARK LORD

H. P. Lovecraft, Kenneth Grant and
the Typhonian Tradition in Magic

PETER LEVENDA

Preface by
JAMES WASSERMAN

IBIS PRESS
Lake Worth, FL

Published in 2013 by Ibis Press
A division of Nicolas-Hays, Inc.
P. O. Box 540206
Lake Worth, FL 33454-0206
www.ibispress.net

Distributed to the trade by
Red Wheel/Weiser, LLC
65 Parker St. • Ste. 7
Newburyport, MA 01950
www.redwheelweiser.com

ISBN 978-0-89254-207-9

Library of Congress Cataloging-in-Publication Data
Available upon requesr

Book design and production by Studio 31
www.studio31.com

[MV]

Printed in the United States of America

Contents

Illustrations

Dancing with the Dark Lord

James Wasserman

17. Now shalt thou adore me who am the Eye and the Tooth, the Goat of the Spirit, the Lord of Creation. I am the Eye in the Triangle, the Silver Star that ye adore.

18. I am Baphomet, that is the Eightfold Word that shall be equilibrated with the Three.

23. I am the hideous god, and who mastereth me is uglier than I.

27. Whom I love I chastise with many rods.

— *Liber A'ash vel Capricorni Pneumatici*

Tʜɪs ɪs ᴀ ᴡᴏʀᴋ ᴏꜰ ʜᴇʀᴇsʏ, a book meant to challenge. What else would the reader expect from that Dark Lord who inhabits the most primal and hidden depths of the unconscious? The Lord of the Shadow Realm, whose very existence has been hysterically lambasted as an evil aberration, who has been conceived as blasphemous and terrifying since people first sat around campfires near the openings to their caves, whose devotees have ever been feared and hunted. The Enemy, the Other, the Adversary, He who inhabits the undiscovered territory which must be charted and mapped by any who wish to consider themselves worthy explorers of the psyche. Lovecraft has warned us against these dark mysteries in the most dramatic terms. Crowley assumed the mask of the Beast 666 to frighten away the shy, the reticent, the cowardly. Kenneth Grant celebrated this archetype in an almost frenzied literary oeuvre that straddles the lines between scholarly discourse, imaginative fiction, and poetic invocation.

In *The Dark Lord,* Peter Levenda, has, once again, applied his considerable erudition and creative mind and pen to the unity of various streams of consciousness. Describing what he calls "the tip of an eldritch iceberg," Levenda posits a mystic alliance between the thematic content of the fiction of H. P. Lovecraft and the magical writings of Aleister Crowley, and makes a compelling case for the confluence of events that existed in real time between their efforts.

Crowley is known as the Prophet of the New Aeon, inaugurated in 1904, the founder of the magical system and religion of Thelema. His sweeping intellect and spiritual exaltation allowed him to explore and synthesize all the world's then-known sacred beliefs and practices and distill their essence into his own system of Scientific Illuminism—the Method of Science, the Aim of Religion. Scientific Illuminism has proven to be a perfect paradigm for our modern world, in which images and information travel with the speed of the electron, and the established religions have become increasingly irrelevant.

The dimensions explored by Lovecraft's fevered imagination continue to haunt and resonate in popular culture nearly a century later. Lovecraft's words and phantasms are a staple of derivative modern fiction, graphic novels, art, film, and music. The extraordinary popularity of Simon's *Necronomicon* (over one million copies in print since 1977!) is a case in point. The talented painter H. R. Geiger has brought Lovecraft's terrifying visions to life in his own artistic Necronomicon. The brilliant Australian artist Rosaleen Norton, whose compelling painting of the Dark Lord is featured on the jacket of this book, was another adept of the Darkly Splendid Worlds.

Kenneth Grant, the British writer and occultist, shared Levenda's fascination with both Crowley and Lovecraft. Grant is celebrated the world over for his biographies of Aleister Crowley and Austin Osman Spare—who each served as teachers and guides to the young magician. Yet it is Grant's writing on the Typhonian Gnosis that captures Levenda's attention in these pages. Grant's embrace of the hidden byways of imagery and symbolism, and the obscure and antinomian practices of widely divergent peoples the world over, evoke the darker dimensions of the shadow-self of humankind.

Levenda conducts a veritable symphony with strains of religious and esoteric knowledge as he explores the roots of the beliefs and doctrines Crowley utilized to develop his system of Thelema. The reader may expect to be introduced to Yoga and Buddhism, Tantra and Gnosticism, Kabbalah, Alchemy, and Egyptology, Confucianism, Daoism, and Afro-Caribbean magic, as well as the more-familiar Judaism, Christianity, and Islam. You will walk through ancient Sumerian temples of the third millennium BCE, participate in the magical circles of the nineteenth century Golden Dawn, and witness contemporary rites of the Typhonian Order. You will learn details about the shadow side of myth that never quite made it into your copy of Larousse or Bullfinch. Nor is Levenda's discussion of Tantra what your mother understood as the ritual of the "five M's."

This book will be of interest to people across a variety of disciplines. Fans of Lovecraft will find his worldview explored in ways that may shock or frighten. They will learn that Lovecraft's fearful fantasies may have a greater connection to reality than they might have hoped. Certainly, readers of Kenneth Grant will be delighted to have the mysteries of his writings made more clear by Levenda's penetrating explication and high regard for Grant. One can imagine Grant himself smiling with satisfaction in the Field of Reeds as he reviews Levenda's analysis of the complex ideas he worked so hard to communicate during his lifetime. Students of Crowley are in for a whirlwind ride of speculation, insight, historical, mythic, and spiritual associations that will enlighten and entertain, as they may also stimulate intense disagreement. (Since Levenda discusses *The Book of the Law* quite openly, those with the strongest objections are free to identify him as a "centre of pestilence" and thereby recover their serenity.) In my opinion, there is more here for Thelemites to learn than to reject.

Peter Levenda and I have known each other for so long our hair was jet black when we met. Larry Barnes, the publisher of the *Necronomicon,* introduced me to Simon, the book's translator and editor, in 1977. Larry proposed that I design and produce the book for Schlangekraft/Barnes Graphics. This would become my first project in Studio 31. Simon introduced me to Peter, who acted as his literary agent and production editor: proofreading various iterations of the typography and dealing with the ever-frenetic Larry. Yes, Simon meticulously scrutinized the seals we had commissioned to be redrawn for publication based on his original and precise felt-tip pen renderings. Simon also paid particular attention to proofing the language of the spells themselves. But Peter handled the bread and butter day-to-day progress of the book. This was well before the days of personal computers so Simon's manuscript needed to be totally retyped by the typesetters, a process offering limitless possibilities for errors. We were all very busy indeed.

Unlike Peter, I am a member of what he refers to as the "Caliphate" O.T.O. (I call it "the O.T.O.") To be fair to the storm of critics who may question my presence in these pages, let me begin by saying that Peter is my friend. Furthermore, he is one of the best researchers into the world's religions on the literary scene today. His *Stairway to Heaven* and *Tantric Temples* are two of my favorites of his books. His quest for human dignity forced him to also look into some of the darkest political conspiracies of our time, such as those recorded in *Ratline*, his recently-published history of the Nazi escape routes following Germany's defeat in World War II. I am thus honored to play a small part in *The Dark Lord*, despite the fact that Peter and I may part company on a number of important issues.

However, when a religion or creed is successful, it opens itself to a broader exposure and discussion in the wider culture. Certain forms of doctrinal exegesis may, of necessity, be confined to those who identify themselves most closely with the specific writings and magical system under discussion. But aspects of the system will make their appearance in literature, music, art, and philosophy in an "unsupervised" manner. While some will undoubtedly reject excursions by those outside the confines of established orthodoxy, such thinking may well herald the death of innovation and the establishment of dogmatic rigidity.

One conclusion that is inescapable here is that the author brings much intelligence to his subject. He shares his vast scholarship of the religious traditions of all times and places in his exploration of the congruence of the archetype vibrated and celebrated by Aleister Crowley, popularized and feared by Howard Phillips Lovecraft, and researched and embraced by Kenneth Grant. Here is a book to study and explore, to weigh and consider, one that will serve as a basis for additional study, exploration, and discussion. It is also a book to enjoy. The author is an excellent writer with a subtle wit and sense of humor that have become his literary trademarks.

The Dark Lord presents perhaps the most compelling and encyclopedic compilation of this archetype—the nightmare figure of humanity's earliest and most persistent childhood fears.

Yet, at the end (and this is the point) when we do at last encounter Him, who will we meet but ourselves?

> 15. I have hidden myself beneath a mask: I am a black and terrible God.
> 16. With courage conquering fear shall ye approach me: ye shall lay down your heads upon mine altar, expecting the sweep of the sword.
> 17. But the first kiss of love shall be radiant on your lips; and all my darkness and terror shall turn to light and joy.
> —*Liber Tzaddi vel Hamus Hermeticus*

INTRODUCTION

The Beast in the Cave

The creature I had killed, the strange beast of the unfathomed cave, was, or had at one time been a MAN!!![1]

As is probably well-known to readers of this study, Crowley was in Cairo in the spring of 1904 when he received *The Book of the Law*.

What is not so well known is that—during the very same period—a young man of high school age was composing a short story, one of his earliest, and it would reflect so completely a vision that was experienced thousands of miles away at the same time that the coincidence is indeed uncanny.

The writer was H. P. Lovecraft, considered by many to be the father of the modern gothic horror story. And this early attempt at writing supernatural fiction was entitled "The Beast in the Cave."

As we know, Crowley called himself the Beast, and identified with the Beast in the Book of Revelation. In Lovecraft's story— written when he was only fourteen years old—the Beast is at first thought to be some sort of monster living in the bowels of the earth but is instead revealed to be a human being—a man.

As Lovecraft's stories often involve dream communications and the transmission of information by psychic means or through the visions of artists and other sensitive souls, could it be possible that Lovecraft—an artist himself, of course, as a writer of imaginative fiction—"picked up" the events of Cairo that were taking place at the very same time he was composing and writing his story about a Beast who was really a man? As outlandish as this suggestion may seem, it is reinforced by further evidence in Lovecraft's own stories, as we shall see. But before we dive into the strange and

---

1 H.P. Lovecraft, "The Beast in the Cave."

otherworldly material of Lovecraft, Crowley, and the British occultist Kenneth Grant, we should set the stage for what is to follow.

There are two sides to existence, to life itself. There is a bright side, where we live and work every day; and there is a dark side, what Kenneth Grant calls the "nightside" of the Kabbalistic Tree of Life.

Spies know this. Criminals and the police who fight them know this. Sexual predators know this. Serial killers know this. Business people know this. Politicians know this.

And occultists know this.

Everyone who has a secret they desperately want kept secret knows this.

There is a dark side to everything from politics to religion. And it is in the dark side that the most tangible, the most basic elements of life can be found. The *prima materia*. The *fons et origo*. One cannot truly know life without knowing the dark side, without peering into its depths, for it is in the dark side that seeds are planted, that sustenance is taken, that dreams are born and take root in the damp recesses of the sunken cellar of the human soul: the cave wherein the Beast resides, the Beast that is—as Lovecraft tells us—a Man.

In average human beings, this dark side is to be found in their unconscious minds, unrecognized and unacknowledged without extensive depth analysis (the term "depth" is instructive); but its impulse can be sensed in their darkest conscious desires, the ones they keep secret from society at large and from their closest loved ones. It is not only sexuality, although sex can be the doorway to knowing the dark side. Freud knew this. Wilhelm Reich knew this. Jung knew this and trembled at its power. Kabbalists knew this, and called it the *Sitra Ahra*, the realm of the damaged gods they called the *qlippoth*. The Tantrikas know this. And Kenneth Grant knew this.

In our lives today we have been ceding the territory of our unconscious little by little: to reality television, to social networking sites, to CCTV cameras on every street corner, to our credit card transactions, to vulgarity in cinema and entertainment generally, to even casual use of the Internet. Electronic databases may know more about our lives and our desires than we can remember ourselves. Profiles can be established that delineate our personalities and plumb the depths of our unconscious using clever algorithms that manipulate the electronic trails we leave behind in our passage through cyberspace—like electromagnetic snails on silicon glass. In this environment it becomes harder and harder to function secretly, either as members of secret societies or as individuals. (Are there any true secret societies left; any society that has the maturity to avoid broadcasting itself on the Internet?) Our inner lives are in danger of being ripped open, a process that began in the 1950s when some G-scale doctors and imbecilic psychiatrists pried open the black box of consciousness like sorcerers's apprentices in a Grade-B horror film.

Perhaps it began even earlier, at the dawn of the twentieth century, in a small apartment in Cairo where an English couple were spending their honeymoon cruising the Nile, visiting museums, and talking to gods.

This is a dark science, this occultism of the nightside. The word "occult" means "secret," "hidden," "dark." There is no occultism without darkness. There is no religion without darkness, either, but that is one of the secrets that religion keeps to itself. Religions are of the daylight, of the Sun, of society and community, of public rituals and private anxieties. But any religion that speaks only of the Sun and its Light is lying: to others and to itself.

For religion is nothing more than the refuge of failed magicians.

We erect edifices of ritual and dogma against the darkness and call it faith, call it religion. But the most useful element of any religion is its ability to exorcise demons. It is a practical ability, one with observable and measureable results. Everything else, all sacraments, depend on faith and the suspension of disbelief: penance, baptism, Holy Orders, Extreme Unction, matrimony, even Holy Communion. But a possessed person is a fact, and the successful exorcism of the demon is another fact. Many otherwise lukewarm individuals have been brought to the faith after having witnessed demonic possession. It is a great recruiting tool for the Church, if nothing else. Sacraments may bind one to the community, reinforce the bonds between the individual and the group. They are rituals of identity. But exorcism ... well, that's another story. Exorcism is not a sacrament. It's a tool, something useful, something with an easily definable mission. It is the place within religion where true magic lies, as if in wait. It is the essential contradiction in religion, this axis of possession and exorcism, of cause and effect. It is the strongest connection in religion to ancient knowledge of the dark side of human experience. It reveals what religion wants kept hidden. Secret. Occult.

Thelema calls itself a new religion, and at the heart of this new religion is the very darkness of which we speak. There is a general desire among some believers to represent Thelema as a religion of the Sun, of the ancient Egyptian deities Osiris, Isis and Horus, of Thoth and Sekhmet.

But it is not.

As we shall see, the very creed of the Gnostic Mass—the ritual designed to be the public face of Thelema to the world—speaks of a god called Chaos. And Chaos is the code-word for Set.

The Dark Lord.

> The interrelationship of the concepts Tutulu, Cthulhu, Oz, Zaa, Yezid, AL, L, Nu-Isis, etc., demonstrates unequivocally the essential identity of the Necronomicon (555) and the Therionic (666) Currents. Oz as the Manifesto and Manifestation of Man are equated in the Necronomicon Gnosis: "The Power of Man is the Power of the Ancient Ones. And this is the Covenant."
> —Kenneth Grant, *Outer Gateways*, p. 14

The above correspondences link irrefragibly the Necronomicon, Kamite, and Thelemic currents, showing the three strands as a continual linear development, in both a chronological and a magical sense.

—Kenneth Grant, *Outer Gateways*, p. 92

In the above two citations from the work of Kenneth Grant we are faced with a bold—if outlandish—concept.

Grant—the late head of the Typhonian Order in England and an intimate of Aleister Crowley—has insisted throughout many books that the magical current represented by Crowley's Thelema and that represented specifically by the "Schlangekraft recension" of the *Necronomicon* (sometimes referred to as the "Simonomicon") are not only compatible but in fact are identical. He refers to the Necronomicon Gnosis—a system representative of not only the Necronomicon itself but also of the stories that fall under the heading of the "Cthulhu Mythos" and which include works by H.P. Lovecraft as well as by his friends and imitators—as a credible magical doctrine and practice. He makes numerous references to Lovecraft, Cthulhu, and the Necronomicon throughout his later works in order to substantiate and justify his position on themes as disparate as the magical methods of Austin Osman Spare, the UFO phenomenon, the visions of Crowley, Jack Parsons, and Charles Stansfeld Jones (Frater Achad), Afro-Caribbean cults, Tantric rituals, and much, much more.

What does all this mean?

Thelema is a Greek word meaning "will" and was used by Crowley to refer to his new religion, one developed through the practice of magic (or "magick" as he preferred to spell the word in order to differentiate it from other forms), and established upon the concept that the world is entering a major new phase of spiritual evolution, a phase he called the Aeon of Horus. The previous age was the Aeon of Osiris: the slain and resurrected god that prefigured that of Mithra and of Jesus, among others. The age before that was the matriarchal Aeon of Isis. The present Aeon of Horus is to be the age of the Child: the offspring of Isis and Osiris, and thus a Magickal Child.

The seminal text of this new religion is the Book of the Law—or *Liber AL vel Legis* to give it its Latin title—received by Crowley in a series of communications obtained in Cairo, Egypt in April of 1904. In order to promulgate his new faith, Crowley enlisted the aid of a German secret society called the Ordo Templi Orientis or Order of the Eastern Temple. This Order exists today in several forms and on virtually every continent. It is comprised of a series of degrees of initiation, and its members are called Thelemites, or followers of Thelema. The Order rituals are based on the idea that the Knights Templar of the Crusader era formed a kind of alliance with a Muslim secret society from which they obtained initiations. Indeed, today the Islamic influence is felt not only in some of the Order rituals but also in the fact that the American-based version of the Order often is referred to as the "Caliphate"—a word that is used in Islam to describe the legitimate successors to the Prophet Muhammad.

This is not so strange as it may appear. The theme of European mystics going to the Middle East to obtain secret knowledge is an old one and can be seen in the origin legend of the Rosicrucians (Christian Rosenkreutz, their putative founder, went to the Middle East in search of wisdom). The German founders of the Ordo Templi Orientis itself also claimed to have visited Muslim lands where they obtained secret initiations. It has been shown by historians that Helena Blavatsky herself—the founder of the Theosophical Society—had links to the Brotherhood of Luxor, an Egyptian-based secret society. Thus, this is a tradition among European occultists that has a long pedigree.

The Necronomicon—the grimoire or magician's workbook to which Kenneth Grant refers in his writings—also has a Middle Eastern pedigree. According to the stories created by gothic horror author H. P. Lovecraft, the book was written by a "Mad Arab" in the eighth century CE. It contains themes and invocations that are the heirs of a Sumerian tradition: the same tradition that Crowley claimed to be rediscovering in his own magical development. Indeed, the English translation of the *Necronomicon* is dedicated to Crowley himself.

Thus of the two basic texts to which Kenneth Grant refers in his books on Thelema—*The Book of the Law,* and the *Necronomicon* —the first was received in Egypt, and the second has its origins in Mesopotamia.

The Middle East is the birthplace of the three great monotheistic religions: Judaism, Christianity and Islam—sometimes called the Abrahamic religions after their common ancestor, the prophet Abraham. But is also where some of the world's oldest recorded religions were born, millenia before the birth of Moses, the founder of the Jewish faith: the Egyptian religion with its plethora of gods and goddesses ... the religions of Sumer and Akkad and Babylon ... and of some even stranger cults, as we shall see.

This insistence on ancient origins is a key factor in reading Grant. In fact, Grant is not satisfied with the antiquity of even these religions but points to an older, more distant, set of ancestors. Even ancient Egypt—the "Kamite" of the second quotation given earlier, is not old enough. The oldest—in Grant's chronology—is that of the Necronomicon and of its associated Sumerian Tradition. To Grant (as well as to Crowley) the tradition that is represented by Thelema had its origins in Sumer, and from Sumer to Egypt, and from there to Aleister Crowley's stunning communications with an alien intelligence in Cairo in 1904.

There is another element to Grant's thesis that is difficult to overlook, and that is the importance he places on sexuality as a method to be employed for the evocation of these dark powers and as a means of entering the mysterious realm he calls the "Mauve Zone." His liberal use of Tantric terms and concepts is a hallmark of Grant's work, and his intimations that unorthodox forms of sexual congress be employed towards magical ends is a theme that runs through his books. There has been much nonsense written about "sex magic" in the literature of the New Age; Grant's specific descriptions of the complex psycho-sexual processes involved should make it clear that "sex magic" does not mean normal coitus performed while meditating or burning scented candles. The fact that the Ordo Templi Orientis itself is considered to be a repository of this type of information should make one aware that a more sophisticated if not more strenuous approach to the use of sexuality in ritual is required.

That said, Kenneth Grant has been criticized by occultists and members of various Orders for a number of reasons. In the first place, he once claimed to be the head of the Ordo Templi Orientis (O.T.O.) upon the death of previous chief (actually the Order's treasurer) Karl Germer. This was hotly contested by the American (Grady McMurtry) branch of the Order known as the "Caliphate." In the end, Grant decided that the title wasn't worth the fight although many of his fans considered him to have been the rightful heir to the throne. Instead, he founded what he called the Typhonian Order: a magical group more in line with the discoveries he and his followers were making and which was based on the identification of Typhon[2]—the Dark Lord—as the operative Power of what he termed the "Mauve Zone" on the hidden side of the Kabbalistic Tree of Life and the place from whence all true magical power originates.

In the second place, Grant was in many ways his own worst enemy when it came to explaining his doctrines. His works are impossible to understand unless one has a deep grounding in Kabbalah, Asian religions, Afro-Caribbean religions, Egyptology, and the rituals and grade structures of the Golden Dawn, the Ordo Templi Orientis, and the Argentum Astrum ... to name just a few. His gematria—the system of Kabbalistic analysis that uses numerological equivalents for Hebrew (and Greek) letters—is off the charts, and so internally inconsistent that it seems more like stream of consciousness than it does numerical or numerological evidence.

---

2 Typhon is referred to by Grant as either male or female, depending on the context. To the Greeks, Typhon was male, but Grant often identifies deities across cultural lines and subsumes their genders according to his system.

To read Grant is to become aware that he is not communicating in a linear, methodical fashion but after the style of a James Joyce: magic as art, art as magic.

Nevertheless, there is buried in the heavy text of Grant's hypothesis a profound and passionate belief in what he is saying and what he has discovered. And rightly so: for if what Grant says is in any way "true," our entire perspective on human history will have to be reconsidered from a terrifying vantage point.

For what Grant is saying is that *all religions and especially all antinomian cults have their origin in a single cult, a single magical order, that has its origin not on earth but in the stars.*

It is this belief—this *discovery*—that finds itself in line with the most cynical of Lovecraft's horror stories concerning a race of alien beings that once colonized our planet and which will come again to reclaim it, a race whose religion is the mother of all cults.

And it is this belief—this doctrine—that finds itself hidden within many of the most important texts of Aleister Crowley's Thelema.

It is at the heart of the current fascination with "ancient aliens" and "alien archaeology" and all those Discovery Channel and History Channel specials about the theories of von Danniken and Zecharia Sitchin, for example. It is central to fears about the coming of the Antichrist, the prophecies of Nostradamus, and the chiliastic panic about the Mayan calendar and the end of the year 2012.

> Other ugly reports concerned my intimacy with leaders of occultist groups, and scholars suspected of connection with nameless bands of abhorrent elder world hierophants. These rumors, though never proved at the time, were doubtless stimulated by the known tenor of some of my reading ...[3]

The purpose of this book is to deconstruct and decode the works of Kenneth Grant as much as possible, at least insofar as the

---

3   From H. P. Lovecraft, "The Shadow Out of Time."

Necronomicon Gnosis and the Typhonian Current are concerned. To do justice to the entire Grant *ouevre* would be a major task outside the scope of this work. What we will do instead is try to understand how the Necronomicon Gnosis fits in with the Thelemic Current, and how both of these together inform Grant's Typhonian hypothesis.

Before we begin, however, it is necessary to address three important points:

In the first place, the author is not a member of the OTO or, indeed, of any magical order or group and never has been. His previous membership in various churches of the "wandering bishop" classification is public knowledge, including at least one church that gave apostolic succession to the Gnostic Catholic Church: an auxiliary branch of the OTO. But that is as far as the association goes. Therefore nothing the author writes about here is to be considered official OTO doctrine nor does it have the blessing, *nihil obstat,* or *imprimatur* of that or any Order.

In the second place, there has been much drama over the Simon Necronomicon, most of which concerns the identity of Simon himself rather than the substance of the book. Simon has addressed these issues in his own *Dead Names: The Dark History of the Necronomicon*, and I have addressed them in various interviews over the years. One may or may not believe in the "reality" of the *Necronomicon*; what is germane to this book is the fact that Kenneth Grant—an occultist, occult author, and occult leader of no small importance—found the book essential reading and took it very, very seriously indeed.

In the third and final place, many of the issues we will discuss will be considered anathema or heretical by doctrinaire Thelemites—such as the works of Frater Achad, A. O. Spare, and even Jack Parsons. While "normative" Thelema (if by that we mean the OTO of the Grady McMurtry line) may be likened to the official Church, it is possible that later generations will consider the writings of Frater Achad, Spare, and Parsons (among others, and possibly including the works of *Necronomicon* editor Simon himself) to be "gnostic" versions of the official gospels, much the way one approaches the Nag Hammadi texts or the Dead Sea Scrolls. It is not my place to defend any of these ideas on doctrinal grounds. Indeed, in that I have little or no interest. My usage of them in this place only reflects Grant's own incorporation of them in his Gnosis, and should be taken to reflect no agenda of my own.

With these caveats in mind, then, let us proceed to an investigation of one of the most-neglected theses in the history of modern occultism: the nature of the Typhonian Current and its relationship to Aleister Crowley's Thelema and H. P. Lovecraft's Necronomicon.

Let us approach the throne of the Dark Lord.

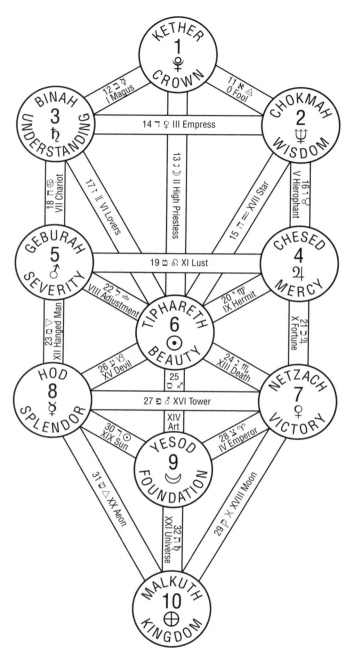

The Tree of Life. Its ten spheres or Sephiroth *are identified with the planets, the twenty-two paths with the letters of the Hebrew alphabet. This one follows Crowley's attributions for the paths of* Hé *and* Tzaddi.

CHAPTER ONE:

Strange Aeons

That is not dead which can eternal lie, And with strange aeons even death may die.

—H.P. Lovecraft

This child Horus is a twin, two in one. Horus and Harpocrates are one, and they are also one with Set or Apophis, the destroyer of Osiris. It is by the destruction of the principle of death that they are born. The establishment of this new Aeon, this new fundamental principle, is the great work now to be accomplished in the world.

—Aleister Crowley

Let not the reverence for the God of thy self cause thee by a misconception to lose thy reverence for the Gods who live for ever—the Aeons of Infinite Years.

—The Golden Dawn, "The Symbolism of the Admission of the Candidate"

THE CONCEPT OF THE AEON may seem like an odd place to start this discussion, but the idea that humanity has entered a new phase of existence—of evolution, perhaps—is central to the belief-system called Thelema and to Crowley's theology in general. For if Crowley's new religion was of a piece with everything that had preceded it, there would be no point to it, or to discussing it at any great length except as a curiosity.

A contemporary of Crowley, the author of gothic horror stories H. P. Lovecraft, had his own idea about Aeons: that they represented enormous lengths of time, and that the contemplation of them (and what life-forms may have evolved during them) would drive a normal person insane, as would the contemplation of the vast distances of space between the Earth and the stars. Yet, as with Crowley, he wrote that in certain cases, and with certain Aeons, "even death may die," or will result, as Crowley wrote, in "the destruction of the principle of death." This conquering of death has been a focus of virtually every major religion in the last five or six millenia (probably beginning with the Egyptians). This represents hope for Crowley but absolute horror for Lovecraft; for if death is overcome for some, it would be overcome for all: mass murderers, serial killers, fiendish dictators ... and the anthropoid monsters of the writer's feverish imagination.

Thus we should begin with a look at the concept of the Aeon. It has been a fractious subject among Thelemites for one of Crowley's colleagues had proposed a different schema for the Aeons, one that would have reduced Crowley's own structure significantly. Also, the idea that the end of the world is near—vide the Mayan calendar, the Nostradamus prophecies, and other chiliastic concerns—lends more significance to any discussion of the Aeons, the New Age, and the astronomical ideas they represent.

Aleister Crowley (1875–1947) claimed to be the Prophet of the new age, the Aeon of Horus, and the Book of the Law its scripture. Received over the course of three afternoons in Cairo, Egypt in April of 1904, Crowley himself rejected it at first. Some of the language is offensive, particularly when it comes to describing the world's great religions. The vehemence with which Christianity, Islam, Buddhism, etc are denigrated seems far from what we have come to expect of spiritual literature. However, a re-read of the first few books of the Bible would be educational in this regard, for the God of the Jews was just as vehement in his attack on all other gods, all other religions. A re-read of the Book of Revelations (also known as the Apocalypse) would reinforce this impatience of the God of Christians and Jews with any and all other forms of religious expression. This vehemence was often backed up with military force, and the massacres of hundreds of thousands of men, women and children was the bloody result. Thus the anger and hatred for earlier faiths shown in the Book of the Law is consistent with Old and New Testament attitudes, if nothing else, and seems of a piece with the contemporary world's religious polarization.

The structure of the Book of the Law is that of three chapters, each devoted to a different Egyptian deity or deities and each represented as the speech of that deity via a praeterhuman intelligence or spiritual intermediary called Aiwass, a being that Crowley later claimed was his Holy Guardian Angel. This occurred as a series of inspired or channeled scriptures over the course of those three days from April 8 to 10, 1904. The readings began after Crowley's wife—Rose Kelly—alerted Crowley to the immediacy of the contact during a visit to the Boulaq Museum in Cairo on the vernal equinox that year, at which time she drew his attention to a stele numbered 666, now known to the faithful as the "Stele of Revealing." This particular stele was a burial plaque for a priest of the Egyptian god Mentu. The priest's name was Ankh-ef-en-khonsu. Each session took place in their apartment between the hours of 12 and 1 pm. (It is possible that the dictations occurred at the precise hour of the mid-day call to prayer, and that they would have heard the muezzin's cry outside their hotel room window right before, during or after the séance.)

It could be considered natural that the scripture would have an Egyptian coloration, considering all the external circumstances. However, the character of Crowley's own previous initiations into a British secret society known as the Golden Dawn would also have an impact on the terminology (if not the philosophy) of the text as we will see. So what we will look at first in this chapter is the nature of the "Egyptology" of the Book of the Law and its relation to the concept of the Aeons.

Egyptian Trinities

The three chapters are the utterances of the Egyptian gods Nuit, Hadit, and Ra-Hoor-Khuit (respectively). Structurally, this seems consistent with Egyptian practice. The Egyptian religion contains many such "trinities" of supreme gods at the head of the various pantheons. One of the oldest is that of Ptah, Sekhmet and Nefertum; another would be that of Amun, Mut and Khonsu. The most famous is perhaps that of Osiris, Isis and Horus. In each case, we are presented with a male god, a female goddess, and a child god. In other words, a nuclear family. We rarely, if ever, come across this type of configuration in the Tantric pantheons of Tibet and India, for instance, where the emphasis is usually on a male and a female deity; while there are offspring of these unions, they are rarely depicted as a family unit in the way of the Egyptian examples.

However, the trinity Nuit/Hadit/Ra-Hoor-Khuit is not a typical one in Egyptian texts. Nuit is a star goddess and the mother of Set and Nephthys. Hadit—according to the Book of the Law and to Crowley's subsequent writings—is either a star within that empyrean or a solar disk; as the sun is a star this is not as inconsistent as it might appear. The third god, Ra-Hoor-Khuit, has much more in common with forms of Horus—offspring of Isis and Osiris—rather than with any conceivable union of Nuit and the lesser-known Hadit (which is itself a form of Horus). We may venture to say that this combination is unique to Crowley and to the Book of the Law.

Yet, there is another deity specifically mentioned in the scripture, and that is Khonsu. Crowley, in his role as scribe of Aiwass and of the gods, is given the title Ankh af-n-Khonsu after the name of the priest whose burial plaque was the Stele of Revealing. The two terms ankh and Khonsu bear some further investigation.

Ankh, of course, is the iconic symbol of the Egyptian idea of immortality. The word *ankh* means "life" and is found on temples and tombs everywhere in Egypt with the associated idea of immortality and life after death. Egyptian pharaohs as well as deities are often depicted holding an ankh, sometimes also called the *crux ansata* or "cross with handle."

Khonsu, however, may not be as well known. It is the name

of another child god, sacred to the moon. This god was usually depicted in mummified form, but with the lock of hair on the right side of his head typical of Egyptian children of ancient times. This is used to emphasize the youth of the god with the implication that he is pre-pubescent. His mother was Mut (not to be confused with Maat), a self-created mother goddess whose symbols were the vulture and the lion and whose name means "mother." In northern Egypt, she became identified with the lion goddess Sekhmet and, at various times, with the cat goddess Bast. Khonsu's father was Amun (sometimes Amen or Amoun), the mysterious self-created god of whom Ra was often considered to be the external image, hence the composite form Amun-Ra.

While Khonsu was a lunar deity, and often depicted as a child, he also had warrior tendencies in the Egyptian religion. He was believed to be a defender of the king, who destroyed his enemies by removing their internal organs and presenting them to the king for nourishment. This odd mythologem gave rise to one epithet of Khonsu as the "king's placenta" and, indeed, he later became identified with childbirth (just as Set would later be identified with miscarriage and abortion).

This idea of Khonsu as the king's defender shares some ideas in common with Horus, who avenged the murder of his father, Osiris. Often, Khonsu is depicted with a hawk's head—recalling Horus explicitly—with a lunar disk and crescent above it to identify him more carefully with the moon, as opposed to the more solar aspect of Horus. In addition, Khonsu was also depicted in a very suggestive way at his temple in Karnak: as "a ram-headed snake who fertilized the cosmic egg."[4] This identification of Khonsu with the Cosmic Egg of creation will have resonance later, as the vision of the Egg comes to play in the Amalantrah Working of Crowley and

---

4 Geraldine Pinch, *Egyptian Myth: A very short introduction*, Oxford University Press, 2004, p. 52.

associates,[5] as well as with the "Blue Egg of Harpocrates" in the rituals of the Golden Dawn.

But it is the presentation of Khonsu as a child that has relevance for the Book of the Law. Khonsu is referred to in Egyptian mythology as the "Moon Child," which would become the title of one of Aleister Crowley's novels. This same image—of a child god—is found in the statues and bas-reliefs of Harpocrates, a form of Horus and, indeed, this form is mentioned in the Book of the Law several times.[6] Crowley, as a "priest of Khonsu" deliberately makes the association with a child-god who is also a martial deity, a defender of the king. In the case of Khonsu's father—Amun—we have the archetype of the "Hidden God" that figures so prominently in the work of Kenneth Grant and to which we will return from time to time.

The first chapter of the Book of the Law consists of the words of Nuit, the goddess of the night sky, who is often depicted with her feet in the west, her hands in the east, and her body thus gracefully arched over the earth, and dotted with stars.

The second chapter reveals the words of Hadit, the Heru-Behdeti of the Egyptian pantheon, called Haidith in Greek. Hadit was recruited by Thoth (the Egyptian god of magic, writing, and wisdom) to assist Horus in the latter's famous battle with Set. Hadit represents a single point of light, a single star in the empyrean of

---

5   A ritual that was conducted between January 14 to June 16, 1918 by Crowley and a number of others, but mostly including Roddie Minor, known as Soror Achitha 555. It should be noted that 555 is the number most closely associated with the *Necronomicon*, as it is the value of the word in its original Greek. Grant associates this number with the Necronomicon Current, just as 666 is identified with the Thelemic Current.

6   For instance, AL I:7: "Behold! it is revealed by Aiwass the minister of Hoor-paar-kraat." AL II:8, "Who worshipped Heru-pa-kraath have worshipped me; ill, for I am the worshipper," and AL III:35, "The half of the word of Heru-ra-ha, called Hoor-pa-kraat and Ra-Hoor-Khut." *Hoor-pa-kraat* and *Heru-pa-kraath* are both original Egyptian forms of the later Greek *Harpocrates*. The name also figures prominently in the initiation rituals of the Golden Dawn.

Nuit. If Nuit is visualized as a circle, then Hadit would be the point in the center. In the Thelemic universe Nuit and Hadit also may represent different forms or ideas about infinity, perhaps infinite expansion and infinite contraction respectively.

The third chapter consists of the revelation of Ra-Hoor-Khuit, or Ra-Herakhty in Greek recension. This is a deity composed of two different ideas: Ra and Horus. The translation of Ra-Herakhty is "Ra, Horus on the Horizon." Thus there is the sense that Ra— the quintessential Sun god of the Egyptians—manifests as Horus when on the horizon, i.e., when the sun is rising or setting. Horus is the son of Osiris and Isis and is the god who battled Set (in one version of the story) to avenge his father's murder. Thus, there is the implication that the identity of Horus is inextricably linked to his parentage, and that Horus's purpose as the Avenging Son thus connects him eternally with Set: a union not of love, but of war. This "unity" of Horus with Set is an idea that Crowley embraced and which appears several times in his published work.[7] Ra-Hoor-Khuit is mentioned frequently throughout all three chapters of the Book of the Law, and is obviously the focal point of the scripture.

It is thus Horus—and especially the form of Ra-Hoor-Khuit— who will occupy most of the attention of Thelema, for he is the symbol of the New Aeon that replaces the earlier Aeon of Osiris. However, there is a darker—more mysterious and to some an extra-terrestrial—aspect to the New Aeon, and it concerns the interme-diary between Crowley and the gods of the Book of the Law: the entity known variously as Aiwaz or Aiwass.

Crowley himself referred to this being as Set-Aiwass or Shai-tan-Aiwass in some of his writings,[8] thus linking it with both the

---

7   See, for instance, Aleister Crowley, *The Equinox of the Gods*, Chapter 8: "This child Horus is a twin, two in one. Horus and Harpocrates are one, and they are also one with Set or Apophis, the destroyer of Osiris. It is by the destruction of the principle of death that they are born."

8   See for instance his statement linking Aiwass with the Shaitan of the Yezidi: "Aiwaz is not a mere formula, like many Angelic names, but it is the true, most ancient name of the God of the Yezidi, and thus returns to the highest antiquity.

Egyptian god of "Evil"—Set or Seth—and with the Middle Eastern name for God's (or humanity's) "Adversary": Shaitan, more
popularly known as Satan (but "reclaimed" by the Mesopotamian
sect of the Yezidis in a rehabilitated form, about which more later).
This refers to a very early, predynastic (i.e., 3500–3000 BCE), form
of Egyptian religion that identified Set as a god of the desert, of
storms, and of rage. Much later, the Greeks at the time of the historian Herodotus (c. 484–425 BCE) identified Set with their own
sea monster, Typhon. (It was this Typhon that gave its name to
Kenneth Grant's new form of Thelema, the Typhonian Order, representing what he called the Typhonian/Stellar Current.) Set was
also said to reside in the Great Bear constellation, and served to
aid the souls of the dead to attain immortality by allowing them to
climb Set's "stairway to heaven."[9] Like most Egyptian deities, Set
originally had both a positive and a negative nature but in the end
the negative aspect of the god won out due to popular attribution.
As the sworn enemy of Horus, Set was seen as the eternal Evil
One and the murderer of Horus's father, Osiris. He was also said to
have been born unnaturally, ripping himself through the belly of his
mother, the sky goddess Nut or Nuit who figures so prominently in
the Crowley scriptures. Thus, he could be seen as an initiatory force.

Indeed, Set's role in the New Aeon could be described as that
of the Grand Initiator of humanity. However, this type of initiation
will be violent and imposed from outside, rather than the relatively
serene form experienced by Crowley himself during his sojourn
with the considerably more sedate Golden Dawn. We can see this
type of violent and involuntary initiation prefigured in the psycho-

---

Our work is therefore historically authentic; the rediscovery of the Sumerian
tradition." In Kenneth Grant, *The Magical Revival*, Friedrich Muller, London,
1972, p. 52

9 The Great Bear constellation figures prominently in both the Schlangekraft
recension of the Necronomicon and in Kenneth Grant's work. The importance
of this constellation—often neglected by western occultists—is detailed in the
author's own *Stairway to Heaven: Chinese Alchemists, Jewish Kabbalists and the
Art of Spiritual Transformation.*

logical experiments of the world's intelligence agencies beginning in the 1950s with the phenomenon of the "Manchurian Candidate" of the Korean War era that contributed to the creation of mind control, behavior control, and psychological warfare programs that sought to unpack the secrets of the human mind by using unsuspecting innocent men, women and children as test subjects and guinea pigs.[10]

Thus we have a rather paradoxical relationship in which Set-Aiwass communicates the text of the Aeon of Horus (his sworn enemy) to Crowley in Cairo. Crowley elevated the status of Set far above that which obtained in dynastic Egypt, and saw in Set the type of force necessary to bring in the new Aeon. This may be considered an "initiated" view of traditional Egyptology which understands Set and Horus as implacable foes. If the myths concerning Set were little more than libels created by followers of the newer gods Osiris and Horus, what was the truth? What did Set really represent, and what is Set's relationship to the Aeon of Horus?

As Crowley's understanding of the Book of the Law matured, so did his understanding of Aiwaz, whom he declared to be none other than his Holy Guardian Angel[11]: a concept developed by the Golden Dawn, the secret society that had initiated him into magic. The Holy Guardian Angel or HGA can be conceived of as one's "Higher Self" or as the apotheosis of one's own spiritual identity; conversely, one's self is seen as a manifestation (one among many) of the Angel. In Crowley's case, he viewed Aiwaz to be one of the gods of ancient Sumer, thus pre-existing the Egyptian civilization

---

10 See the author's trilogy, *Sinister Forces: A grimoire of American political witchcraft* (Trine Day, Walterville (OR), 2005, 2011) in particular volume 3, chapter 17: "Voluntary Madness," for a more detailed explanation of this connection.

11 See, for instance, *The Equinox of the Gods*: "I lay claim to be the sole authority competent to decide disputed points with regard to the Book of the Law, seeing that its Author, Aiwaz, is none other than mine own Holy Guardian Angel, to Whose Knowledge and Conversation I have attained, so that I have exclusive access to Him. I have duly referred every difficulty to Him directly, and received His answer; my award is therefore absolute without appeal."

and their oldest known divinity, the desert god Set, who might then
be considered an avatar or emanation of the original Sumerian
archetype.

In addition, Crowley proposed a composite Set-Horus "current"
that would represent the combined tension of the two antagonists
as a single force emblematic of the New Aeon. This was typical of
Crowley's tinkering with the known Egyptology of the day. It did
not reflect any new discoveries in the field, but was rather informed
by his occult insight into the play of spiritual forces represented
by "god forms" and ideas associated with the Egyptian gods in the
consciousness of the Western mind of the early twentieth century.
As we have seen, he also combined Set, Shaitan and Aiwaz into
a single concept representing not only his own HGA but also a
deity or devil from the little-known civilization of Sumer.[12] Thus,
we have the Egyptian Set, the Semitic Shaitan, and a Sumerian god
identified only by the word Aiwaz or Aiwass—which has no meaning in the Sumerian language—all lumped together without regard
for individual religious or social contexts. From the point of view
of mainstream religious studies or anthropology—especially post-
modern anthropology—this is a car wreck of a proportion equivalent to a major highway pile-up.

It is perhaps relevant to point out at this juncture that one
cannot refer to any of Crowley's writings as representative of formal Egyptological theory or research. Crowley is not an academic
source for this type of material. Rather, he was an interpreter of the
Egyptological discoveries of his day, such as those by Gaston Mas-
pero (1846–1916) and most especially of the amateur Egyptologist
Gerald Massey (1828–1907), whose fanciful—and esoterically-
oriented—descriptions of the ancient world were never taken seriously by mainstream archaeologists but which were embraced by

---

12 "I now incline to believe that Aiwass is not only the God or Demon or Devil
once held holy in Sumer, and mine own Guardian Angel, but also a man as I
am, insofar as He uses a human body to make His magical link with Mankind,
whom He loves, and that He is thus an Ipsissimus, the Head of the A∴A∴"
Ibid.

occultists. The theories of Massey still exert an important influence over occult authors today, regardless of the fact that they are considered in error (at best) or wholly imaginary (at worst).

Crowley's interpretations—like those of Massey—were free-form, conforming to his own experiences as an occultist and magician. The occultism of the nineteenth and early twentieth centuries largely was indebted to universalist ideas of "common origins," a worldview which in its extreme form took as a given the existence of an Ur-cult or Ur-religion in the remote past that provided the inspiration and basis for all future cults. Thus, the religions of Sumer and Egypt had a source in common with those of India and China, and even the Aztec and Mayan religions of Latin America. Symbols that were discovered in several vastly different locales—such as the Dragon—were believed to represent a single, common idea regardless of whether the Dragon symbol was carved on a stone block in England or seen on a porcelain fragment in China. This idea—that same or similar symbols were evidence of a single belief or cultural phenomenon—was taken to its logical conclusion by the Nazis who raced to find evidence of the swastika on ancient remains around the world, thus supporting their contention that a single, Aryan race was responsible for all of human civilization.[13] We can see a similar trend in the present era with all the talk of ancient aliens having "given" the human race its science, its architecture, and its religions. In a sense, this is close to Lovecraft's idea that an ancient race from the stars once inhabited the Earth.

In Crowley's day, however, this approach was exciting and encouraged a great deal of amateur speculation on the history of the ancient world. While universalism has been discredited by the philosophers of the Frankfurt School and their associated postmodern approach to theories of knowledge and interpretation, with its fetishism of cultural differences and uniqueness, some elements of its worldview stubbornly remain. Rather than throw out the

---

13 See *The Master Plan* by Heather Pringle, or the author's own *Unholy Alliance* and *Ratline* for more details on the anthropological fantasies of the Nazis.

proverbial baby with the bathwater, it can be acknowledged that certain aspects of the human condition—birth, death, sexuality—are identical among all members of the human race, and that while different approaches may be taken to sacralize or otherwise interpret these aspects they are nonetheless "universals" and their comparison across ethnic, racial and environmental lines may contribute to a better understanding of the human condition.

So, when Crowley wrote—seemingly recklessly—about a "Set-Horus" current in occultism, or identified Set with Shaitan and with a Sumerian Aiwaz, he was not referring specifically to these ideas as they are understood by scholars or were understood by the indigenous peoples who contributed them to the world's body of knowledge. Instead, he was emphasizing certain perceived qualities that he deemed cognate, without overmuch regard for their historical context. At the same time, one should not infer that Crowley's "Egyptology" needs to remain at odds with normative Egyptology. On the contrary, by supplementing Crowley's writings on the subject with recent scholarship in the field many advantages accrue and discoveries occur and, where necessary, corrections may be made.

A further defense of Crowley's Egyptology may be made in light of the fact that the Egyptian religion itself went through many changes over the course of its roughly three thousand—four thousand years of history. Gods and goddesses changed attributes over time, changed rulerships and characteristics, and even parentage. Their sacred sites were moved, or renamed. Their effigies defaced as new cults emerged. Often gods were merged with other gods to form new, composite forms. Thus one could make the argument—perhaps only slightly frivolously—that the Book of the Law represents a new iteration of the Egyptian religion and continues the developmental process begun in the pre-Dynastic era.

Another factor to be taken into consideration is one that is frequently ignored, even by those who claim a certain degree of expertise in this area, and that is the fact that Crowley had been initiated into the Golden Dawn and framed much of his magical and esoteric worldview within the Golden Dawn structure of rituals and instructions. Thus, we first come across Hoor-par-kraat, Osiris, Isis, Nu, Maat and many of the other Crowleyan references in this context: in the Golden Dawn rituals themselves, the ones used to initiate Crowley, which had a profound affect on his consciousness and his intellectual and spiritual development. In fact, certain phrases in the Book of the Law make no sense whatsoever without reference to those very rituals.

As an example, we can refer to the very first chapter wherein it is written:

> Abrogate are all rituals, all ordeals, all words and signs. Ra-Hoor-Khuit hath taken his seat in the East at the Equinox of the Gods; and let Asar be with Isa, who also are one. But they are not of me. Let Asar be the adorant, Isa the sufferer; Hoor in his secret name and splendour is the Lord initiating. (AL I:49)

In his "New Comment" to the Book of the Law, Crowley himself clearly states:

> The general allusion is to the Equinox Ritual of the G∴D∴ where the officer of the previous six months, representing Horus, took the place of the retiring Hierophant, who had represented Osiris.

Thus, the replacement of Osiris by Horus—i.e., the old Aeon by the New—was already prefigured in the rituals with which Crowley was completely familiar, but which would have been incomprehensible to an outsider. In that ritual Horus was represented by the officer known as the Hiereus (or "priest"). Osiris was the Hierophant (or "high priest"), and another of the important officers was the Hegemon ("leader" or "guide"), which was the Goddess Maat, and indeed the hall of initiations in the neophyte ceremony was called the Hall of Maat. (In the verse from the Book of the Law

cited above, Asar is Osiris and Isa may be Isis or Jesus.[14]) Thus, the
gods of the Book of the Law were speaking to Crowley in a Golden
Dawn context (since the allusions make no sense outside of the
very specific Golden Dawn rituals). They were using his initiation
as a channel through which to communicate, to make their words
known and understood.

What this means is that the cultus of Thelema and the organizations that grew out of it—the A∴A∴, Grant's Typhonian
Order, etc.—have the Golden Dawn system as their base. (The
OTO does not have any connection to the Golden Dawn, either
through its earliest founders or its ritual structure.) Intellectually—if not spiritually—Thelema can be truly understood only
within that system and is thus (from a historical point of view)
a development of what began as the Golden Dawn in nineteenth
century England. Crowley's own organization, the Argentum
Astrum or A∴A∴, is a "perfection" of the original Golden Dawn
system of grades, with the addition of the three degrees representing the three spheres at the top of the Tree of Life: the ones not
assigned by the Golden Dawn itself since they were believed to
be outside the understanding of normal human beings. Crowley
claimed to have attained each of those degrees, and then set about
reforming the Golden Dawn system by making Thelemic adjust-
ments to all of the degree rituals, and by adding Asian mystical
practices to the curriculum: including Hatha Yoga and Buddhist
meditation methods and terminology.

---

14 "Isa" is the Arabic form of the name "Jesus," and thus "Isa the sufferer" is an
apt description but may not be what the Speaker intended. The Golden Dawn
mudra for Isis specifically refers to her as "mourning," and the characteristic
of the Book of the Law is overwhelmingly Egyptian. While Crowley believed
that Isa was a reference to Jesus, it is possible that he is mistaken in this regard.
It should also be noted that the preferred pronounciation of "Isis" is "ee-set" or
"ee-sa."

Egyptian Aeons

Even so, Thelema was designed to be a revolutionary spiritual movement, at once as grounded in science as in faith. It would overthrow Western ideas of spirituality, of morality and ethics, by replacing them with a worldview very similar in some respects to that of Buddhism. The death of the Ego is a familiar Buddhist concept; but at the same time Crowley calls for an end to the "limitation of the Mind by Reason." In Crowley's theology, as in some forms of Zen Buddhism, one must transcend both faith and reason in order to attain the highest illumination. Yet, paradoxically perhaps, both faith and reason are tools in the arsenal of the Thelemic magician.

How, then, is Crowley's system different from Buddhism?

In terms of Aeons, there are similarities. In Buddhist cosmology, there is the great measurement of time, or *mahakalpa*, which is divided into four *kalpas* or aeons. Each kalpa is extraordinarily long in terms of the human measurement of time and can take hundreds of thousands, or even millions or billions, of years to pass. The four basic kalpas are *Vivartakalpa* (the Aeon of evolution in which creation occurs), *Vivartasthayikalpa* (the Aeon of duration of evolution), *Samvartakalpa* (the Aeon of dissolution), and finally *Samvartasthayikalpa* (the Aeon of the duration of dissolution). These are similar in concept to the Hindu system of *yugas*, described below, and are based on an idea that creation begins in a perfect or pure state—"*in illo tempore*"—and then gradually disintegrates through the passage of time. But there is a judgemental aspect to both the Buddhist and Hindu concepts of the Aeons, and Crowley was not immune to this concept. He characterized the Aeon of Isis as considerably more pleasant than the Aeon of Osiris, and the Aeon of Horus as a kind of necessary corrective which would culminate in an Aeon of Maat that would wipe the slate clean and start all over again.

Yet while Crowley praised Hindu and Buddhist forms of meditation, yoga, and their corresponding methods of attainment of altered states of consciousness, and instructed his students to become proficient in all of these, he rejected many of the doctrines of Buddhism—as he had all previous manifestations of religion—as superceded by his own cultus. He had difficulty accepting the core concept of Buddhism, that all existence is sorrow and that sorrow proceeds from attachment. Crowley embraced life in all its forms and could not bring himself to refrain from tasting every flavor it offered. In this he could claim to have transcended attachment by indulging in all forms of sensation, accepting none and rejecting all in the process. Yet Crowley's approach to Buddhism—as it was to all previous forms of religion, spirituality and magic—was purely mechanical and pragmatic. The previous religions were viewed as possessing technologies that could be mastered, and not faiths to believe in. Certainly their theologies were rejected as obsolete and even dangerous. As his famous couplet states:

We place no reliance on virgin or pigeon
Our method is science, our aim is religion.

Paradoxically, however, Crowley frequently refers to Asian religious concepts in his writings and indicates that he values what they represent. He speaks of samadhi, anatta, advaita, the chakras, Kundalini, lingam and yoni, and other Buddhist and Hindu concepts with approval. He strives to attain samadhi, for instance, and reprimands himself for clinging to attachment. One could be forgiven for seeing in Crowley's diaries, his *Confessions*, and his letters a western man attempting to dominate eastern mystical practices. However, if this was all Crowley was—a New Age proto-hippie in search of enlightenment in the hashish parlors of Nepal or the yoga studios of midtown Manhattan—then we would not be interested in him. For Crowley, these Asian systems are just that: systems. Systems to be worked. Methods to be employed. For all his attraction to Asian ways of thought and culture—perhaps starting with his friendship with Alan Bennett, the Bhikhu Ananda Metteya and one of the first Englishmen to bring Buddhism to the United Kingdom—Crowley was still a western man. He did not take the vows of a Buddhist monk, as did his close friend Bennett. He did not work under a Hindu, Buddhist or Daoist teacher or guru. It was his mission to make these disparate forms of religious experience—Asian, European—work for him, become elements of his own philosophy. The "double-wanded" power that he wrote about so frequently could be construed as Crowley himself, uniting both Asian and European paths to God in a single system. This insistence on bringing together both hemispheres to produce a "syzygy"—to use the Valentinian Gnostic term (see below)—is typical of Crowley's mindset. Indeed, he even insists that Horus is really a twin: Ra-Hoor-Khuit and Hoor-par-kraat, Horus and Harpocrates, the Avenging Son and the Babe of Silence, respectively—as if unable (or simply unwilling) to commit entirely to a single identifiable entity.

The Aeon of Horus, then, is the Age of the Child. The child will try anything once, will test boundaries, will explore each sense to its fullest capacity. The infant does not *believe*: it has not yet reached that point where belief is necessary as a technique of avoiding confrontation with an unpleasant reality. The infant has no ideology to restrain it, to force it to choose one path over another. As Crowley himself writes in this regard:

> The child is not merely a symbol of growth, but of complete moral independence and innocence. We may then expect the New Aeon to release mankind from its pretence of altruism, its obsession of fear and its consciousness of sin. It will possess no consciousness of the purpose of its own existence. It will not be possible to persuade it that it should submit to incomprehensible standards; it will suffer from spasms of transitory passion; it will be absurdly sensitive to pain and suffer from meaningless terror; it will be utterly conscienceless, cruel, helpless, affectionate and ambitious, without knowing why; it will be incapable of reason, yet at the same time intuitively aware of truth.[15]

---

15 Aleister Crowley, *Confessions*, p. 399

But before we investigate the Aeon of Horus—and Frater Achad's Aeon of Maat—in greater detail, we must first understand what an Aeon might be.

The usual meaning of the term is that of a period of time, usually a very long period of time, but the precise length varies from culture to culture, from context to context. It's root comes from an ancient Greek word meaning "life" and is thus conceptually related to the Egyptian *ankh*.

In Gnosticism—the spiritual tradition embraced by many occultists of the nineteenth and early twentieth centuries in Europe and the Americas— the word aeon refers to an emanation (or characteristic) of God. Thus, the Gnostic aeons include such concepts as *Arche* ("the beginning") and *Proarche* ("before the beginning"), among other designations, with their associated references to Time. The term aeon can also be used to refer to the fullness of God perceived as an emanation itself.

Perhaps the closest in meaning and sense to Crowley's use of the term is that of the Valentinians, an early (2nd century CE) Gnostic sect for whom the aeons were created in male/female pairs called syzygies of which there were fifteen,[16] for a total of thirty aeons. It is important to realize that these aeons were emanations from God and therefore divine themselves, much in the way the Jewish mystics perceived the emanations that became the *sephirot* of the Tree of Life.

As they were emanations, their existence took place in Time. Until that process of emanation took place, God was silent and creation had not yet begun. (This is similar to the Indian tradition that the world was not created until Parvati seduced the otherwise

---

16 The number fifteen is suggestive. Grant understands it to be the number of female secretions known as *kalas*, which will be discussed later. Taken as a male/ female pair, however, we are at the point of understanding the central secret of the OTO as well as of western esotericism generally.

monastic and celibate Shiva. In this view, God has to be urged to create.)

When the emanations began, Time also began. This may explain the relationship between the concept of Aeon as "emanation" and Aeon as "period of time." They are linked, and one presumes the other. This is what we find in Crowley's schema of the Aeon of Isis, proceeded by the Aeon of Osiris and then to the present-day Aeon of Horus. They reflect periods of time (similar to the precession of the equinoxes that has given us the "Age of Aquarius") but they are also *personified* periods of time. They are periods in which the designated God or Emanation rules.

Specifically with Valentinianism, the Aeon known as Sophia ("wisdom") caused creation as we know it to take place. Sophia is feminine, the youngest of all the Aeons. She wished to know the Father and went on a quest to find God. She may be thought of as an analogous figure to that of the Shekinah in Jewish mysticism: a feminine figure removed from the Source of creation who is then reunited with God in a mystical marriage. In the Valentinian version, she became "divided"[17]: one aspect of Sophia was caught down in the lower realms, in physical creation, separated from God. Another aspect—her original self—remained in the upper realms. The two aspects were separated by something called "the Limit," which was a border between the fullness of God in the Pleroma and God's creation in the material world. This Limit[18] was personified

---

17 Cf: Liber AL I:29 "For I am divided for love's sake, for the chance of union" for a Thelemite analogue. In this case the speaker is the goddess Nuit.

18 From the Greek *horothetes*, the "giver of limit." Had it been Aramaic, however, the word *horos* would imply "father" as in *hor, horah*. There is some dispute on this issue. But it becomes more interesting in light of the fact that Crowley—in at least one place—confuses the Aeon of the Father with the Son. In his *Confessions*, in a chapter entitled "The Historical Conception on Which the Book of the Law is Based" he writes: "To recapitulate the historical basis of *The Book of the Law*, let me say that evolution (within human memory) shows three great steps: (1) the worship of the Mother, continually breeding by her own virtue; (2) the worship of the Son, reproducing himself by virtue of voluntary death and resurrection; (3) the worship of the Crowned and Conquering Child

by the Valentinian concept known as *Horos*, which some scholars believe is the Gnostic interpretation of the Egyptian god Horus: the same Horus who figures so prominently in the Book of the Law. Interestingly, this concept was enshrined in the very origin of the Egyptian Horus, as described in the Coffin Texts and as explained by Mordechai Gilula in an article published in the *Journal of Egyptian Archaeology*:

> Coffin Texts, Spell 148 narrates the birth of Horus. Having been delivered of her son, Isis addresses him in these words: *Bik s3.i Hr hms r·k m t3 pn n it·k Wsir m rn·k pw n bik hr(y) znbw hwt 'Imn-rn,* "O falcon, my son Horus, dwell in this land of your father Osiris in this your name of Falcon who is on (or 'above') the battlements of the mansion of Him-whose-name-is-hidden" (CT II, 221c-e). This is the actual naming of Horus who, until his birth, is referred to as Bik (219b).[19]

What is striking about this information is that Horus at his birth is associated with "the battlements of the mansion": i.e., he rests atop the border between the celestial and the earthly worlds, which is precisely what the Gnostic Horos represents: the Limit. In addition, the "mansion" referred to in the Coffin Text is that of "Him-whose-name-is-hidden," in other words, the Hidden God— the *Deus Absconditus* or Amun—which is the title of one of Ken-

---

(the Aeon announced by Aiwass and implied in His Word, Thelema." (Reproduced in Aleister Crowley, *Magick*, p. 703) In this case Crowley has once again emphasized the now-disproven chronology of matriarchy-patriarchy, but more importantly he states that the Aeon of Osiris was the Aeon of the Son (i.e., of Jesus and other slain gods; Osiris may be considered in the same category of dead and resurrected god, but in what way can Osiris be considered a "son"?). The concept of patriarchy would seem to have been replaced—in at least this single instance in Crowley's published work—by a filiarchy.

19 Mordechai Gilula, "An Egyptian Etymology of the Name of Horus" in the *Journal of Egyptian Archaeology*, p. 259, Vol. 68. (1982), pp. 259–265

neth Grant's studies of the Typhonian Current.[20] This "limit" may
be thought of in terms of Victor Turner's concept of liminality[21]: a
boundary between two modes or states of being, i.e. the sacred and
the profane. In this sense, Horus represents a liminal figure, one
who crosses over from one state to another and thus has some of the
characteristics of an initiator.

Further, the figure of Isis is cognate with a number of other
feminine deities who give birth without having been impregnated
in the usual way. The husband of Isis—Osiris—had been slain by
his brother Set and, according to one version of the legend, cut up
into fourteen pieces.[22] Isis went in search of those pieces and reas-
sembled her murdered husband in order to impregnate herself and
give birth to Horus. We recall that Mary, the Mother of Jesus, was
characterized as a virgin and the birth of Jesus a "virgin birth," a par-
thenogenesis. Her Son became the intermediary between humanity
and the invisible, hidden God, and was executed on a cross. The
symbol for the Gnostic Horos was also a cross, identified astro-
nomically as the place where the ecliptic and the zodiac meet. In the
Gnostic universe, the Aeon Sophia also attempted to give birth to a
child parthenogenically, i.e., without benefit of intercourse.

In India—locus of much of Grant's attention as well as considerable study by Crowley—we have another instance of creation
having been the result of abnormal conception. Shiva is portrayed
as a monastic living in the wild who spends most of his time in
meditation. He is aroused by his wife, Uma (or sometimes Parvati), to engage in sexual intercourse. However, Shiva has enormous
stamina and the couple engage in intercourse for millenia until the

---

20   Kenneth Grant, *Aleister Crowley and the Hidden God*, Friedrich Muller,
London, 1973.
21   See Victor Turner, *The Ritual Process: Structure and Anti-structure*. Aldine,
Chicago, 1969
22   The number is interesting, and recalls the number of the Stations of the
Cross in Roman Catholic churches which always number fourteen and which
represent the crucifixion, i.e., a slain God.

gods can take the sound of it no longer and distract Shiva so that he withdraws from Uma at the moment of ejaculation. Uma takes his seed—either in her mouth, or in her hand depending on the text—and impregnates herself with it, thus conceiving the created world.[23] This sounds suspiciously similar to the way in which Isis conceived Horus except that in the Egyptian version the husband of Isis has been murdered, while in the Indian version, Shiva is still very much alive. Both Isis and Uma, however, give birth to sons who may be considered avengers, Uma/Parvati giving birth to Skanda,[24] commander of the Devas in battle with the demon Taraka.

In India, where periods of time are inordinately huge, we are believed to be living in the *yuga*—or "age"—of Kali. This is a period of hundreds of thousands of years (according to some sources) which is said to have begun in the year 3102 BCE. It is the last of four yugas or ages: *Satya* yuga, *Dvapara* yuga, *Treta* yuga and *Kali* yuga. The Kali yuga is ruled by the demon Kali (not Kali the goddess), a symbol of strife and conflict, a fearsome creature sometimes depicted carrying a huge sword or other weapon.

Thus, even in India, an Aeon can be identified with a supernatural being. The names of the previous three yugas can be translated as Truth (Satya), Double (Dvapara), and Triple (Treta). These are designations that don't appear to have specific deities attached to them by name, but the ages themselves do reflect the actions of various deities in the relevant Indian texts, such as the Mahabharata. In the Indian system, the chronological order of the yugas reflects a degeneration of the quality of spirituality, from the perfect

---

23 This episode is discussed more fully in the author's *Tantric Temples: Eros and Magic in Java*, Ibis Press, Lake Worth (FL), 2011. For a more Crowleyan context, one should refer to his notes on The Paris Working (a series of occult rituals devoted to Jupiter which took place in that city from Dec 31, 1913 to Feb. 12, 1914) in which he writes: "The name of this Phallus is Thoth, Hermes or Ma. Ma is the god who seduced the Phallus away from the Yoni; hence the physical Universe. All worlds are excreta; they represent wasted semen."
24 A word which, incidentally, means "spilled seed."

age in Satya yuga to the increasingly vice-ridden ages of Dvapara and Treta, to the thoroughly corrupt Kali yuga: an age in which Lord Krishna has completely withdrawn himself from humanity. This is paralleled in the Buddhist cosmological system of the kalpas, mentioned above.

Obviously, Crowley's concept of the Aeons is slightly more optimistic and a lot simpler. There is no specific sense of an ongoing spiritual degradation or degeneration; there are, in fact, no clear moral judgments being made at all about the spiritual quality of each Aeon; only that the processes they represent are inevitable and inescapable. Although the Aeon of Horus is identified with warlike imagery, it also represents the flowering of individual freedom through the abandonment of ideas of sin and restriction. Rather than devolve from Aeon to Aeon, human potential is reawakened in different ways, leading to an ultimate perfection. Indeed, the concept of perfectibility—so crucial to understanding western alchemy with its processes of transformation—is central to Crowley's initiatory scheme. It is the Aeon of Horus that provides the avenues through which the human population in general (rather than an elitist handful of adepts) attains this perfection. In this very important sense, Crowley's philosophy is at odds with Asian ideas of kalpas and yugas. While Buddhism, for example, provides the techniques for a dedicated individual to attain nirvana and defeat the endless cycle of rebirth, it does not propose that all of humanity will—or can—do so at once, or during a single two-thousand-year period of time, but only through many millions of years with the assistance of Boddhisattvas: human beings who have attained all but the ultimate stage of complete enlightenment but who have taken a vow not to complete the initiatory path until all sentient beings have done so first. This type of self-sacrifice is presumably anathema in Thelema, a holdover from the previous Aeon of Osiris in which a god suffers for the sake of humanity.

Crowley's scheme does reflect some controversial anthropological theories current at the time, however, proposing that there was a matriarchal society that preceded a patriarchal one. This concept was popularized in the early 20th century by such authors as Marija Gimbutas, Robert Graves, and by Margaret Murray in her influential—though heavily-criticized—works on the alleged European witchcraft cult, *The God of the Witches* and *The Witch-Cult in Western Europe,* and even earlier by the Swiss anthropologist J. J. Bachofen in his *Myth, Religion and Mother Right* (1861). Thus, Crowley posits a matriarchal Aeon of Isis that precedes the more patriarchal Aeon of Osiris. This matriarchal-patriarchal chronology has been largely discredited. It should be noted that there is no real historical precedent for this as an Egyptological scheme, and it does not appear in any standard works by archaeologists or other specialists in Egyptian history and religion. It comes, instead, directly from the Book of the Law.

As mentioned above, however, the Book of the Law owes much to the initiatory system that produced Aleister Crowley, that of the Golden Dawn. In this system, one of the more important and revealing initiation rituals is the very first, the Neophyte initiation ritual. Within this ritual may be discovered elements of all the succeeding ones. It is here that Maat—as *Themaist,*[25] and as Hegemon—first appears. It is also here that one gets the first glimpse of

---

25 This word has given some newcomers to Thelema a headache, for it seems it can be found nowhere else except in Crowley's work. A tour through the usual search engines shows up nothing. However, the term Themaist appears in the Golden Dawn rituals with some associated detail, and in several different forms, thus illustrating once more how essential it is for an understanding of Thelema and of Crowley's *ouevre* to have access to the Golden Dawn material as a basis. See for instance Israel Regardie, *The Golden Dawn*, St Paul, Llewellyn, p. 339 "The Enterer of the Threshold": "Before the Face of the Gods in the 'Place of the Threshold' is the name of Hegemon, and She is the Goddess Thma-Ae-St having the following Coptic forms: Thma-Ae-St ... Thma-aesh ... Thmaa-ett..." etc., and for the same names written in Coptic script, see p. 352 Ibid. On page 375 of the same work we find four different versions of the name Thma-Est (this time) associated with the four letters of the Divine Name, YHVH with the further clarification "In the Equinox ceremony, the Hegemon is Air, Spirit, and the principal officer. She reconciles from East to West, and from North to South, and in a circular formulae."

what an Equinox of the Gods might entail, and of how the Crowleyan Aeons were conceived.

The Golden Dawn rituals were published by an initiate—Francis Israel Regardie (1907–1985)—who was an intimate of Aleister Crowley (during the period 1928-1932), and thus had a ring-side seat for much of what was taking place in the western occult world at the time. Regardie joined the Stella Matutina (a successor to the Golden Dawn that used its rituals) in 1934 and eventually (1937-1940) published their secret rituals and other material in a four-volume hardcover set, an action for which he was heavily criticized by members of the Order.

The Equinox ritual, published in Regardie's *magnum opus* includes a number of temple officers representing Egyptian gods, and the uttering of a password for the season. The ceremony is based on the point at which the days and nights are of equal length—the "equal night" or *equinox*—that takes place on the first day of spring and on the first day of autumn, the vernal and autumnal equinoxes respectively. According to the Golden Dawn ritual, a Word is changed from one equinox to the other with a corresponding change of Hierophant. This idea of an Equinox of the Gods, with a change of the guard as it were, and the creation or utterance of a new Word is central to the Book of the Law and to Crowley's entire Thelemic worldview.

The Book of the Law saga begins with Crowley and Rose Kelly (his first wife) visiting Cairo, Egypt in March of 1904. Sylphs appearing to the couple in the King's Chamber of the Great Pyramid on March 16, followed by a stream of cosmic messages to Rose during the next few days, convinced Crowley that Horus was in fact addressing him directly through Rose—his first Scarlet Woman. She demanded he "break all the rules" and helped him design an invocation of Horus that he successfully performed on the Spring Equinox, March 20. Now known as the "Supreme Ritual," this is the invocation that ushered in the New Aeon, the day when "the world was destroyed by fire," the "Equinox of the Gods." Rose's identification of the image of Horus (Ra-Hoor-Khuit) on the

Stele of Revealing (exhibit number 666 in the Boulaq Museum!) as the communicating Intelligence was the final proof for Crowley. Although the Book of the Law would not be received until weeks later, from April 8 to 10, Crowley imagines that the vernal equinox was the real starting point of the new Aeon of Horus. Of course, it is the day when—according to the Golden Dawn rubric—Horus takes over from Osiris as Hierophant, sitting on Osiris's throne in the East. In Crowley's case, what was performed ritualistically for decades within the temples of the Golden Dawn and its successors occurred in reality on March 20, 1904. If one reads the Book of the Law in this context, it all begins to make sense.

But it also raises many other questions. Many contemporary occultists, esotericists, and New Agers by definition believe that we are on the cusp of a new phase of human existence. From the rather vague concept of an Aquarian Age of peace and harmony to Doomsday predictions of mass extinction, what these ideas have in common is their lack of specific focus on the individual. Crowley's Cairo revelation—while similar in many respects to both the dreamy New Age version of a renewed humanity to the Doomsday predictions of war and violence—shifted the emphasis from general redemption and/or general holocaust to one of individual empowerment. Individual identity—and the survival of that identity—seems to be important in the Thelemic scheme of things. After all, as it is written in the Book of the Law: "Every man and every woman is a star." (AL I:3) Thelemites believe they have something to do with creating or facilitating the New Age. This may reflect the means through which the New Age was revealed to Crowley, i.e., in the context of a secret society of magicians rather than on a mountaintop in Sinai or a cave in Saudi Arabia. It took place in a rented apartment in the city of Cairo, and was revealed to an Englishman. There thus was no specifically ethnic context to the revelation. It was not Moses among the Jews, Jesus among the Jews, or Mohammed among the Arabs. It was not even Buddha among the Indians or Lao Ze among the Chinese. The revelation came out of nowhere, to two Brits on their honeymoon in Egypt. Certainly, the deities who spoke to Crowley were Egyptian, and Crowley was in Egypt. But Crowley himself was not Egyptian, nor was his wife. Why was the revelation not made to indigenous Egyptians? Was it because, as Muslims or Coptic Christians, they presumably would not have been open to such a message? The implication is that Crowley's prior exposure to Egyptian material in the context of the Golden Dawn initiations provided the appropriate channel for the Egyptian deities to manifest, and his presence in Cairo—in the shadow of the pyramids, the Sphinx, and the Valley of the Kings—made it that much easier. Further, the manifestation of the pre-Islamic Egyptian gods in the middle of Islamic Cairo would anticipate some of the more controversial statements in the Book of the Law concerning Jesus, Mary, and most especially Mohammed:

> I am in a secret fourfold word, the blasphemy against all gods of men.
> Curse them! Curse them! Curse them!
> With my Hawk's head I peck at the eyes of Jesus as he hangs upon the cross.
> I flap my wings in the face of Mohammed & blind him.
> With my claws I tear out the flesh of the Indian and the Buddhist, Mongol and Din.
> Bahlasti! Ompehda! I spit on your crapulous creeds.
> Let Mary inviolate be torn upon wheels: for her sake let all chaste women be utterly despised among you! (AL III: 49–55)

These sentiments were as revolting to Crowley at the time they were written as they may be to us today. The vitriol with which other faiths are attacked in these passages—in the mouth of Ra-Hoor-Khuit, the Avenging Son of Osiris—may reflect the tension that exists in Egypt over the presence of so many ancient, but pagan and polytheist, monuments in a predominantly Muslim country during an era of Islamic resurgence and identity conflict. Indeed,

at the time this book is being written we are informed of certain
radical Islamic groups in Egypt[26] that want the pyramids and other
ancient edifices destroyed in the name of the faith, in much the
same way the Taliban destroyed the famous Buddha statues of
Bamiyan, Afghanistan in early 2001. Thus, in the eyes of some radical religionists, it is time for a New Aeon of Islam with Arab characteristics to utterly remove all traces of pre-Islamic (i.e., non-Arab)
religion anywhere they can be found—something the followers of
the Prophet Muhammad attempted to do to the pyramids and the
Sphinx on their drive through Egypt in the mid-seventh century
CE. On November 17, 1997 there was a massacre of foreign tourists
at the Temple of Hatshepsut, coincidentally at the very site where
the Stele of Revealing was first discovered in 1858 by the French
archaeologist François Auguste Ferdinand Mariette. The master-
mind of the attack was Ayman Al-Zawahiri, at the time head of
the terrorist group Al-Gama'a al-Islamiyya and presently the leader
of Al-Qaeda after the death of Osama bin Laden. More recently,
there is the ongoing destruction of Timbuktu in Mali by Islamic
radicals in that country. One should remember that one of the first
official acts of the Prophet Muhammad was the destruction of the
pagan shrine in Mecca that had housed 360 idols, a shrine that he
transformed into the Ka'aba.

This is a pattern of behavior that, while repugnant to liberal-
minded lovers of religion and culture everywhere, is represented—
at least philosophically, or even ideologically—in the Book of the
Law with its insistence on the destruction of the old faiths. The
difference is only in the nature and character of the religion doing
the destruction, and the violence with which it is attended. While
there are no Thelemites charged with the destruction of Christian
or Buddhist iconography—even though the titular head of the

---

26 Leaders of Egypt's Salafi party as well as some more extreme members of
the Muslim Brotherhood, who began the call after the election of a Muslim
Brotherhood candidate to the Egyptian presidency after the ouster of Hosni
Mubarrak in 2012.

largest and most visible OTO organization is referred to as the "Caliph"(!)—the appearance of these lines in the Book of the Law conceivably could be used to signal just such a holocaust if Thelema and its followers ever get the upper hand in a country or region. We have seen how similar passages in the Qur'an have been used to justify violence against the Jews, for instance.

However, Crowley's entire life and writings are devoted to a syncretic approach to religion and spirituality—making use of whatever works from whatever culture or religion or occult practice is available—whereas the worldview of Islamic radicals is viciously opposed to such syncretism and insists on a purely Muslim-Arab interpretation of all spirituality. It is perhaps ironic that the world's most populous Muslim nation—Indonesia—is opposed to the monolithic, mono-cultural Arabist approach of Middle Eastern radicals and embraces its own multi-cultural—Hindu, Buddhist, indigenous—religious heritage as part of its national as well as its religious identity, demonstrating in real-time a syncretic approach that does not diminish their Islamic faith but seems instead to strengthen it.

While Crowley's scripture spoke of a new Aeon that would abrogate all previous Aeons, paradoxically it came in the mouths of ancient Egyptian gods. For Crowley, the Aeons are Egyptian. There is a certain element of cultural fetishism where ancient Egypt is concerned (especially among occultists and New Age followers), and in the west Egyptian crazes come and go. The American fascination with the traveling King Tut exhibit in 1976–1977 is one example, and occurred at the time that the Schlangekraft recension of the Necronomicon was being prepared for publication. So, while the New Aeon insists that "the rituals of the old time are black," (AL II:5) it appears that incorporation of elements from one of the oldest of old religions is exempt from this critique.

The surviving liturgies of ancient Egypt—the so-called Book of the Dead and the Coffin texts, for instance—are focused on the prime concern of the Egyptians: the survival of the individual identity after death. They are focused, therefore, on Osiris who represents the totality of that meme: a dead (murdered) and resurrected god whose example promised immortality for human beings—a clear prototype of the Christian scheme that would appear thousands of years later. Horus, while an extremely important player in these events and in his cosmic battle with Set, is not the focus of his own rite with the same intensity of purpose and elaboration of ritual as his father, Osiris ... at least, not in the surviving corpus of ancient Egyptian literature. If we characterize Aeons by their namesakes— the way the Gnostics did, and particularly the Valentinians with their Aeon of Jesus, Aeon of Sophia, etc—then it stands to reason that there would be an Aeon of Horus. However, the rituals and form of worship are missing, if they ever existed. (Imagine a cult of Saint Peter or Saint Paul, or even of Emperor Constantine who legitimized the worship of Jesus in the Roman Empire.) Horus was part of the cult of Osiris, was integral to it. What Crowley's scripture seems to indicate is that Horus is by now well and truly annoyed at this state of affairs and is intent on creating his own cultus, his own liturgies, his own heroic narrative. Furthermore, it is one that does not necessarily represent death and resurrection in the way we have all come to understand that concept but is another take on the human condition entirely. It is a credit to the Egyptians that they were able to provide enough raw material—real, imagined, or purely speculative based on bits and pieces of monuments, statues, and stelae—to fuel any dozen new religions, new approaches to spirituality, new techniques for becoming ... perfect.

For comparison, we may reference the revelation received by Joseph Smith on another Equinox of the Gods, the *autumnal* equinox of 1823 during which time he caught a glimpse of the golden plates on which were inscribed, in "Reformed Egyptian"(!), the Book of Mormon. This scripture claimed it was the record of a Jewish tribe that had escaped to North America at the time of the fall of Solomon's Temple to the Babylonians. Joseph Smith was not Jewish and he did not pretend to be Jewish. Smith, however, was a magician, and the discovery of the golden plates came as the result of magical ceremonies conducted at that site by Smith using essentially the same rituals and the same texts that would form part of the Golden Dawn curriculum fifty years later. The revelation came in North America—upper New York State, to be precise—and not in Israel or in Egypt. The parallels with Crowley's revelations could not be stronger: two Anglo-Saxon males—one born in America, the other in England, both magicians—receive spiritual revelations that command them to form new religious movements, yet neither are of the race (Jewish or Egyptian) from whom the revelations are received, and both involve Egyptian texts. In Smith's case, the golden tablets were written in "Reformed Egyptian" (which does not exist), and in Crowley's case the revelations began with the discovery of a stele written in Egyptian hieroglyphics (which had the obvious advantage of being written in genuine Egyptian).

Prior to the Smith "discovery" there was another Egyptian discovery, this time by the mysterious Count Cagliostro (1743–1795). Napoleon had invaded Egypt, and one of the earlier forms of the perennial Egypt craze had begun. In Cagliostro's case, it resulted in the Egyptian Rite of Freemasonry. Cagliostro claimed to be able to initiate into those mysteries and created his own Masonic lodges based on this "Egyptian" style, replete with ceremonial robes adorned with hieroglyphic embroidery. In the case of both Joseph Smith and his precursor, Cagliostro, there was safety in the fact that no one knew how to translate Egyptian hieroglyphics. The Rosetta Stone (discovered in 1799 and its code "broken" in 1822 at the earliest but not officially formalized until years later) had not yet yielded its treasures. People could say whatever they wished about the Egyptian writing and claim to be able to read and translate it.

By the time Crowley appeared on the scene, however, Egyptian writing had been decoded for eighty years and no one could claim special mystical knowledge about their contents. Egyptology had become a scientific field of study involving the new disciplines of linguistics, archaeology and anthropology, among others. Yet still the allure of the Egyptian religion remained, perhaps even stronger than before once it was revealed what all those hieroglyphics really said about gods, goddesses, rituals of embalming and promises of eternal life.

"Our method," Crowley wrote, "is science; our aim is religion."[27] The translations of the "Book of the Dead" by E. A. Wallis Budge (1895) and others only fueled this particular fire. Thus, while Crowley was a magician in the style of both Cagliostro and Joseph Smith, and claimed Masonic titles and lineages as did both of those men, he had the benefit of access to genuine information about Egypt and Egyptian religious beliefs and practices. He was, in a sense, their apotheosis. He created a new religion—as did Smith—and a new occult order, as did Cagliostro.

Of course, it did not begin and end with Egypt alone. Along the way, Crowley incorporated much Asian religion into his new cult and was advised—specifically in the Book of the Law—to include Afro-Caribbean rites and practices as well.[28] This New Aeon was to be all-inclusive and global in intellectual and spiritual reach. Is this one reason why a young Englishman on his honeymoon in Cairo was selected for this revelation and its new scripture, and not a native Egyptian?

An aspect of the Crowleyan Aeon of Horus that has not been the focus of much attention is the fact that Crowley's scripture and its associated ideas are essentially pagan, if by "pagan" we mean polytheist and even animist. The brunt of the attack of the Book of

27 The slogan "The Method of Science—The Aim of Religion" appears on the title page of every volume of Crowley's occult periodical, *The Equinox*.
28 AL I:37: "Also the mantras and spells; the obeah and the wanga; the work of the wand and the work of the sword; these he shall learn and teach." The terms *obeah* and *wanga* refer explicitly to Afro-Caribbean religions. This is a theme that was picked up and expanded by Grant in association with Michel Bertiaux, a Chicago-based magician who developed a system of magic out of elements of Haitian voudon. This will be discussed in greater detail in the chapters that follow. Crowley had access to some of this material through his friendship with the author and adventurer William Seabrook, but seems not to have made use of it. His interpretations of these words as published in his New Commentary are wholly implausible and ignore their obvious Afro-Caribbean meanings. Why?

the Law against other religions is concentrated on two of the three Abrahamic faiths: Christianity and Islam. Both Jesus and Mohammad are singled out for blinding. Mary "inviolate" (by which we understand the mother of Jesus) is to be torn on a wheel. The flesh of Hindus, Buddhists, "Mongol and Din," are to be torn out, but oddly not of their gods. (One imagines a list of all the Hindu gods to be blinded would have taken too many pages.) Crowley assumes "Mongol" to represent Confucianism,[29] and "Din" by an even longer stretch to represent Judaism. His "New Commentary" to the Book of the Law is explicit in his admiration for Islam as a manly religion, devoid of what he sees as the cringing, craven quality of a religion—Christianity—that is based on accepting the sacrifice of someone else for one's sins. But the blinding of Mohammad is as necessary as that of Jesus because both prophets had the wrong

---

29 Confucius (551–479 bce) was not a Mongol, but a Han Chinese of Shandong Province. "Mongol" may be a reference to the religion of the Mongolians which was an indigenous religion known as Tengriism (the worship of the Mongolian deity Tengri). One will find elements of Buddhism, shamanism, and even Islam among the Mongols at various times. But at the time the Book of the Law was written, most Mongols were Buddhists and had been for centuries; alongside their indigenous religion of Tengriism which was already dying out and would be gradually replaced by atheism, introduced by the Chinese at the time of the Communist revolution. Thus, there is no legitimate way to connect Confucius with the term Mongol. "Din" is an even more difficult reference. Crowley attempts to connect it to Judaism—the Hebrew word *din* meaning "judgment"—but the attribution is unworthy of him, as "Din" in this context is clearly referring to another race, i.e., "Mongol and Din." Another option is to assume that he heard the phrase incorrectly, and that "Mongol and Din" was really "Mongol ad-Din." *Ad-Din* is an Arabic term for "of the faith," and in this context the entire line may be read as "With my claws I tear out the flesh of the Indian and the Buddhist, Mongol ad-Din" or "...the flesh of the Indian and the Buddhist Mongol of the Faith." As the Mongols were Buddhists, it may be a reference to a specific cultus or a specific personage within the cultus. There were several Muslim military leaders with the surname "ad-Din" and "al-Din" who fought the Mongols during various invasions. This is, however, a fanciful suggestion but is more logical than assuming "Din" is a reference to the Jews. Even the Islamic leader prominent in Templar lore was named Saladin, which is a Europeanization of the name Salah ad-Din. .

"perspective." He further claims that Hinduism "metaphysically and mystically comprehensive enough to assure itself the possession of much truth, is in practice almost as superstitious and false as Christianity, a faith of slaves, liars and dastards. The same remarks apply roughly to Buddhism." Thus two important points are made: Hinduism and Buddhism both possess "much truth," but their practices are corrupt. This enables Crowley to retain Hindu and Buddhist rituals, techniques, and terminology within his Thelemic framework—essentially looting a burning building. His general respect for Islam enabled him to refer in correspondence to his successors as "Caliph," a term—from the Arabic *khalifah*— that represents the successors to the Prophet. Indeed, the initiation rituals of the OTO in the lower degrees use an Arab framework from the Crusader era as the template for the rites, much the way the Golden Dawn used an Egyptian temple motif. Thus, the Book of the Law seems to reserve its strongest opprobrium for Christianity: the religion in which Crowley was raised and which he despised for most of his life.

Another potential conflict arises, though, when one considers that the organization at the forefront of Thelema is the Ordo Templi Orientis, or Order of the Eastern Temple, an order identifying itself with the Knights Templar. The Templars were, of course, a Roman Catholic religious and military organization devoted to the capture of the Holy Land from Islamic control. One might think that this represents some accommodation with Christianity in a Thelemic context, but one would be mistaken. For the mythology of the Knights Templar characterizes it as a secret society with mystical elements that found itself opposed to mainstream Christianity and which, indeed, was suppressed by the Catholic Church in the fourteenth century, its famous Grand Master—Jacques de Molay—burned at the stake on false charges of heresy. Thus, identifying with the Templars does not make one a Christian in any normative sense of the word, and this would have appealed to Crowley as well as the libel associated with the Templars, that they engaged in deviant sexual practices as well as idol-worship. Crowley took as his Order name the word Baphomet, which was supposedly the name of the (non-Christian) idol that the Templars worshipped. While much scholarship recently has thrown many of these assumptions about the Order into serious doubt, the association of Templarism with the mysterious Orient of the Saracens, as well as with sexual mysticism, is the idea with which Thelema most closely identifies.

Since the Aeon of Horus is focused on individual responsibility and freedom—where "Every man and every woman is a star"—it stands to reason that its greatest foe would be Christianity, at least the Christianity as understood by Crowley himself, a faith of "slaves, liars and dastards." Indeed, as the "Beast 666" Crowley set himself in firm opposition to the organized Church by identifying with its Apocalyptic enemy and claiming as his bride the Whore of Babylon (in Crowley's numerology renamed "Babalon"). The anti-Christianity of Crowley is obsessive, and one wonders why he even bothered. The Book of the Law has an Egyptian framework and motif; it was received in Cairo, during sessions surrounded by the cry of the muezzin from the minarets of the city's fabled mosques. Why bother bringing up Christianity at all, much less incorporating some of its elements into the Thelemic *gestalt*? Because, to Crowley's way of thinking, Christianity represented the old and now discredited Aeon of Osiris *par excellence*. For such a well-traveled and intelligent man, it seems odd that he would think that way considering that most of the world—especially the world he traveled in, Asia and the Middle East—was not Christian and never had been Christian. How was the Aeon of Osiris represented in China, for instance? Or in India?

This may seem like nit-picking to some, but it goes to the heart of an important point, one that forms the essence of the Grant-Lovecraft theme that we will take up shortly. Crowley's interpretation of the Book of the Law could be described as—if not Eurocentric then—Occident-centric. It focuses almost exclusively on western ideas about religion and spirituality, and especially on resisting any form of Christianity. It is a kind of spiritual colonialism: the ransacking of Asian religions and practices for anything of value to a system that is almost wholly focused on defeating a western obsession with sin, restriction, and the cupidity of its priests. It is quite similar to the anxiety some in the west feel over the prophecies of Nostradamus and the Mayan calendar, signalling the End of Days and an Armageddon-like final conflict. There is no such sense of this in the East. There is no such anxiety there. Their calendars are different, their religious context entirely dissimilar, their fear of an Anti-Christ non-existent. The end of the world that the west fears so much may be just that: the end of the *western* world as we know it, but not of "*the* world" … not the "whole enchilada."

For the Aeon of Horus to be an Aeon for all it needs to respond to all, to the anxieties of all and to the desperation of all. It has to make as much sense in Beijing as in Boston, in Jakarta as in Jersey City, in Tokyo as in Tunbridge Wells. In Chennai as in Chicago.

The importance of the Kenneth Grant material, therefore, lies in his attempt to create a more global character for Thelema by incorporating as much Afro-Caribbean and Asian elements in far more detail and with much greater insight than was available in the Crowley writings. In some cases, this meant taking the work of former Crowley colleagues and initiates far more seriously than had been done previously. It also meant that Grant would delve into the darker aspects of Thelema and of what Thelema was insinuating: that at the heart of the cultus was an acknowledgement of humanity's more sinister roots, roots that went back to pre-Dynastic Egypt and even further, to the oldest civilization for which we have any texts at all: Sumer. Crowley's writings assumed that his readers already had a strong background in comparative religion, the rituals of the Golden Dawn, and the Kabbalah. In fact, today we have far greater access to this material than Crowley did. We have the ability to develop the basic themes of Thelema in much greater depth and with a wider scope. Grant was the first proponent of Thelema to recognize this, and while many Thelemites find his writings either obscure, or heretical, or both, his research and his dedication cannot be denied.

One of Grant's fixations concerns one of Crowley's most famous disciples and critics. While Crowley believed himself to be the prophet of this new, post-patriarchal Age, the Aeon of Horus, one of his followers went on to proclaim yet another Aeon, one that began only forty-four years after the start of the Aeon of Horus.

This was Charles Stansfeld Jones (1886–1950) —known as Frater Achad—and his Aeon was proclaimed the Aeon of Maat or sometimes Ma-Ion. At first glance, this would seem to be an inconsistency if not an impossibility. How could a new Aeon begin when the last one—Crowley's Aeon of Horus—had hardly begun? Yet, as we will soon discover, this concept does have precedents.

Ma-Ion

As mentioned, Jones was one of Crowley's most important disciples and followers, a man who Crowley once claimed was his "magical son," but who nevertheless broke with Crowley on several points of doctrine and who became a convert to Roman Catholicism, thus abandoning Thelema entirely.

According to Jones—known under a variety of occult names and mottoes but most famously as Frater Achad ("achad" being the Hebrew word for "one")—a new Aeon began on April 2, 1948 which he called the Aeon of Maat. This would be an era of peace and love, a kind of counterpoint to Crowley's Aeon of Horus which is characterized as the era of the Crowned and Conquering Child, a somewhat more warlike image.

Achad's Aeon of Maat was named after the Egyptian goddess of the Balance. The weight of the human heart after death was measured against a single feather of Maat's headress. If the heart weighed more than the feather, the soul was doomed to an unpleasant afterlife. Thus, Maat symbolized Justice as well as Equilibrium. One could say with some justification that Maat was a more likely icon of the "Age of Aquarius" than a warlike Horus, but that depends on how one views an implacable force of Justice!

The problem with the Maat proposal is that one does not know
with any certainty how long a Crowleyan Aeon is supposed to last.
If one takes the traditional Western view, an Aeon is roughly equivalent to an astrological Age which corresponds to the length of time
it takes for the Sun's passage through the vernal equinoctial point
in one of the zodiacal signs, a process known to astronomers as the
precession of the equinoxes. The precession of the equinoxes takes a
total of 25,800 years; thus, the length of time of each Age—corresponding to one of the 12 zodiacal signs—is about 2,150 years. This
idea that the Age corresponds to the equinoctial point is reflected
in many Thelemic writings and rituals, such as the title of Crowley's
own occult magazine, *The Equinox*, and his commentary on Liber
AL, *The Equinox of the Gods*.

However, Crowley postulated that the Aeon of Horus began in
1904—the year he received the Book of the Law. The problem with
this date is that it is not consistent with the scientific calculation
of some astronomers regarding the Age of Aquarius. They declare
it will not actually begin until about 2600 CE. On the other hand,
many astrologers and occultists believe otherwise—proposing start
dates ranging from the fifteenth century CE to a thousand years
from now. In this cluttered field, Crowley's "Aeon of Horus" is only
one among many contenders for the title of "current Age" and as
such is perhaps just as valid as any other.

But how long does a Crowleyan Aeon last?

This is also a contentious area, for Crowley himself was not
clear or consistent in his calculations. While he seemed inclined to
accept the standard precessional length of time of 2,000 to 2,150
years he was not committed to it. How could he be, when a 1904
start date was inconsistent with both astronomical *and* astrological
literature? In his various writings he admitted the possibility that an
Aeon could be measured in as little as a hundred years or as many
as thousands of years, stipulating that the experience of Time by the
gods was not identical to human conceptions.[30] Thus, when Frater

---

30 For instance, in the "Old Comment" to The Book of the Law in *The Equinox*, volume 1 number VII: "Following him will arise the Equinox of Ma, the

Achad proclaimed the Aeon of Maat as beginning only forty-four years after the beginning of the (presumably 2,150 year long) Aeon of Horus, there theoretically was some wiggle-room for insisting on such a shortened "Aeon." Crowley's adoption of the precessional idea of the Aeons or Ages seems pro forma, as if he accepted the 2,150 year "age" as a given rather than basing it on any specific revelation or calculation on his part, the way he accepted the matriarchal-patriarchal sequence long since abandoned by scholars. It is obvious to even the most cursory examination that two thousand years prior to 1904— i.e. the year 96 BCE—could not have been the beginning of the patriarchal Age of Osiris. The worship of Osiris had predated this period by thousands of years; further, the two thousand years prior to 96 BCE could by no stretch of the imagination be considered a matriarchal age.[31]

This was not Achad's only creative adjustment to the Kabbalistic system embraced by Crowley. He also went on to redesign the Tree of Life and to assign different variables to the spheres and to

---

Goddess of Justice, it may be a hundred or ten thousand years from now; for the Computation of Time is not here as There." He further explains this in his *Confessions* when he writes, "I may now point out that the reign of the Crowned and Conquering Child is limited in time by *The Book of the Law* itself. We learn that Horus will be in his turn succeeded by Thmaist, the Double-Wanded One; she who shall bring the candidates to full initiation, and though we know little of her peculiar characteristics, we know at least that her name is justice." p. 399. (*Thmaist* is a variant of Maat used by the Golden Dawn and not found elsewhere, presumably a conflation of *Themis*—the Greek goddess of Justice—and *Maat*. Crowley explicitly identifies Thmaist with Maat, for instance in his *The Book of Thoth* where he identifies the 'double-wanded one' of AL III:34 as " Maat, Themis, the Lady of the Balance": Aleister Crowley, *The Book of Thoth*, Samuel Weiser, York (ME), 1974, p. 25)

31 This is a point that has been brought up by J. Daniel Gunther in his *Initiation in the Aeon of the Child*, where he states "These views are irreconcilable with historical evidence, and should therefore be reconsidered. If we are truly to understand the progression of the Aeons, it must be done by studying empirical evidence, not by static adherence to traditional interpretations. The Method of Science cannot be hamstrung by the Aim of Religion." (Gunther, p. 166.) Gunther is a member of Crowley's A∴A∴ and is considered an expert on Thelema. This same attitude should be applied to all of the Crowley material, of course.

the paths on the Tree that connect the spheres. This type of tinkering could have important and far-reaching consequences for those brought up under the Golden Dawn, A∴A∴ and OTO systems for it rendered all sorts of symbolic language inoperative and inoperable.

The Tree of Life is the primary template for the magical system that came out of the Golden Dawn. The initiatory degrees are based on the spheres of the Tree, and the corresponding instructions in magic, kabbalah, astrology, Tarot, etc are all related to the paths that connect the spheres. Thus, any re-arranging of this scheme would be anathema and would possibly question the occult attainments (or at least their analysis and interpretation) of those who had already passed through the degree system to any extent. This would include Crowley himself, of course. Achad was aware of this problem, and mentioned it briefly in the Preface to his *The Egyptian Revival*.

> One great Authority, however, while admitting that many of the ideas are brilliant, says that he cannot accept this Reformed Order in the face of several hundred years of the old tradition, and maintains that the previous arrangement is the correct one.
>
> While I realize that great changes in the recognized Systems of Initiation in certain Orders might be necessary if the Reformed Order of the Paths were adopted, and while recognizing the importance of the Authority mentioned above, I still maintain that this New Arrangement is worthy of the most careful consideration and study.[32]

Thus, what Achad was doing was redesigning an entire occult system that had taken years to produce and fine-tune, and in which hundreds of people had already been initiated and trained. There is nothing inherently wrong with this, of course, for the Golden Dawn system itself was a novel approach towards uniting a great many occult ideas into one comprehensive methodology with a

---

32 Frater Achad, *The Egyptian Revival*, Samuel Weiser, NY, 1974

flexible and internally-consistent magical vocabulary. Even the idea of assigning the twenty-two Tarot Trumps to the twenty-two paths on the Tree of Life (corresponding to the twenty-two letters of the Hebrew alphabet) was no older than the nineteenth century, a legacy of the French occultist Eliphas Levi (of whom Crowley believed himself to be the reincarnation). The power and sheer beauty of that system to anyone who previously had spent years poring over the grimoires and other medieval instruction books on magic is obvious. Achad's ambition was to supplant that older framework: after all, it had been created decades before the Book of the Law revelation and thus could be considered inoperative in the Aeon of Horus.

This extended, evidently, even to the arrangement and chronology of the Aeons themselves. This type of creative interpretation of Crowley's *ouevre*—including various approaches to the Book of the Law—infuriated Crowley, and prompted him to issue a famous "Comment" on the Book of the Law in November, 1925 from his then-current base in Tunis in which he forbade completely any open discussion of the Book or its contents. He demanded that he and his writings be regarded as the sole authorities, and that each person should have recourse only to those two sources and to no other. (Of course, with Crowley's death in 1947, one of those two sources was rendered unavailable.)

So how could Achad's system be consistent in any way with that so painstakingly created by the Golden Dawn and developed further by Aleister Crowley, one of the Golden Dawn's most famous initiates? This question becomes more important once one realizes that Crowley considered Achad his "magical son," the one prophesied in the Book of the Law.[33] There have been a number of possible solutions put forward by defenders of Achad, but defending Achad is a thankless task. Aside from Grant and his followers,

---

33 The relevant citation is from AL I:54-56: "Change not as much as the style of a letter; for behold! thou, o prophet, shalt not behold all these mysteries hidden therein. The child of thy bowels, *he* shall behold them. Expect him not from the East, nor from the West; for from no expected house cometh that child. Aum!"

there has been very little interest in Achad's writings and theories from mainstream Thelemites. Achad is considered a heretic in the Crowley world, but before he went off the reservation he did make several important contributions to Thelema including an important "decoding" of a significant element of the Book of the Law, which is why he was anointed as Crowley's magical son.

Obviously, the most glaring challenge to Crowley's system was the inauguration of the Aeon of Maat in 1948, just five months after Crowley's death and two years before Achad's own demise. To a literal-minded observer, Achad's insistence on a new Aeon so soon after the birth of the previous one seems insane. Yet, the nature of Aeons is such that there is a precedent for Aeons running concurrently and the proof of this is in the Gnostic, Hindu and Kabbalistic traditions so beloved of Crowley himself.

In the first place, according to Valentinian Gnostic belief, the Aeons were created in male/female pairs, called syzygies. Thus every male Aeon had a female counterpart, a consort or spouse. Again, we must be clear that we are speaking of Aeons as divine emanations and not necessarily as lengths of time. However, the Egyptian Aeons as understood by Crowley were also divine emanations. They were, in fact, gods. What Achad did was to include the Aeon of Maat as a kind of "sister" or "spouse" of the Aeon of Horus, according to some commentators. While this seems at odds with Crowley's own writings on the subject it is nonetheless consistent with the Gnostic Aeons. Why should this matter? Because the main vehicle for regular Thelemic worship is something Crowley created called the Gnostic Mass.

Gnosticism is understood by many to be a mystical form of Christianity, incorporating many pagan and Greco-Egyptian elements. It is an "initiated" form of the religion, and Valentinian Gnosticism in particular fits this description quite capably. Crowley's development of the Gnostic Mass—based, he claimed, on a Divine Liturgy he witnessed in Moscow[34]—and its regular celebra-

---

34 The author, who has long personal experience of Eastern Orthodox liturgics and especially those of the Russian and Slavic churches, finds this explanation

tion by his Gnostic Catholic Church would seem to imply that he approved of Gnosticism, at least in some forms. The theme of the Aeons is central to most Gnostic writings, and he would have been familiar with the condemnations of it by the early Church Fathers (which fact alone would have made it attractive to Crowley).

In fact, the Gnostic teachings include a creation of the world through the illegitimate sexual desires of the last and youngest of the thirty Aeons, Sophia. It is this same Sophia that is called in some Gnostic texts "the Whore." In different versions of the myth, Sophia is either without a consort—that is, not a member of a syzygy—or abandons her consort in the search for God the Father. She learns that the Unbegotten One has Himself begotten the Pleroma (the rarified spiritual realm where all the Aeons reside), and she wishes to imitate him by producing an offspring herself, without benefit of intercourse. This she does, but it is a monster: in some texts described as an "abortion" or as a "miscarriage." In others as simply "the Void of Knowledge" and "the Shadow of the Name." It is her illicit desire to become a God that results in the creation of Anger, Fear, Despair and other negative impulses which in turn create the world as we know it.

In another version of the story—mentioned above—Sophia falls far and fast from grace and is nearly out of reach of the other Aeons until she comes up against the Limit (*horos*) and is saved. The Limit stands between the Pleroma—the fullness of God—and the outer darkness. She then becomes reunited with her Aeon and the Pleroma is right again. The problem is, however, that her unholy Intention caused a tremor in the Pleroma and it together with her Passion is cast into the outer darkness, i.e., the Pleroma rejects this

---

suspect as Crowley's Mass has much more in common with Roman Catholic versions of the same than with Orthodox forms. And, especially, no Orthodox clergyman or lay person would refer to the Divine Liturgy as a "Mass" which is strictly a Roman Catholic term from the Latin *missa*. (The Orthodox churches do not use Latin.) However, the apostolic succession of the Gnostic Catholic Church owes more to renegade Orthodox lineages than to normative Catholic ones.

new creature and it becomes the infamous "abortion" or "miscarriage" mentioned above, a "formless entity" that requires that the Limit be erected in order to keep it away from the Pleroma, and to preserve the Pleroma from its polluting aspect. It is this entity that becomes the created world.

Eventually—according to the Valentinian Gnosis—the other Aeons become worried over their newly-perceived vulnerability. In order to quiet the Aeons and restore some sense of harmony and stability, two new Aeons are created: Christos (male) and the Holy Spirit (female). Christos has the advantage of being able to operate on both sides of the Limit, both in the Pleroma and in the outer darkness. Eventually, the Aeon of Jesus is formed and this Aeon functions solely outside of the Pleroma.

It is interesting that the two qualities that cause the Limit to be erected in the first place are precisely Intention and Passion, corollaries of Will and Love, the two determining qualities of the Thelemic system.[35] Thus, as Kenneth Grant will later expound, there is an ontological link between the beliefs of Thelema concerning Will and Love on the one hand, and with the Outer Darkness on the other. And in the middle of them stand Sophia (the Whore) and the Limit (Horos, vide Horus).

These Aeons all run simultaneously, i.e., they are divine emanations and as such have no beginning or end save in the mind of God. There is a chronology which begins with an Ogdoad (an initial group of eight Aeons) and which is then augmented by ten Aeons and then twelve additional Aeons for the total of thirty original Aeons, thus suggesting a kind of sequential order but with no fixed length of time involved and, anyway, these Aeons exist in the Pleroma and are inaccessible by mere mortals. The Aeons of Christos and Jesus, however, *do* impact directly on the created

---

35   As represented in the famous Thelemic greeting, "Do what thou wilt shall be the whole of the Law" and its response, "Love is the law, love under will," both taken from the Book of the Law.

world—the world formed from the monstrous stillbirth of Sophia. This world, composed of negative elements from Sophia's reckless quest for equality with God, is in need of Aeonic assistance and that is why—according to the Valentinians—Christos, the Holy Spirit, and Jesus were formed in order to bring order into the realm beyond the Pleroma.

A complete discussion of the Gnostic Aeons is far beyond the scope of this book and interested readers are urged to consult any of the standard works on Gnosticism, perhaps starting with Hans Jonas and his *The Gnostic Religion*, which covers the Valentinian Gnosis in some detail. There has been much new work done on the Valentinians (and other Gnostic groups) since the Jonas book was first published but access to a good university library or database is usually required. There will be further discussion of the Aeons in the chapters that follow, but they will be based on the information already given.

What we should take away from this chapter, however, is the fact that the Gnostics were the first to talk about Aeons in an esoteric sense, and to do so in a very detailed and complex manner reminiscent of the later books of the Jewish mystics and particularly of the Kabbalah. The Gnostics understood the Aeons in both senses of a length of time that may not be measurable in human terms, and as the emanation of a particular deity or divine characteristic. To apply this reasoning to the Crowleyan Aeon of Horus we may say—in the spirit of Gnosticism—that such an Aeon would have the characteristics of Horus (however they may be described) as well as a specific (but probably unknowable) length of time or chronology. And, most importantly, from the best available data on record we know that while the Gnostic Aeons were created in a kind of chronological order, in the end they all ran *concurrently*. They all existed at the same time and not in any kind of consecutive order with one ending as another began. This could be applied to the debate over the Aeon of Horus versus the Aeon of Maat; there does not need to be a "versus" at all.

But if that alone was not enough to allow an Aeon of Maat to run concurrently with the Aeon of Horus, there was yet another option.

In the Indian system of yugas or great ages we are told that they sometimes "overlapped" as in this citation from the *Bhagavata-purana*:

> Suta Gosvami said: when the second yuga overlapped the third, the great sage [Vyasadeva] was born to Parasara in the womb of Satyavati, the daughter of Vasu." (*Bhagavata-purana*, 1.4.14)

Thus there is a precedent, even in Hinduism, for overlapping yugas so why not for overlapping Aeons, their cognates? To be sure there are several different calculations for the lengths of the respective yugas; yet this implies (a) they are not based on the precession of the equinoxes through the astrological signs which most experts agree are of regular length and (b) that the yuga of one system will necessarily overlap the yuga of another, which is not a bad thing, but which gives rise to further calculations and refinements of the chronological system. And, according to the citation above, great things can happen when yugas (or Aeons) overlap.

The final approach that could be taken with respect to the Aeons is a purely Kabbalistic one, but one of which Crowley does not seem to have been aware. This system is elaborated in the *Sefer ha-Temunah* or the "Book of the Image," a text that is usually dated to the thirteenth century. The "image" of the title refers to the shape of the Hebrew letters which were believed to contain certain secrets. For our purposes, however, the other value of the book is in its discussion of the *shemittot* (sing. *shemitta*) the "cosmic cycles" of the encoded Torah.

Years were counted in multiples of seven, which were themselves multiplied by seven, so that a cycle consisted of 7 x 7 years or 49 years in total. The next year—the fiftieth year—was a "jubilee" year, a year in which the sins and errors of the previous 49 years were erased and the slate cleaned and the cycle begun anew.[36] This was one cycle, or *shemitta*.

Using this framework as a starting point, Bible and Kabbalah scholars have tried to ascertain the age of the universe. Each cycle of 7,000 (7 x 20 x 50) years is considered a Kabbalistic "age" and is related to one of the seven lower *sefirot* on the Tree of Life. The number 7,000 comes from a line in the Talmud[37] that states the world will exist for 6,000 years and that for the 1,000 years thereafter it shall be "desolate." According to some Kabbalists we are living in the second age, that of *Gevurah* or "Severity."

Using the Jubilee formula, then, 7,000 years times 7 would equal 49,000 years which would be the age of the universe. If we are living in the second cycle, that would imply that Adam was created somewhere around 7,000 years ago (depending on where we are in the second cycle, the beginning, middle, or the end).

However, using a citation from the *Midrash*, "A thousand years in your sight are but as yesterday" it is indicated that a thousand human years equals only one Divine day, thus the ensuing calculations would reveal an age of the universe as something closer to 15 billion years (if we are living in the last Kabbalistic age) which—coincidentally—matches the latest scientific estimates of the age of the universe.

There are two implications pertinent to this study that can be found in the *Sefer ha-Temunah*. The first is that Kabbalistic ages can be identified by a series of sefirotic references. Thus, the very first year of the cycle is named after Chesed—the first of the seven sefirot below the Abyss on the Tree of Life and the only ones used for these calculations by the rabbis—which also gives its name to the entire first cycle of 7,000 years, and that the second year would be Gevurah, then Tiferet, etc. Thus, year two is the year Gevurah of the greater cycle year Chesed. But, of course, the interlocking ages

---

36 There is some debate over whether the Jubilee year is the 49th year or the 50th year.

37 Sanhedrin, 97A.

do not end there and can be continued indefinitely down to the smallest unit of time.

This system is mirrored in the table of astrological hours used by ceremonial magicians, in which the first hour of Sunday—for instance—would be the hour of the Sun, the first hour of Monday would be the hour of the Moon, and so on for the seven days and the seven philosophical planets. These planetary hours are equivalent to the sefirotic attributes, for Chesed is considered the sphere of Jupiter (and hence of Thursday), Gevurah of Mars (and Tuesday), Tiferet of the Sun (and Sunday), etc. One could then just as easily take the magician's astrological hours and expand them to include years, multiples of years, etc. to arrive at corresponding planetary Aeons.

The point of this exercise is that time periods have subsets, and that these subsets have the same qualities as the various time periods themselves albeit with modifications. For example, the period Sun in the greater period Saturn (for instance) would not have the same quality of action as the period Saturn in the greater period Saturn, or the period Saturn in the greater period Sun. This system is actually used by Vedic (Indian) astrologers in their calculation method known as *antardasas*.

Using this as a theory, could there be an Aeon of Maat *within* the greater Aeon of Horus, as a subset of Horus?

As complicated—perhaps unnecessarily complicated—as all this sounds, we should be reminded of a statement by Crowley himself, when he writes:

> … Aiwass, uttering the word Thelema (with all its implications), destroys completely the formula of the Dying God. Thelema implies not merely a new religion, but a new cosmology, a new philosophy, a new ethics. It co-ordinates the disconnected discoveries of science, from physics to psychology, into a coherent and consistent system. Its scope is so vast that it is impossible even to hint at the universality of its application. But the whole

of my work, from the moment of its utterance, illustrates some phase of its potentiality, and the story of my life itself from this time on is no more than a record of my reactions to it.[38]

Thus, a new cosmology is required, and it is entirely possible that this new cosmology would have at its heart a re-interpretation of all that has been written concerning the Aeons: their nature, their number, their chronological order, and their periods of time. One stands in awe at the scope of Crowley's project for this New Aeon, and at the same time one measures it against the words of one of his contemporaries:

> The sciences, each straining in its own direction, have hitherto harmed us little; but some day the piecing together of dissoci-ated knowledge will open up such terrifying vistas of reality, and of our frightful position therein, that we shall either go mad from the revelation or flee from the deadly light into the peace and safety of a new dark age.[39]

Thus, Lovecraft himself was aware of the possibility of uniting the same sciences—Crowley's "disconnected discoveries" and Love-craft's "dissociated knowledge"—and was terrified that it would one day occur, and that the Aeon of Horus would become a "new dark age."

Which leads us to the second implication contained within the *Sefer ha-Temunah* and in the deliberations of its sages: the idea that the world has already been created and destroyed several times over. The seventh 1,000 year period of each cycle is a time of "desolation" in which all life of the previous 6,000 years is wiped out. Depending on where we are in the great scheme of things—with experts offer-ing opinions anywhere from the second cycle to the seventh—the

---

38 Crowley, *Confessions*, p. 398
39 H. P. Lovecraft, "The Call of Cthulhu."

world may have been destroyed at least once, and as many as six times already. This gives rise to the possibility that the 2,000 year cycle known to the astrologers could be replaced by the 7,000 year cycle known to the Kabbalists, meaning that the Aeon of Osiris (which ended, according to Crowley, in 1904) actually began in 5,096 BCE, and that the Aeon of Isis began in 12,096 BCE. Using these somewhat larger values gives us the historic coordination we need, for 5,096 BCE places us much earlier than pre-Dynastic Egypt and allows for the possibility that an Aeon of Osiris began at that time, and that there was a pre-historic matriarchal age beginning in 12,096 BCE for which there is no written record but for which circumstantial evidence in the form of goddess statues and the like may be offered to support it.[40]

In any event, the Typhonian understanding of the Aeons is much closer to the Gnostic concept. Each Aeon is an emanation, a manifestation of a particular God, and they all exist concurrently as separate forms of awareness, of consciousness. One could go to great lengths to try to "prove" Achad's system—the above few paragraphs give an idea as to how much calculation and speculation would be involved—but to Grant this is not necessary. The mere fact that we have imagined an Aeon of Maat is sufficient to claim its existence. To adhere to the idea of the Aeon of Horus as being exclusive to this time and place ignores the essential nature of the gods themselves as being beyond all considerations of space and time. If a middle-aged white man can sit in an ashram in Goa and commune with Kali, or a teen-aged girl can stand naked in a circle and draw down the Moon, then it is probably safe to say that Maat

---

40   Using this scheme, the Aeon of Horus began in 1904 and the first sub-period of Horus lasted 42 years before entering the "desolation" phase from 1946-1952 during which time Frater Achad proclaimed the Aeon of Maat. This would have been the Maat sub-period of the greater Horus period. Interestingly, 1946 plus 49 years gives us the year 2001, the year when everyone says "the world changed."

can be approached and her influence experienced in the present Age.

Grant's anxiety—as expressed in *Nightside of Eden* and in his other works—is that the Earth is being infiltrated by a race of extraterrestrial beings who will cause tremendous changes to take place in our world. This statement is not to be taken quite as literally as it appears, for the "Earth" can be taken to mean our current level of conscious awareness, and extraterrestrial would mean simply "not of this current level of conscious awareness." But the potential for danger is there, and Grant's work—like Lovecraft's—is an attempt to warn us of the impending (potentially dramatic) alterations in our physical, mental and emotional states due to powerful influences from "outside." This "extraterrestrial" race has already been here, already made itself known (and hence the antiquity of the Typhonian Tradition, according to Grant), and is returning to the planet in greater numbers than before and with an agenda that only the adepts would be able to divine. This concept is emphasized in the Schlangekraft recension of the Necronomicon, where it is stated:

> … for thou can never know the Seasons of Times of the Ancient Ones, even though thou can tell their Seasons upon the Earth by the rules I have already instructed thee to compute; for their Times and Seasons Outside run uneven and strange to our minds, for are they not the Computors of All Time? Did They not set Time in its Place?[41]

Thus, once again it can be shown that the Necronomicon, Crowley, and Grant are in agreement on certain specific points of interest concerning the advent of the New Aeon. The idea that the human race is not the first on the planet is one that has been picked up and developed into an entire mythos by H. P. Lovecraft and expanded upon by Kenneth Grant. It is linked to the Lovecraftian idea of the

---

41   Simon, *Necronomicon*, p. 217.

Great Old Ones, gods—or alien creatures, or both—who came to
the earth in "aeons past" and who will return again. The recurring of
the Aeon of the Great Old Ones is cognate with Crowley's recurring Aeons of the Egyptian gods. It is also connected to another
Lovecraftian theme, the idea that there are people on earth who
are in secret communication, usually telepathically but also through
ritual, with the Great Old Ones and are preparing the way for their
return.

> *Let my servants be few & secret: they shall rule the many & the
> known.*[42]

---

42 AL I:10

CHAPTER TWO

GODS, THE BEAST, AND MEN

A church of magic does not exist.
—Emile Durkheim, *The Elementary Forms of the*
Religious Life, p. 43 (emphasis in original)

ONE HESITATES TO REFUTE or contradict the father of modern sociology, but at the time the above classic was published—in 1912—there already *was* a church of magic. In fact, there were several. Durkheim's statement reflects his understanding that magic is not amenable to rituals of group worship, since the approach to the sacred that is undertaken by the magician is a "delicate operation that requires precautions and a more or less complicated initiation ..."[43] This did not stop the French magicians Jules Doinel (1842–1903) from creating (in 1890) and Papus (Gerard Encausse, 1865–1916) from joining (in 1892) a "Gnostic Catholic Church"; nor did it stop Crowley from using a version of the Gnostic Catholic Church as his vehicle for Thelema, writing a Gnostic Mass in 1913 (a year after Durkheim's work was published). Whether or not such a church is an effective tool for magic and the goals of magic remains to be seen, however. Anyone witnessing some of the celebrations of the Mass by members of the Gnostic Catholic Church at various times over the previous five decades or so would have recognized obvious differences in style from those of normative Christian denominations. It may be argued that magicians are not priests by nature—they are individual, solitary persons devoted more to their own spiritual development than to the spirituality of a group. Further, a magician's approach to a public, communal ritual may leave something to be desired, particularly when the magician takes as his or her template an established ritual like the Catholic Mass

---

43 Durkheim (1912) p. 39

with nearly two thousand years of history behind it and its celebration and then proceeds to alter it considerably to suit what can only
be described as an opposing theological *weltanschauung*. At best,
you have an imitation of the original, a kind of "cover" version that
may leave one yearning nostalgically for the original. At worst, the
results can range from the scandalous to the hilarious ... to the just
plain sad. Given the options, one easily prefers the scandalous.

The scandalous might have been Crowley's intent in the early
days of the twentieth century but now, in the early days of the
twenty-first century, what Crowley saw as challenging and provocative hardly constitutes cause for censorship or suppression (except
perhaps by the religious Right, but they are easily inflamed). Crowley wanted to institutionalize (and make popularly accessible) the
religious and philosophical precepts underpinning his new faith of
Thelema. He saw the Mass—and the Gnostic Catholic Church—as
the vehicle for doing this, much in the way the Catholic Mass can
be seen as the vehicle for proclaiming and celebrating the doctrines
and theology of Roman Catholicism. But Crowley was a magician,
first and foremost. His teachings are couched in magical language
and magical references. Virtually all of his writings were designed
for those belonging to one or both of his most important magical
societies, the A∴A∴ and the OTO, neither of which were designed
with communities of worshippers in mind but which are predicated
on the idea of individual (not group) attainment.

His theology is easily summed up in the familiar "Do what thou
wilt shall be the whole of the Law" and "Love is the law, love under
will." It was antinomian, authoritarian, and transgressive. After one
exhorts everyone to do their will, that every man and every woman
is a star, there is not much else to the theology or the doctrine. The
core of Thelema is in the work itself, the Great Work of uniting
oneself with one's Holy Guardian Angel (to use the Golden Dawn
and A∴A∴ terminology), and that is an individual and not a group
endeavor.[44]

---

44 There are other attainments beyond the Knowledge and Conversation of
the HGA, and they will be discussed as they come up.

The famous Biblical Ten Commandments—handed down to Moses from God—consists of three commandments concerning sins against God and seven commandments prohibiting sin against the community. There is no identification of sins against one's self. It is as if God and community were all that mattered spiritually; that if one abides by the rules of God and family then one has already avoided sin against one's self. What Thelema does is question that assumption: in other words, is it possible to sin against one's self? The Thelemic answer is a definite "yes." If one obeys the commandments concerning God and community to the detriment of one's self then one is sinning against one's self. What Crowley does is turn the assumptions implicit in the Abrahamic religions on their head by insisting that the individual matters more than the community or, to be more precise, that the salvation or preservation of the community is dependent upon the spiritual growth of its component individuals. This, of course, is the magical worldview and always has been, ever since the bifurcation between the needs of the individual and the state took place sometime in misty antiquity.[45] What Crowley had attempted to do was to codify the magical worldview as a religious worldview, applicable to all.

Thus the tension between the magical worldview and the requirements of an organized church contributes to confusion concerning the liturgics. Crowley's religion has sexual mysteries at its heart, and Crowley—as a magician—was devoted to its prosyletizing. He understood the sacrament of the Mass—and most especially the rite of transubstantiation—as a Gnostic rite of transformation, and it can be argued that this is so, or certainly can be interpreted that way. The problem remains, however, how to teach this concept to the general public if it has no background in religious studies, Gnosticism, or Tantrism, much less Kabbalah or ceremonial magic?

---

45 Evidence for this may be found in the Sumerian *Maqlu* text, the "Burning" grimoire that consists of spells against "witches" which may be taken to mean independent spiritual experts who work on behalf of individuals—for love, money, power, etc—rather than for the group. An abbreviated form of this text appears in the Schlangekraft recension of the Necronomicon.

A further difficulty is raised by the unitary form of the Catholic Mass and its single priest-celebrant. This dynamic was transformed by the Crowley church into a dual priesthood of a man and a woman, a priest and a priestess. On a very basic liturgical level this presents problems in conceptualization, but most importantly, in the identification of two individuals with the appropriate transformative Power which must take place simultaneously and in harmony. There are other, more easily organized, rituals that involve male and female participants which could have been used instead (or simply invented), but it was Crowley's intention to use the Catholic Mass as the basic structure, possibly with a view towards forcing the public to understand the sexual component of a rite with which they were already familiar—albeit in a different context—and thus providing a kind of legitimacy of lineage, much in the same way pagan shrines in Europe were converted into Catholic holy places by the building of churches on the same spots.

All of this, however, is predicated upon Crowley's religion and its understanding of the nature of the Gods.

Central to most descriptions of religions is this concept of a God or Gods. While the word "religion" is relatively new, and is in fact problematic in some cultures which do not recognize this artificial distinction between spirituality and other areas of culture, we can assume for the sake of this essay that religions (popularly understood) rely upon the existence of some kind of supernatural Power, Creator or Cosmic Judge we call a God.

One of the most bewildering aspects of Thelema to outsiders is the near-chaotic assembly of gods, goddesses and techniques from religious traditions spanning the globe and the centuries. We have seen some of this in the previous chapter. While the Book of the Law is focused on Egyptian gods, by the time one is finished with even a cursory look at Crowley's writings, one realizes that Egypt is not the only cultural touchstone for the movement.[46]

---

46 Crowley's approach can be characterized as *bricolage*, after its use as a term of art in cultural studies and anthropology, notably by Claude Levi-Strauss (*The*

Crowley's own self-identification with the Beast of the Book of Revelation—and his *soror mystica* as the Scarlet Woman or Whore of Babylon (Babalon, to use his spelling)—seems at first glance to be out of synch with the rest of his philosophy. After all, the Beast 666 and the Whore of Babylon are characters specific to the Christian Bible. How does one rectify the Biblical personalities with ancient Egyptian or Sumerian archetypes?

Crowley's early childhood was spent in the somewhat lethal embrace of a Christian sect called the Plymouth Brethren. In fact, he attended schools run by the Brethren for most of his childhood and adolescence, only escaping the denomination by the time he enrolled at Trinity College, Cambridge in 1895. As a child, his mother would refer to him as "the Beast" with its obvious Biblical connotations and it seems Crowley took the appelation to heart, particularly as he got older and began to question Christianity. He never abandoned the Beast nomenclature, however, for he seemed to feel that this was an aspect of his identity—not only as a human being, as his mother's son, but—as a magician and a prophet of the New Age. Thus, in order to overthrow the Old Age he came to identify himself with its anti-god, the Beast of Revelation. This would predate any exposure Crowley had to the rich fabric of Egyptian spirituality.

It was most likely his introduction to the Golden Dawn that gave Crowley his background in Egyptian religion and in the names of their gods. As we have seen in the previous chapter, he took those names to heart and they resurfaced in his Book of the Law and in

---

Savage Mind, 1962). This refers to a method of taking whatever is useful at the time from whatever source and building a system or a philosophy out of the assembled parts. Anyone reading Crowley's vast published work will readily come to the conclusion that Crowley indeed was a *bricoleur par excellence*. Of course, central to the ritual environment of the Golden Dawn—the occult society that gave Crowley his first initiations—was the doctrine of correspondences, in which disparate religious and spiritual elements were given equivalence through the medium of the Kabbalistic Tree of Life. This, in a sense, was *a systematized form of* bricolage.

the Holy Books: names such as Hoor-paar-kraat, Ra-hoor-khuit and Thma-est (which spellings are not found in popular works on Egyptology) make their way into Crowley's religion, as well as the concept of the Equinox of the Gods and the associated rotation of its divine officers throughout the year.

But he also added a liberal dose of Greek and Roman concepts as well as some Asian ideas. While the Golden Dawn had a few Asian-inspired documents—such as instructions concerning the *tattwas* (Indian elemental forms) and some basic yoga exercises—it was rather more focused on western esoterica than "Orientalia." This may be due to the example of the Theosophical Society, which began as a repository of western occult and hermetic ideas but which rapidly switched its focus to India and to Buddhism and indigenous Indian religions (normally grouped under the rubric "Hinduism"). Blavatsky's growing obsession with India and Tibet changed the characteristics of the Theosophical Society to such an extent that there was really very little room for Hermetica or western esoterica in general. Kabbalah was ignored, as was ceremonial magic. These were areas that were picked up and developed to a greater degree by the Golden Dawn and its Masonic creators, thus filling a void that had been created by the Theosophical Society's abandonment of its western esoteric roots.

Crowley, therefore, represented a bridge between both societies. While his initiations and instruction in spirituality began with the Golden Dawn, and he never really left the embrace of its initiatic structure,[47] he did absorb some of the Asian techniques that were the focus of the Theosophical Society. He advocated practices such as *pranayama* (breath control), *asana* (yoga postures), and the attainment of *samadhi* (a higher state of consciousness reached through intensive meditation, analogous to a non-dualist state of awareness in which subject and object are one).[48] He recognized *samadhi* as an

---

47 He used the Golden Dawn grade system as the template for his own A∴A∴. Both degree systems are based on a version of the Tree of Life of the Kabbalists.
48 Crowley's instructions to his disciples on these techniques form the substance of his *Book Four* which is completely focused on yoga and which—in

essential element of his own personal development and encouraged the pursuit of this enlightened state of consciousness among his followers.[49]

But this did not mean that he was a Buddhist or a "Hindu" by any stretch of the imagination.[50] In fact, he broke with his good friend Alan Bennett (the Bhikku Ananda Metteya) over this issue. He was more than willing to take what he could from the super-market of religious ideas, but he was not loyal to any one brand. In this, perhaps, he was typical of the stereotypical New Ager, who is a spiritual dilettante and who picks over ancient religious tradi-tions like a shopper in a fruit and vegetable stand ... but with one important and crucial difference: unlike many of today's New Age spiritual seekers, Crowley did not skim the surfaces of the traditions he investigated but dived in completely. He had to know and to experience what these traditions offered, and he subjected himself to strenuous physical and intellectual pursuit of this knowledge. The fact that he was at leisure for much of his early life, due to an inheri-tance from his father's estate, contributed to his ability to wander the world and devote himself to spiritual pursuits. He would incor-porate significant amounts of these traditions into his own occult orders and into his religion of Thelema, and while we may argue

---

Crowley's system—became an important adjunct to the more western ceremo-nial practices of the Golden Dawn. Along with *Book Four* were his *Eight Lectures on Yoga* in which he develops these ideas even more specifically. In a sense, the yogic methods were the missing element in the grimoires which simply gave the rituals as recipes to be followed by those already trained in yoga (or in some cor-responding form of mental and physiological control represented in the western, European systems by fasting, celibacy, prayer, etc.).

49 This may be due to the emphasis put on samadhi in *The Yoga Aphorisms of Patanjali*, a Hindu text of which Crowley was fond and which he recommended to his followers. It is also an essential aspect of Buddhist meditation, and refer-ences to it can be found in the Sikh religion as well.

50 This excerpt from Crowley's *Book Four* is illustrative of his contempt for Buddhism: "The vulgarism and provincialism of the Buddhist canon is infinitely repulsive to all nice minds; and the attempt to use the terms of an ego-centric philosophy to explain the details of a psychology whose principle doctrine is the denial of the ego, was the work of a mischievous idiot." (p. 80, footnote)

about his selection process or question the assumptions upon which some of the intellectual material is based, there can be no doubt that there was a strong element of sincerity in Crowley's approach.

Crowley *believed* in his own system, in his role as a prophet, and in the Book of the Law. There can be no other explanation for his life's work than this. Thus, in order to comprehend the ramifications and implications of Thelema—particularly as represented in the Typhonian Tradition—we need to understand Crowley's concept of the Gods.

Apocalypse Now

As mentioned, Crowley's first exposure to religion was in a Christian fundamentalist household, whose members belonged to the sect known as the Plymouth Brethren. Like many Protestant denominations with an extreme view of scripture, this one placed an emphasis on the Book of Revelation, also known as the Apocalypse. This is a controversial text, dealing with the End of Days and the Final Judgement. It is couched in esoteric symbolism, more than any other Biblical text, and defies easy interpretation, but it is within its pages that we come across such famous concepts as the "number of the Beast" which is 666, as well as the Beast himself, and the Whore of Babylon. It is a book that foretells the fall of Rome and/or Jerusalem, and a final, cosmic battle between the forces of Light and Darkness. There are dragons, trumpets, and angels galore and it is beyond the scope of this (or most any) book to give a full and coherent description of its contents or to analyze its meaning.[51] Rather, we shall focus on the handful of elements that meant most to Crowley and which surfaced so prominently in his cultus.

The Book of Revelation virtually overshadows the rest of the New Tesament due to its surreal, cinematic imagery and its prophe-

---

51 One can compare the Biblical Book of Revelation (Apocalypse) with documents discovered at Qumran, such as the Song of the Sabbath Sacrifice, for similar predictions of a great cosmic battle and the loss of the Temple of Solomon in Jerusalem.

cies of doom. Those who focus on this text tend to neglect the message of the Gospels in favor of the more drastic condemnations of the Church's enemies.

One of these enemies is the Beast. According to many theologians, this particular Beast symbolizes Rome and the persecution of Christians by the Roman emperor. The number of the Beast is 666, but no further clarification of this number is given in the text. Some believe it is a coded reference to the emperor Nero. In any event, that number has come to be synonymous with evil incarnate and is frequently cited as a reference to the Devil itself.

It is important to note that there are *two* beasts mentioned in Revelations. The first comes out of the sea—the abyss—and the second from out of the earth. They are each empowered by the Dragon, to whom they evidently owe their allegiance. Thus, there is some confusion in Thelemic circles as to just what Beast Crowley was referring to, and why. Of course, he favored the 666 designation, making him the Beast of the Earth, known to readers of the Bible as the "False Prophet."

Crowley would adopt the number as his own, and offer pages of Kabbalistic-style analysis of its meaning. He was able to show that the Greek term *To Mega Therion* or "the Great Beast" added up to 666 when using Greek numerology, or gematria.[52] Gematria is a system of numerology in which letters (of the Greek or Hebrew alphabet) equal numbers. When a word has the same numerical value as another word, then a relationship between them both is assumed to the extent that one word may clarify or justify the other. (This fascination with gematria has bedeviled Thelema for much of its existence to date; it became a focus of Frater Achad's symbol system and, later, of Kenneth Grant's analysis of Thelema which would take gematria to near ridiculous lengths. The idea that the Bible contains coded information is central to Kabbalistic exegesis

---

52 More properly referred to as "isopsephy" when applied to the Greek language and alphabet.

as well as more recent textual analysis such as *The Bible Code* and its heirs. It is by no means unique to Thelema.)

The fact that there are two Beasts in Revelation, plus one Dragon, begs the question: could there be, or have there been, other contenders in Thelema for these available designations? Was there a human Beast of the Abyss? More importantly, perhaps, was there a physical/biological Dragon in a Thelemic context? The answers to both of these questions has to be a somewhat qualified "no." Crowley was not taking the entire text of Revelation as a blueprint for his own religion, but only that section of it that he believed seemed to refer to himself. But one has to wonder if Crowley ever considered that there might be another human manifestation from Revelation. This will lead us to the example of Jack Parsons, who famously identified himself with the Anti-Christ, and we will look at that in another chapter.

Why Crowley would identify himself with the Devil is an important point and one which will lead us directly to the concept of the Dark Lord. For Crowley, the Devil is something more ancient and more respectable than the caricature we come across in normative Christian imagery. The Devil represents everything the Church wants to suppress, and this includes most especially expressions of human sexuality.

Crowley's view of Satanism and Devil-worship would have been colored by the Continental obsession with the Black Mass. This ritual famously blasphemes the Catholic Mass, but in order to do so makes use of sexual elements. Thus, a woman is used in place of the altar; coitus is performed on the woman in place of the transubstantiation of the bread and wine.[53] These are all the

---

53 This idea would be adopted and elaborated upon by the cult around Crowley's contemporary, Maria de Naglowska (1883–1936) in Paris, as well as by the German offshoot of the original OTO, the Fraternitas Saturni and even the groups around the Italian mystic and fascist ideologue Julius Evola (1898–1974). The influence of these groups on the OTO and eventually on Thelema cannot

scandalous aspects of the Black Mass as it was popularly understood through such vehicles as J. K. Huysmann's best-selling novel,
Là-Bas or "Down There." In this context, sexuality is transgressive.
It is used to attack the Church at its most delicate and important
point: the sacrifice of the Mass itself, the central ritual of the faith
that is normally celebrated by celibate priests. Crowley would take
up this theme in his own Catholic-inspired Gnostic Mass in which
the sexual elements are once again represented, albeit in a more
sedate way than in the rapacious rituals of the nineteenth-century
French esthetes.[54]

To Crowley, the restrictive attitudes of the Church were themselves sinful. As it is written in the Book of the Law: "The word
of Sin is Restriction" (AL I:41). This is a subtle play on words, for
the exact meaning of the term "religion" is derived from the Latin
religio, itself probably derived from the verb *ligare* which means "to
bind" (as in the modern English *ligature*). The meaning of the sentence to a Thelemite is clear: it is religion that is sinful, religion that
"binds." Such restriction is anathema to a doctrine whose central
affirmation of faith is "Do what thou wilt shall be the whole of
the Law." Thus Crowley, by identifying with the great enemy of
the Church—the Beast 666—is aligning himself with the enemy
of restriction, and therefore with the free expression of all forms
of human sexuality: the ultimate example of sin and an important
target of the Abrahamic religions. This is emphasized by the rest of
the verse quoted above:

---

be discounted or ignored, and even may contribute to a fuller understanding of
Thelema, as well as an expansion of its major themes. See Chapter 5.

54   Another French depiction of a Black Mass can be found in the twentieth century novel by Georges Bataille, *L'histoire de l'oeil*—"The History of the
Eye"—which is concerned with sexual as well as religious transgression. It was
published in 1928, and contains scenes in which sexual fluids are intermingled
in such a way as to suggest some of the deeper mysteries of the western Tantric-
influenced cults.

The word of Sin is Restriction. O man! refuse not thy wife, if
she will! O lover, if thou wilt, depart! There is no bond[55] that can
unite the divided but love: all else is a curse. Accursèd! Accursèd
be it to the aeons! Hell. (AL I:41)

This emphasis on love rather than law as the touchstone for
human relationships is one element of Thelema that sets it apart
from mainstream religion. When love goes, according to the verse,
then so should the lover. This dissociates the act of love from legal
considerations, whether of religion or of secular government. It is
most especially—given the context—an attack on the sacrament of
matrimony and on religiously-sanctioned marriage. If marriage is
subtracted from the equation, what is left? Either pure eros—sexuality as a form of human relationship—or something even deeper:
a relationship based not only on sexuality popularly understood,
but on emotional attraction and attachment the way many adoles-
cents experience it—without a legal or a religious context, something approaching Jungian ideas of archetypes or Freudian ideas
of repressed erotic feelings for one's parent. As Crowley himself is
known to have had both male and female lovers, married and unmarried, this seems consistent with his worldview. But it is inconsistent
with the mainstream religions of his time, and he would be moved
to see in the Beast a force of resistance against the strictures of
the establishment, of the status quo, because he perceived them as
obstacles to a fuller knowledge of the Self. It is this tension between
the Self and Community (particularly in the sphere of sexuality and
human relationships) that is the focal point of Thelema, at least as
understood by some of its most prominent apologists such as Kenneth Grant. It is also the point at which Lovecraft balks, pointing

55 The word "bond" in this context expands upon the definition of *religio* and
ligare, given above, but more importantly it may reflect a modern iteration of
Giordano Bruno's revealing text, *De vinculis in genera* ("Of Bonds in General").
Here Bruno identifies the "bond" as love or eros, and especially in a magical
context, thus agreeing completely with AL I:41 in which "bond" is equated with
"love." Bruno was burned at the stake by the Catholic Church in the year 1600
for heresy.

to the transgressive magician and sorcerer as the cause of the community's vulnerability to forces from Outside.

By identifying himself—in a positive way—with the Beast, Crowley was performing a kind of self-therapy. He was taking the suppressed and repressed elements of a personality that had been molded by a normative and restrictive Christian sect and liberating them by means of re-characterizing them as positive values and not negative impulses.[56] It was perhaps more important for Crowley to self-identify this way than it was for his followers, for whom the Beast of the Book of Revelation might have less powerful (even confusing) associations. It marked his independence from Christian—and hence English—society and its expectations of conformity. It was dramatic, certainly, especially for the time. But was there more substance to the image than that?

To answer that question we must visit another powerful image of the Book of Revelation, the Whore of Babylon.

This personality is as complex and mysterious as the Beast. It is obviously a coded reference that made a lot of sense at the time, and in the millenia since the Book of Revelation was written there have been numerous attempts to analyze and identify the Whore in contemporary contexts. Where Crowley was concerned, the Whore of Babylon could only be a reference to his Consort, of whom he had quite a series that he called "Scarlet Women."

In the Book of Revelation the Whore of Babylon is referred to as "Babylon the Great, Mother of Harlots and Abominations of the Earth" (Revelations 17:3-6). Babylon was a reference to the alien culture that had crushed the Israelites and destroyed Solomon's Temple, and which thus became a code word for the Roman Empire that was the object of scorn of the writer of Revelations.

---

56 In this Crowley was anticipating the revolutionary psychological theories of Deleuze and Guattari in their *Anti-Oedipus*, where they argue that families and society at large conspire to repress desire and act as vehicles of neuroses which are necessary to the smooth functioning of capitalist society. In such a situation schizophrenia is the only logical outcome. See also R. D. Laing, *The Politics of Experience*.

Like Rome, Babylon was viewed as an "evil empire" bent on destroying God's people. At the time the Book of Revelation was being written—about the first century CE—the land of Israel was under Roman domination. Both Christians (at the time little more than a Jewish sect) and Jews were being persecuted as a result of their refusal to obey the edicts of Emperor Domitian, who demanded that everyone in his empire worship him as a god ... or be executed.

The Whore of Babylon is depicted as wearing purple and scarlet robes, and holding a golden cup filled with "the abominations and filthiness of her fornication." She sat on a scarlet beast with seven heads and ten horns, and was drunk on the blood of saints and martyrs. (Purple was the color of Roman royalty and was forbidden to the average citizen, so its inclusion here is instructive.)

Crowley incorporated this personality—one is hard-pressed to refer to her as a god, at least not in her Biblical persona—into his religion as the personification of the female principle of the universe, as Shakti: the female partner to the Beast, who represents the male principle, or Shiva. The cup of "abominations" is an analogue of the commingled male and female essences that are known as amrita in the East. And, just as in Revelation the Beast was subordinate to the Dragon, in Crowley's theological structure the Beast is subordinate to other powers.

In order to clarify these admittedly bizarre relationships it is worthwhile to have recourse to the Thelemic Creed as offered in the liturgy of the Gnostic Mass, written by Crowley:

I believe in one secret and ineffable LORD; and in one Star in the company of Stars of whose fire we are created, and to which we shall return; and in one Father of Life, Mystery of Mystery, in His name CHAOS, the sole viceregent of the Sun upon Earth; and in one Air the nourisher of all that breathes.

And I believe in one Earth, the Mother of us all, and in one Womb wherein all men are begotten, and wherein they shall rest, Mystery of Mystery, in Her name BABALON.

And I believe in the Serpent and the Lion, Mystery of Mystery, in His name BAPHOMET.

And I believe in one Gnostic and Catholic Church of Light, Life, Love and Liberty, the Word of whose Law is THELEMA.

And I believe in the communion of Saints.

And, forasmuch as meat and drink are transmuted in us daily into spiritual substance, I believe in the Miracle of the Mass.

And I confess one Baptism of Wisdom whereby we accomplish the Miracle of Incarnation.

And I confess my life one, individual, and eternal that was, and is, and is to come.

AUMGN, AUMGN, AUMGN.

Readers who were brought up Roman Catholic—like the present author—may be forgiven if they recognize what seems to be a travesty of the Apostles' Creed of their youth. The basic formula is the same:

I believe in God, the Father almighty, creator of heaven and earth.

I believe in Jesus Christ, His only Son, our Lord.

He was conceived by the power of the Holy Spirit and born of the Virgin Mary.

He suffered under Pontius Pilate, was crucified, died, and was buried.

He descended to the dead. On the third day he rose again.

He ascended into heaven and is seated at the right hand of the Father.

He will come again to judge the living and the dead.

I believe in the Holy Spirit,

the holy catholic Church, the communion of saints,

the forgiveness of sins,

the resurrection of the body,

and life everlasting.

Amen.

In both versions—Thelemic and Roman Catholic—the emphasis in the first lines is on a profession of faith in a creator God, termed a Father. That this is different from the "ineffable LORD" in the Thelemic Creed seems clear from the text. Here, the Father is the "Father of Life," and is the vice-regent of the Sun on earth. And, somewhat disconcertingly perhaps, his name is CHAOS. Chaos was, indeed, one of the appelations of the Egyptian god Set and he is referred to as such in the Greek magical papyri.[57] A god with the name Chaos would not be a reference to Osiris, or Horus, or Thoth, or Ra or any of the other more popular deities. Chaos is associated, in Egypt and in the Near and Middle East of the period (first century CE at the latest), with Set and with Set-Typhon. And the Star to which the Creed refers could only be—for Grant and the Typhonians—the Pole Star with its seven circumpolar attendants the Big Dipper (or, as it was known in Egypt, the "Thigh of Set"). The very important statement concerning "one Star in the company of Stars of whose fire we are created, and to which we shall return," implies the extra-terrestrial origins of humanity and by extension its ultimate destination. This "Star" has been identified as the Sun, of whom the Father is the sole vice-regent, but I believe this is a blind (as were the seven "planets" in Mithraism[58]) for the "real" Sun, which is the immortal Pole Star, a sun that never rises or sets but which sits unmoving directly overhead.

The name CHAOS has been interpreted to mean Air and Gas. The first statement of the Thelemic Creed ends with "Air, the nourisher of all that breathes" and is thus connected with CHAOS, the Star, and the Father.

The very next doctrinal statement in the Creed identifies BABALON as "the Mother of us all" and as the Earth itself. We

57 See Jacco Dieleman, *Priests, Tongues, and Rites: The London-Leiden Magical Manuscripts and Translation in Egyptian Ritual (100–300 CE)*, Brill, Leiden (2005) p. 134: "The Greek invocation develops the Sethian elements of the rite further by calling the deity the god of cosmic upheaval, who is hostile to the social order and dwells in foreign countries."
58 Levenda, *Stairway to Heaven*, pp. 135–145.

therefore have the Sky and the Earth— Air and Earth—CHAOS and BABALON as the first divinities enumerated in the Creed. This is followed by BAPHOMET, which was Crowley's name in the OTO.

Thus, we have two Ur-gods—CHAOS and BABALON—followed by the name of the Prophet of the New Aeon, BAPHOMET or Crowley himself. This requires us to look more closely at BABALON since Crowley was fixated on her and on what she represented, clarifying that his succession of (female) magical partners— the Scarlet Women—were but avatars of Babalon.

The three Abrahamic religions—Judaism, Christianity and Islam—do not elevate the female principle to the level of divinity. For that reason they are often referred to as "patriarchal" religions. From the previous chapter, we remember that Crowley—like some of the anthropologists of his day—believed that the patriarchal era was preceded by a matriarchal one. While this theory has largely been disproved on the basis of archaeological and other evidence, it nonetheless remains a strong concept among those professing a New Age worldview. One is tempted to imagine what the world would look like if matriarchal—as opposed to patriarchal—religions were the dominant force in the west.

In the east, however, women—and female representations of godhead—are more common. In India, goddesses are of supreme importance especially among specific sects that worship Kali, Durga, Shakti, etc. In China, among the Daoists and the Buddhists, Quan Yin is an extremely important goddess and believed to be the Chinese version of the Indian Avalokitesvara, the (male) God of Compassion. Even in predominantly Muslim Indonesia, the goddesses Sri, Lara Kidul, and Durga are still important and still reverenced.[59]

Thelemic documents, including the Book of the Law and the Gnostic Mass, reveal the desire to reinstate awareness of the feminine aspect of divinity. Conscious that this is an antinomian position

---

59   See the author's Tantric Temples: Eros and Magic in Java, for many examples of this meme.

to take, the feminine aspect that is most identified and cherished is that of the Whore of Babylon, perhaps the most transgressive female image in all of Christendom.

As Gail Corrington Streete has discussed at some length[60] the Whore of Babylon (*porne megale*) is but one iteration of the "foreign woman" of the Bible, the seducer of Israel who tries to tempt men away from the True Faith. But the "foreign woman" is also the Queen of Sheba, who tempted Solomon himself with the worship of foreign gods; she is Jezebel; and so many other strong yet strange women in the Bible who represent not only "woman" in general but ideas related to foreign-ness, to the alien, and the Other. Like Set, Babalon is a foreign deity. Set may represent ideas of masculine or male chaos where Babalon represents the feminine or female aspect of chaos. They are the Yang and Yin, respectively, of every antinomian and unorthodox belief and practice.

But there is another possible motive for this idealization of the Whore of Babylon and it may rest in the sexual mysteries themselves, the ones that Crowley learned from the OTO of Karl Kellner and Theodor Reuss, which placed an emphasis on the mingling of both male and female sexual excretions. This "sex magic" at the heart of the OTO mysteries is what has been elaborated upon at great length by Kenneth Grant and it forms the initiatic process of the Typhonian Current. In this context, a "whore" is a sexually-promiscuous woman, a woman who has sex for money or other favors, and as such is a threat to other women because of the implied devaluation of sexual intimacy between husband and wife: the characterization of sexuality as a biological function that can be bought and sold like food or water or manual labor rather than as the seal of an emotional and spiritual contract. The whore exists outside of the community of married men and women, of householders, and of upholders of the government, the church, and even of consensus reality. The relationship with a prostitute is a secret relationship; few

---

60   Gail Corrington Streete, *The Strange Woman: Power and Sex in the Bible*, Lousiville (KY), Westminster John Knox Press, 1997.

men boast of going to prostitutes or of having any sort of relationship with them outside of the sex act. In fact, the more established a
man is—the more respected in his community, his government, his
religion, his business—the less likely he is to admit to such a relationship in the public forum. He may go to great lengths to conceal
it, to keep it secret, hidden, and entirely personal. It is, in a sense, an
"esoteric" or "occult" relationship.

In the Book of Revelation, the Whore of Babylon represents
not only the ultimate Prostitute and sexually active Woman, but
also signifies an enemy of the Church. It is in this dual role that
she is important to Thelema; for even as sexual mores have changed
considerably since the Victorian era when Crowley was a youth,
Church and the State are still viable targets for a religion of liberation and freedom.

There is one more aspect to the Whore of Babylon that must be
considered, and that is her stated origin: Babylon. The implication
is clear: a connection, however tenuous, not to Egypt but to Sumer,
Akkad and Babylon itself. The Whore of Babalon (to use Crowley's
spelling based on his rendering of the name to satisfy a gematria of
his own) is thereby a link to the most ancient of the known western
religions, the one that is the focus of Grant's work and one that is
referenced by Crowley, Parsons, and other Thelemic authors and
personalities, and enshrined in the Schlangekraft recension of the
Necronomicon: the Sumerian tradition.

While Crowley's fixation on the Beast and the Whore of the
Christian Bible may have been motivated originally by a desire to
be a "bad boy" and outrage the adults around him, the adolescent
fantasy of transgression became enshrined in a doctrine. The Whore
was lifted out of its Biblical context and re-imagined as "the Mother
of us all" and as a Mesopotamian deity (as was Aiwass). It should be
acknowledged, however, that this theme of transgression applies not
only to the Christianity of the Book of Revelation, but—because of
the destruction of Solomon's Temple by the Babylonians—to Judaism as well. Crowley's alleged anti-Semitism has been the subject
of several investigations and we won't belabor the point here. It may

be sufficient to state that Crowley's philosophy was deliberately provocative and anti-establishment in nature to the extent that he ridiculed most human institutions and therefore treated most people with contempt if they were not converts to his new faith. This might not have been the result of deep feelings of genuine racism, sexism, etc. but was rather what one would expect of someone who set himself up as the Prophet of a new Age, much in the same way that Moses and his followers rained death on their enemies, or the Church in its many inquisitorial purges and crusades, or the anti-Semitic remarks that can be found in the Qur'an and the military actions that took place against non-Muslims during the Prophet's life and those of subsequent caliphates. This is not to say one should enshrine these ill-advised declarations as statements of doctrinal authority, however. They need interpreting; yet a key point of contention in this case is that no one is supposed to interpret Crowley's writings but Crowley himself.[61]

This is one of the inherent contradictions in Thelema, for while Crowley insisted that he be the arbiter of all things Thelemic, his slogan was quite different: "Our method is science, our aim is religion." The "our" is understood not as the editorial or Papal first person plural, but as encompassing all Thelemites. If the scientific method is indeed the cornerstone of Crowley's occult praxis, then it behooves Thelemites to undertake independent experimentation and discovery.

This is precisely what the late Kenneth Grant set out to do, and in the process he made some interesting and possibly crucial discoveries. Among these was the value of different sets of god-forms from different cultures, in particular those with which Crowley himself was not as familiar. While his incorporation of genuine Tantric and Afro-Caribbean data makes his writings worthwhile for anyone interested in what an expansion of Crowley's basic themes would look like—and in particular Crowley's magic—it is Grant's will-

---

61 Naturally, this present volume ignores that stricture! To do otherwise would be, in the words of Liber AL, a "sin."

ingness to look beyond religion and spiritual techniques to other sources of information that place this British occultist upon an entirely different plateau. If Crowley was committed to having his philosophy embraced by the masses—and used every means at his disposal to ensure this, including public performances of his rites, publishing occult novels, and attempting to influence famous celebrities—then Grant's discovery of Thelemic themes in the fictional writing of Howard Phillips Lovecraft should have been welcomed by Crowley's followers enthusiastically, especially as Lovecraft's imagined cultus reflects so deeply Crowley's own revealed religion.

The Beast in the Cave

In 1907, Crowley was writing some of the works that became seminal to the doctrines of Thelema, known as *The Holy Books*. These include *Liber Liberi vel Lapidus Lazuli, Liber Cordis Cincti Serpente*, and other works written between October 30 and November 1 of that year, and *Liber Arcanorum* and *Liber Carcerorum*, written between December 5th and 14th that same year. Lovecraft would have had no knowledge of this, as he was only a seventeen-year old recluse living at home on Angell Street in Providence, Rhode Island, dreaming of the stars. Instead, he later would write of an orgiastic ritual taking place that year in the bayous outside New Orleans, Louisiana, and on the very same day that Crowley was writing the books enumerated above.

The story Lovecraft wrote is entitled "The Call of Cthulhu" and is arguably his most famous work. He wrote the story in 1926, in late August or early September, but placed the action in New Orleans in 1907 and later in Providence in 1925. How is this relevant?

Lovecraft's placement of the orgiastic ritual in honor of the high priest of the Great Old Ones, Cthulhu, and the discovery of a statue of Cthulhu by the New Orleans police on Halloween, 1907 coincides precisely with Crowley's fevered writing of his own gothic prose. In the *Liber Liberi vel Lapidus Lazuli*, for instance, Crowley writes the word "Tutulu" for the first time. He claims not to know what this word means, or where it came from. As the name of Lovecraft's fictional alien god can be pronounced "Kutulu," it seems more than coincidental, as Kenneth Grant himself noted.

However, this is only the tip of an eldritch iceberg.

In Crowley's *Liber Cordis Cincti Serpente*—or "The Book of the Heart Girt with a Serpent"—there are numerous references to the "Abyss of the Great Deep," to Typhon, Python, and the appearance of an "old gnarled fish" with tentacles ... all descriptions that match Lovecraft's imagined Cthulhu perfectly. Not approximately, but perfectly. Crowley's volume was written on November 1, 1907. The ritual for Cthulhu in New Orleans took place on the same day, month and year.

Here are the relevant passages:

From *Liber Liberi vel Lapidus Lazuli*:

1. By the burning of the incense was the Word revealed, and by the distant drug.
2. O meal and honey and oil! O beautiful flag of the moon, that she hangs out in the centre of bliss!
3. These loosen the swathings of the corpse; these unbind the feet of Osiris, so that the flaming God may rage through the firmament with his fantastic spear.
4. But of pure black marble is the sorry statue, and the changeless pain of the eyes is bitter to the blind.
5. We understand the rapture of that shaken marble, torn by the throes of the crowned child, the golden rod of the golden God.
6. We know why all is hidden in the stone, within the coffin, within the mighty sepulchre, and we too answer Olalám! Imál! Tutúlu! as it is written in the ancient book.
7. Three words of that book are as life to a new æon; no god has read the whole.
8. But thou and I, O God, have written it page by page.[62]

---

62 Crowley, *Liber Liberi vel Lapidus Lazuli*, Chapter VII, verses 1-8. Verse six

And in *Liber Cordis Cincti Serpente*:

Then was the Adept glad, and lifted his arm. Lo! an earthquake, and plague, and terror on the earth![63]

And:

Behold! the Abyss of the Great Deep. Therein is a mighty dolphin, lashing his sides with the force of the waves.[64]

And:

Thou art Sebek the crocodile against Asar; thou art Mati, the Slayer in the Deep. Thou art Typhon, the Wrath of the Elements, O Thou who transcendest the Forces in their Concourse and Cohesion, in their Death and their Disruption. Thou art Python, the terrible serpent about the end of all things![65]

And finally:

I trembled at Thy coming, O my God, for Thy messenger was more terrible than the Death-star. On the threshold stood the fulminant figure of Evil, the Horror of emptiness, with his ghastly eyes like poisonous wells. He stood, and the chamber was corrupt; the air stank. He was an old and gnarled fish more hideous than the shells of Abaddon. He enveloped me with his demon tentacles; yea, the eight fears took hold upon me.[66]

---

mentions Tutulu and states that it is written in an "ancient book": Tutulu in an ancient book, and Cthulhu in the *Necronomicon*.

63 Crowley, *Liber Cordis Cincti Serpente*, Chapter I:57. The earthquake is an important element in the Lovecraft story.

64 Ibid, II:37. Cthulhu is a monster of the Abyss of the Great Deep.

65 Ibid, III:30

66 Ibid, IV:33-35. These verses could just as easily be descriptions of Cthulhu.

Compare with relevant passages from Lovecraft's "Call of Cthulhu":

Above these apparent hieroglyphics was a figure of evident pictorial intent, though its impressionistic execution forbade a very clear idea of its nature. It seemed to be a sort of monster, or symbol representing a monster, of a form which only a diseased fancy could conceive. If I say that my somewhat extravagant imagination yielded simultaneous pictures of an octopus, a dragon, and a human caricature, I shall not be unfaithful to the spirit of the thing. A pulpy, tentacled head surmounted a grotesque and scaly body with rudimentary wings; but it was the general outline of the whole which made it most shockingly frightful. Behind the figure was a vague suggestion of a Cyclopean architectural background.[67]

And:

The figure, which was finally passed slowly from man to man for close and careful study, was between seven and eight inches in height, and of exquisitely artistic workmanship. It represented a monster of vaguely anthropoid outline, but with an octopus-like head whose face was a mass of feelers, a scaly, rubbery-looking body, prodigious claws on hind and fore feet, and long, narrow wings behind. This thing, which seemed instinct with a fearsome and unnatural malignancy, was of a somewhat bloated corpulence, and squatted evilly on a rectangular block or pedestal covered with undecipherable characters. The tips of the wings touched the back edge of the block, the seat occupied the centre, whilst the long, curved claws of the doubled-up, crouch-

---

67 H.P. Lovecraft, "The Call of Cthulhu," from the first section sub-titled "The Horror in Clay." A "pulpy, tentacled head" seems to recall Crowley's "He enveloped me with his demon tentacles ..." The term "Cyclopean architecture" is one we will come across again in Thelemic literature.

ing hind legs gripped the front edge and extended a quarter of the way down toward the bottom of the pedestal. The cephalopod head was bent forward, so that the ends of the facial feelers brushed the backs of huge fore paws which clasped the croucher's elevated knees. The aspect of the whole was abnormally life-like, and the more subtly fearful because its source was so totally unknown. Its vast, awesome, and incalculable age was umistakable; yet not one link did it shew with any known type of art belonging to civilisation's youth—or indeed to any other time. Totally separate and apart, its very material was a mystery; for the soapy, greenish-black stone with its golden or iridescent flecks and striations resembled nothing familiar to geology or mineralogy. The characters along the base were equally baffling; and no member present, despite a representation of half the world's expert learning in this field, could form the least notion of even their remotest linguistic kinship.

In *Liber Liberi vel Lapidus Lazuli*, Crowley refers to several of the images with which Lovecraft would be consumed in his stories, but especially in "The Call of Cthulhu." Here we have a buried god that is awakened from a stone, in a coffin, in a sepulchre, and mysterious words written in an ancient book, including Tutulu. And "of pure black marble is the sorry statue" resonates with the black stone on which the statue of Cthulhu squats.

In *Liber Cordis Cincti Serpente* we have an expansion of this theme, beginning with an earthquake (Lovecraft's story is centered around an actual earthquake that took place in 1925), and extending to an Abyss of the Great Deep, the Slayer in the Deep, a Death-star, and the "fulminant figure of Evil" (a stinking, fish-like creature with tentacles). This figure is a messenger of the Gods and, indeed, Cthulhu is not only a god itself but a high priest of the Great Old Ones who will return to earth when "the stars are right." A more paranoid observer than your author may wonder if the statement in Liber AL—"Every man and every woman is a star"—is a decoding of the famous Lovecraft quotation "when the stars are right."

It would imply that when the followers of Thelema (the "stars") are powerful enough, or numerous enough, then the Great Old Ones will return.

This was certainly Crowley's objective, as understood by Grant and as revealed by these excerpts from Crowley's *Holy Books of Thelema*. Crowley believed that the first two books mentioned above were not his writing, but were inspired works dictated to him by his Holy Guardian Angel, the ancient Sumerian personality Aiwass, after Crowley had attained *samadhi* during a course of rituals he undertook with his colleague, George Cecil Jones, in England.[68] Even the undecipherable language of "Olalam Imal Tutulu" has its counterpart in the enigmatic hieroglyphics of the Cthulhu statue and the ecstatic, glossolalia-like cries of the worshippers in the Louisiana swamps.[69] Both men—the American author and the English magician—were dealing with the same subject matter, and indeed Lovecraft had dated the first appearance of the Cthulhu statue *to the same year, month and day* that Crowley began writing these sections of the *Holy Books*.

There is no hard evidence that either man knew of the other, although the author believes that references to an English satanist in Lovecraft's "The Thing on the Doorstep" could be an allusion to Crowley. In any event, to suggest that these two men cooperated or collaborated in any deliberate way would be the height (or depth!) of conspiracy theory. It may actually be more logical to

---

68 "After returning from Morocco, the spirit came upon me and I wrote a number of books in a way which I hardly know how to describe.... The prose of these books, the chief of which are *Liber Cordis Cincti Serpente, The Book of the Heart girt with the Serpent*, and *Libri vel Lapidis Lazuli*, is wholly different from anything that I have written myself. I cannot doubt that these books are the work of an intelligence independent of my own." Aleister Crowley, *Confessions*, Chapter 62, p. 558.

69 The following year—1908—the word "Tutulu" would reappear as Crowley was involved in evoking the Aires or Aethyrs of the Enochian system in North Africa at the time. The word was heard during the invocation of the 27th Aethyr. At that time Crowley admitted that the word was untranslatable. See Crowley, *The Vision and the Voice*.

suggest—as an explanation for some of these coincidences—that darker forces were at work. In fact, it is possible that the same forces of which Lovecraft himself writes—the telepathic communication between followers of Cthulhu and the Great Old Ones—was what prompted him to write these fictional accounts of real events. Either Lovecraft was in some kind of telepathic communication with Crowley, or both men were in telepathic communication with ... Something Else.

This Dark Lord of the *Holy Books* is one of the gods—perhaps the most important god—of the Crowley pantheon. In the Crowley line of succession, this god is at the juncture of Egyptian and Sumerian religion and is thus pre-Judaic. In Lovecraft's succession, Cthulhu is a high priest of the Great Old Ones who came to the planet from the stars aeons ago, long before humans walked the earth. Although dead and buried deep beneath the earth or under the ocean, he can rise again once the "stars are right" and his followers assist in calling him up, in resurrecting him.

This leads us to a slight detour into the Tibetan language.

The word *ku su lu* in Tibetan[70] evokes for us another coincidence, for it refers to a shaman (i.e., a kind of priest) but also to one who was once dead but who has come back from death.[71] This meme—the shaman who has come back from the dead—is a perfect description of Lovecraft's Cthulhu and may provide a means of understanding Crowley's Tutulu as well. According to Kenneth

---

70   Accessed from Rangjung Yeshe *Tibetan-English Dharma Dictionary*.

71   This is a theme familiar to anyone who has studied Siberian shamanism, and reference to this concept can be found in the works of Mircea Eliade (especially his magnum opus *Shamanism*) as well as in books by the present author, such as his *Sinister Forces* trilogy. In this tradition, a shaman is one who has undergone the death and rebirth experience after a long period of meditation and solitary ritual in the forest. The death and rebirth formula is also an integral part of the initiation structure of the Golden Dawn and of Aleister Crowley's A∴A∴, as well as of the third degree of Freemasonry. In that sense one could say that anyone who has gone through these systems can be called a "kusulu," but there is a difference between the formalized rituals of the western esoteric tradition and the intense psychological experience of genuine Asian shamanistic initiation.

Grant, one possible translation of the word Tutulu can be "Who will attain." These are all consistent with the idea presented by Lovecraft of a high priest of the Great Old Ones, dead but "dreaming," who will resurrect from his watery grave to take charge of the earth once more. As noted in the Schlangekraft recension of the Necronomicon, Cthulhu can be rendered in the Sumerian language as *kutu lu* or "the man from Kutu" or "the man from the Underworld." Kutu—the Biblical Gudua, sometimes rendered Kutu or Kuta—was the ancient city of Cutha, sacred to Nergal and the entrance to the Underworld in Sumerian religion. It was also the city in Mesopotamia with special relevance for Islam, for it was the city where the Qureish were from. The Qureish are, of course, the tribe of the Prophet Muhammad, the tribe in charge of the pagan shrine in Mecca known as the Ka'aba or the Black Stone. This was the shrine containing 360 idols, probably of the Moon God Hubal, that the Prophet dismantled and replaced with a shrine sacred to his new religion of Islam.

The death and rebirth theme that is central to Siberian shamanism was also a crucial element of Sumerian and Babylonian religion. The famous narrative of the descent of the Sumerian goddess Inanna (Ishtar) into the Underworld, and her rescue and resurrection three days later, is one of the legends that helped form the Sumerian Gnosis. Indeed, she has sometimes been identified with the Whore of Babylon. When she finally ascended the seven levels of the Underworld to reappear in the world, she was accompanied by a host of demons who had previously been restrained in the Underworld, and who took advantage of her defeat of death to flood out of their subterranean prison and populate the earth. This bears some resemblance to Lovecraft's fictional Cthulhu who is dead but who will be reborn "when the stars are right" and at that time bring his alien gods to the earth to rule it once more. In both cases—the Lovecraft scenario and the Sumerian prototype—the dead require the assistance of the living to effect the resurrection.

This complex narrative is reprised in the Christian example of Jesus who, after his crucifixion, "descended into hell" and rose on the third day. His descent into hell was for the purpose of releasing from the Underworld all those noble souls who had died before he appeared on the earth to redeem humanity from original sin. In the Christian case, the souls that were released were those of the righteous dead; in the Sumerian case, the souls that were released were demonic forces. In the Lovecraft scenario, the gates are opened to hideous alien beings from outer space. Either the Christian case is mere wishful thinking, or a deliberate gloss on the older traditions of the region, or is it something else?

Much has been written in the past hundred years or longer on the subject of the "dead and resurrected god," referencing a whole category of such deities ranging from Osiris to Tammuz, Mithra, and others in the Middle East and North Africa. It is often characterized as evidence of an agricultural society in which seeds are planted (i.e., "buried") in the ground and then "resurrected" in the form of new plants. However, this process could just as easily be the basis for any of a number of sexually-oriented fertility cults as well, and not necessarily the basis for a dead and resurrected god (or goddess, as in the case of Inanna).

Unless, of course, there is a relation or connection between the idea of death and resurrection on the one hand and sexual intercourse and reproduction on the other. In the Gnostic Mass as revised by Crowley, we have the template of a celebration of Christ's Last Supper and the consumption of his flesh and blood by the faithful over which is applied the sexual components of Crowley's cultus. While the sexual aspect of the Gnostic Mass is the most obvious one and the aspect that gets all the attention, the death and resurrection foundation of the Mass is still present and is in disguise. Crowley might have said that his Mass was the "reveal" of the innate sexual message of the original Mass, while the original Mass can be interpreted as the "reveal" of the primary death and resurrection message hidden within the Crowley version. They can be seen as mirror images of each other, if one views them both from an angle slightly off-center, from—as Lovecraft would say—a "space between the spaces."

As in the Catholic Mass, the gods are present in the Gnostic
Mass. They are classified differently, of course, with a totally different emphasis. The reason this much time has been taken for a
look at the Mass, its Credo, and its transgressive characteristics is
because it is the formula that most clearly represents the coherence
of the Thelemic message. That is not to say that the Mass is perfectly
coherent, of course (but, then, neither is the Catholic Mass). But it
can be viewed as a kind of *wayang kulit*, a shadow play conducted
behind a curtain in which the actors are flat, two-dimensional puppets standing in for three-dimensional gods but which—in the case
of the Gnostic Mass—are replaced by three-dimensional human
beings standing in for extra-dimensional entities: those described at
some length by Kenneth Grant, H.P. Lovecraft, and the Typhonian
Tradition of magic.

Like, for instance, Set.

Set–Typhon

> Crowley's *Liber XXXVI*[72] contains a formula for establishing
> contact with the Old Ones through the invocation of Set, son
> of Isis and brother of Horus.
>   —Kenneth Grant, *Beyond the Mauve Zone*, p. 123

As must be obvious by now, Grant's focus throughout his aptly-
named Typhonian Trilogy as well as in the construction and organization of his Typhonian Order always has been the composite figure
of Set-Typhon. Set is the ancient Egyptian god that has long been
associated with chaos, with the desert, with storms, with foreigners
and foreign lands (i.e., the "Other"), and with the murder of Osiris
and the ongoing struggle with Horus, the son of Osiris. Typhon, on
the other hand, is a Greek god who has many of the same attributes
of a god of darkness, storms and chaos. Typhon, like Set, was born

---

72 Liber XXXVI is also known as *The Star Sapphire*, see below. Kenneth Grant,
Beyond the Mauve Zone, London, Starfire Publishing, 1999.

unnaturally from his mother and, also like Set, was the enemy of the pantheon. Thus, it was the Greeks who identified Set as a version of their own Typhon and the form Set-Typhon came to be known in the Mediterranean. There has been much speculation in academic circles that the legends surrounding Typhon are derived from those of ancient Sumer, specifically the creation epic known as Enuma Elish and the episode of the serpent monster, Tiamat, who is slain by Marduk in battle.[73] As we have seen, Grant identified Set-Typhon as a form of Crowley's supramundane contact, Aiwass, as well as of the Shaitan of the Yezidis, and linked it all to Sumer.

Oddly, however, Crowley himself did not seem to focus on Set-Typhon to the extent that his disciple would, except as a kind of twin to Horus as we have seen.[74] Crowley's attention was taken by Horus in his various forms as Hoor-par-kraat and the composite Ra-hoor-kuit, among others. Crowley identified with what he saw as the "solar phallic" nature of Osiris and Horus and, indeed, neither Set-Typhon nor Set himself were major figures in the Egyptian pantheon of the Golden Dawn—where Set appears as the personification of evil in the rituals associated with the idea of the Threshold and represents the "Averse Sephiroth" and the Qlippoth.[75] In this instance, Set would not be identified as a being to whom

---

73 See, for instance, Jean-Pierre Vernant, *The Origins of Greek Thought*, Ithaca, Cornell University Press, 1982, pp. 110-111.

74 One notable exception is his *Liber XXXVI* or *Star Sapphire*, which is a reworking of the Golden Dawn Ritual of the Hexagram, to be discussed below.

75 This is particularly evident in the Golden Dawn's document entitled "Z.1, The Enterer of the Threshold" which is an analysis of the Neophyte initiation ritual. Set-Typhon occupies one of the Invisible Stations in this ritual, where he is described as "*Omoo-Sathan, Typhon, Apophis, Set.* The Evil Persona is a composite figure of the powers arising from the Qlippoth..." The other two stations on this Path—on the Middle Pillar of the Tree of Life, the segment named Samekh after the Hebrew letter—are Hathor and Harparkrat. Hathor is sometimes considered a consort of Set and a partner in his drunken revels; the presence of Harparkrat (Harpocrates or Hoor-paar-krat, the child form of Horus) along with Set and Hathor is a dead give-away as to the true nature of the Aeon of Horus. See Regardie, *The Golden Dawn*, St. Paul, Llewellyn, 2005, pp. 356–357.

worship would be directed. One gets the sense that if a member of
the Golden Dawn were to construct rituals intended to invoke or
evoke Set that it would be considered an act of "black magic," i.e., a
harmful or wholly negative act.

To Grant, however, the character of Set is a rich vein of cosmic
importance and Grant expands on this theme considerably, to the
point that Set—in Grant's scheme of things—overtakes Horus and
Osiris in relevance to the ideas embodied by Crowley's doctrine
of Thelema. Where Osiris and Horus represent the solar aspect of
Egyptian religion, Set and Set-Typhon represent the stellar aspect.
Osiris and Horus can be identified with the rising and setting sun—
and thus with the east and west respectively—but Set is identified
with the circumpolar stars (in particular with the Great Bear or Ursa
Major) and the north, the direction of the sun's nadir beneath the
earth and the realm of Amenta: the Abode of the Dead. The author
has elsewhere shown that the asterism known to us as the Big Dipper was identified with Set in the Egyptian text popularly known
as the Book of the Dead, specifically with the "thigh" of Set in the
crucial Opening of the Mouth ceremony.[76] The Big Dipper is also a
critical asterism in the Necronomicon Gnosis, as the Gates between
this world and the transdimensional realm are opened "when the
Great Bear hangs from its tail in the sky."[77] Grant discovered the
close association between the Egyptian Set and the Necronomicon,
which further reinforced his theory concerning the Tunnels of Set.
These tunnels are hidden pathways on the "nightside" of the Kabbalistic "Tree of Life"—known to Kabbalists as the *Sitra Ahra*, or
"Other Side"—that he associates with the Qlippoth, the "shells" of
a previous creation that was destroyed due to imbalance resulting in
shattered or broken sephiroth, specifically the sephira Gevurah or
"Severity." These shards of an Elder Creation roam the cosmos as
evil spirits or demonic forces, but to Grant these are value judge-
ments made by pious monotheists who ignore their true nature.

76 See his *Stairway to Heaven*, New York, Continuum, 2008, pp. 16-18.
77 *Necronomicon*, Lake Worth, Ibis Press, 2008, p. 124.

But there is more to Set than even all of this. A close examination of Set's importance and character in the ancient Egyptian texts reveal that there is a close correlation between how the Egyptians understood Set and the initiatory process of Crowley's OTO as well as the central thesis of Grant's ouevre.

In recent years there has been much academic investigation and discourse on the nature and identity of Set. This discourse has ranged from the fields of pure Egyptology to studies of Gnosticism and the Kabbalah. Set remains an engimatic figure, a stranger to the rest of Egyptian religion in so many ways. Indeed, the identity of Set's "animal" (the totemic creature or zoötype with which Set is identified in hieroglyphics and Egyptian art) remains unidentified, and even the etymology of Set's name is a source of controversy. While there is no space to go into all of this here, relevant topics will be highlighted so that the reader can appreciate the extent of the Crowley-Grant-Lovecraft concept, characterized by Grant as the Necronomicon Gnosis.

Who is Set?

There are two basic schools of thought concerning the origins of Set. One school claims that Set represents an ancient ruler of Upper (i.e., southern) Egypt who came into conflict with a ruler represented by Horus of Lower (i.e., northern) Egypt. It is this political and military conflict that led to the myth of the warfare between Set and Horus.

This idea has been criticized as there is no historical evidence to support it, although it is true that pharaohs considered themselves rulers of both Upper and Lower Egypt, and that their double crowns were references to the union of Set and Horus.

Another school has it that Set represents a foreign god, and hence a foreign tribe, race, country. This foreign deity eventually became incorporated into the overall religion, representing all those concepts that were considered antinomian, transgressive, and "other." There is some support for this interpretation but it is by no means conclusive.

The name "Set" defies translation, just as his totemic animal defies identification. The hieroglyphic representing the word for Set can be pronounced in various ways, depending on the area of Egypt (Upper or Lower) and the relevant dynasty.[78] Variations such as "Setah," "Sut," "Seth," and of course "Set" have been put forward as alternatives.[79] The determinative form has been used in words denoting storm, thunder, roaring, chaos, illness, nightmares, darkness, and a host of other dangerous phenomena. One theory is that Set represents that which separates or divides. Set is the god of alien lands (alien to Egypt and thus, by extension, the "Other") and the desert, and as such is a liminal figure, a god of the Threshold, the guardian at the Gate to the Underworld as the Golden Dawn rituals testify.

This may be due to (at least in part) the identification of the Set "animal" as an ass or donkey, specifically *Equus africanus* or the African wild ass, a species that is today nearing extinction but which still survives in the deserts of Somalia and Ethiopia having once been common in the Egyptian desert as well. This species thrives in desert places and is largely identified with the sere wastelands outside of the ancient Egyptian cities. (Indeed, one of the magical spells that appear in the Papyrus London-Leiden magical manuscripts specifically instructs the magician to use the blood and head of a donkey in order to evoke Set-Typhon.)[80] It is claimed that the sound the donkey makes—its peculiar braying—gave rise to one of the most common utterances to be found in Crowleyan (and, indeed, most Gnostic and Greco-Roman occult) literature: *Iao* or

78 For this and most of the other references in this chapter to Set's origins, names, etc. see H. Te Velde, *Seth, God of Confusion: a study of his role in Egyptian mythology and religion*, Leiden, Brill, 1967.

79 Ibid., pp. 3–7.

80 As shown in Jacco Dieleman, *Priests, Tongues, and Rites: The London-Leiden Magical Manuscripts and Translation in Egyptian Ritual (100-300 CE)*, Leiden, Brill, 2005, pp. 130–138.

Io, both of which were considered names of the Egyptian god Set in the Greco-Roman literature and serve as invocations of that god.[81]

Set has been associated with foreign countries and their inhabitants. Thus, the peoples of Libya in the west were considered (by the Egyptians) to be followers of Set. The Semitic peoples of Mesopotamia in the east were also considered to be Set-worshippers and their god, Baal, was identified often with Set. Crowley's prime female deity, Babalon, also is obviously Babylonian and authors have tried to identify the famous "Whore of Babylon" of the Biblical Apocalypse as the Babylonian Ishtar (Sumerian Inanna). This would seem to justify to some extent Grant's (and Crowley's) insistence that the source of the Thelemic testament, Aiwass, was Sumerian and that he might have been a priest of an Ur-form of Set-Typhon. If this could be supported by other evidence, then it is clear that Thelema owes a great deal of its identity to the influence of that exemplar of the transgressive forces of the universe ... and that Lovecraft's horror of the high priest of the Great Old Ones, Cthulhu or Kutulu, was at least in some measure justified!

In addition, it is tempting to see the Semitic word *satan* שטן as a form of the Egyptian Set. They have the consonant sounds "s" and "t" in common, and they both seem to represent evil beings. Actually, while the relationship is hypothetical at this point, the two words do have a lot in common. Add to that the general reluctance of Egyptian scribes to write out the name of Set phonetically[82]— but who instead chose to use his hieroglyphic signifier in texts—and you have an apt comparison to the avoidance of pronouncing the initial consonant of Shaitan's name by the Yezidis. Both, incidentally, begin with the same consonantal sound: the initial *s̀* or *s̆* sound used for the name of Set in transliterated Egyptian is believed to be identical to the sound *s* in Satan and *sh* in Shaitan, respectively.

---

81 For this rather startling revelation, see Jarl Fossum and Brian Glazer, "Seth in the Magical Texts," in *Zeitschrift für Papyrologie und Epigraphik* 100 (1994) 86–92.

82 H. Te Velde, op. cit., p. 4.

The Hebrew word *satan* comes from a root meaning "adversary" or "to resist" as well as "enemy," "obstacle," or "obstruction," depending on whether the word is used as a noun or a verb. It may come from the word *sut* שׁוט which means "to fall aside or away," or the word *set* שׁט which means "one who revolts." The final "n" in the Hebrew *satan* indicates an emphasis on the root for the purpose of personification, and thus "he who falls aside," or "he who revolts," or "he who obstructs." We remember that one of the earliest suspected pronounciations for Set is indeed *Sut*.

If it can be shown that Semitic ideas of Satan derive from the ancient Egyptian god Set, then Grant's hypothesis that Set-Shaitan-Typhon are one and the same takes on increased importance. By identifying Aiwass with this signifier we may understand the Book of the Law a little better, particularly its controversial third chapter which sets the New Aeon in complete opposition to the world's religions in a dramatic and even violent way. The message of Liber AL then becomes a message consistent with the personality and objectives of Set, the Dark Lord.

On the other hand, there is a scene from the Book of Coming Forth by Day (more commonly known as the Egyptian Book of the Dead) in which Set is shown at the prow of Ra's barque, fighting the serpent god Apophis. In this setting, Set is protecting the Sun God, Ra. If Set is "evil" as is often claimed, how is it that he also can be depicted defending the pantheon? Indeed, some pharaohs even took the name Set as their own or added it to their titles.

Set as Tantric God

A recurrent theme in all of Grant's work is that of sexuality, especially within a ritualistic context. The OTO is said to be a repository of the sexual secrets discovered by its German founders a century ago, and the OTO's debt to the sacred spirituality advocated by the African-American mystic Pascal Beverly Randolph has been detailed elsewhere.[83] Tantra forms the main context for Grant's elaboration of the sexual mysteries at the heart of Thelema and Thelemic magic, and indeed Grant went much further than Crowley in his description of these mysteries and their relevance to Tantra and in particular to Vama Marg Tantra or "Tantra of the Left Hand Path" as it is often—erroneously—characterized. Grant's Tantra is not the New Age, feel-good, Tantra of the West, but the transgressive Tantra of the Nath Siddhis, the Kaula circles and other traditions that view the human body—male and female—as both laboratories and temples combined. Tantra according to this approach is a technology of spirituality, spiritual power, and tremendously altered states of consciousness which has as its goal communion with supramundane beings ... in other words, precisely what Lovecraft described when he depicted the orgiastic rites in the swamps outside New Orleans in his short story "The Call of Cthulhu."

While many readers will be familiar with the legend of Set murdering Osiris, and Isis giving birth to a child, Horus, who will avenge his father's death in battle with Set, what is not so well known is the sexual component to the myth. For decades this aspect has remained somewhat hidden from the non-academic world and buried in obscure Latin phrases and euphemisms and generally ignored. That Set was understood to be either homosexual or at least bi-sexual will seem strange to those who have always believed Set to be the personification of pure evil and murder, a kind of Jungian "Shadow" archetype. But Set as representative of "the Other" in almost everything also represents sexual transgression, the perhaps ultimate expression of "Other-ness" and a natural characteristic of the type of Tantric sexuality that is the focus of Grant's thesis.

83   See Joscelyn Godwin, Christian Chanel, and John P. Deveny, *The Hermetic Brotherhood of Luxor: Initiatic and Historical Documents of an Order of Practical Occultism*, York Beach, ME.: Samuel Weiser, 1995 and T. Allen Greenfield, *The Story of the Hermetic Brotherhood of Light*, Beverly Hills, Looking Glass Press, 1997.

To understand this—and its relevance to Grant's Typhonian magic—it is necessary to know how Egypt described the origins of Set.

According to one of the cosmological systems of the ancient Egyptians, the supreme or eldest god, Atum, gave birth to the world by self-propagating his two children, Shu and Tefnut, who in turn gave birth to Geb the earth god and Nut the sky goddess. These in turn gave birth to Osiris and Isis. However, they also gave birth to Set and Nephthys, which disturbed the order of the cosmos as, until that time, the system had been established whereby one male-female pair gave birth to only one other male-female pair, essentially what the Gnostics would refer to as syzygies. Further, it was claimed that Set was not born via the usual method but essentially tore out of his mother's side on his own volition in an untimely season and violent manner. Thus it appears—though is not specifically stated—that Set did not have a childhood per se but entered life fully-grown. Even the word for "birth" is not used in the Egyptian texts in connection with Set's origins. Indeed, his own mother refused him and his sister/wife Nephthys was also in horror of him. Isis, whose brother/husband Osiris was slain by Set, lived in fear of him as well, especially during her pregnancy with Horus. It was believed that Set (due to his unnatural birth) caused abortions and that he would "open the womb" of pregnant women so that they would miscarry or abort. And even though each of the male-female pairs of gods would go on to beget other male-female pairs, Set and Nephthys did not have children and Nephthys was characterized vulgarly as the one with the "useless" vagina. Nephthys runs to Isis in fear of Set, or to console Isis after the murder of Osiris, a situation more fit for a *telenovela* than the gravitas of Egyptian religious mysteries. Thus the Set and Nephthys couple or dyad represent the disorder of the universe; evil enters into the cosmos through their unnatural entrance into the pantheon and the carefully-crafted structure of the created world is ripped apart.

Thus Set is the ultimate (and perhaps the original) anti-hero. His birth and early years are models of rejection, abuse, and violence: rejected by his own family, he turns to the abuse of them and their offspring and violently attacks and kills Osiris and then waits to do the same to Horus, his biological nephew.

But not before sodomizing the Crowned and Conquering Child.

There is little doubt today among Egyptologists that Set was characterized as a homosexual god, and that the famous "Contendings of Horus and Set" contain an account of Set's attempt to sodomize his nemesis. In fact, this attempted act of sodomy is the foundation for such an iconic Egyptian motif as the Eye of Horus. These associations were not generally known in Crowley's time outside a small circle of specialists. Had they been familiar to Crowley, they might have elicited a great many more musings on such themes as sexual magic, the mysteries of the Aeons, and the degree structure of the Ordo Templi Orientis. They certainly do lend support to such claims by later Crowley devotees that the New Aeon would be a "homosexual" Aeon, the males under the aegis of Typhon and the females under Maat.[84]

It was the mother of Horus, Isis, who suggested to her son that he avoid penetration by Set through the use of his fingers to cover his anus, thus capturing Set's semen in his hand whereupon he flung the seed into a river. Set believed he had sodomized Horus successfully, and in a strange turnabout Horus deposited his own semen on a leaf of lettuce (Set's favorite food). Set ate the lettuce and thereby was "penetrated" (orally, we observe) by Horus.

When Set bragged to the gods that he had sodomized Horus, the semen that Horus had thrown into the river spoke out and denied Set the satisfaction of his boast. At that time, Horus claimed that he had penetrated Set, and to prove it the semen that Set had consumed issued forth from Set's forehead as a white disk.

---

84 From a letter written by Michael Bertiaux dated October 10, 1987 and cited in Peter Koenig, "XI°—Per Aftera Ad Astra, Anal Intercourse and the O.T.O."

Before the enraged Set could grab the disk it was seized by Thoth, the god of Wisdom, Magic, and Writing, and placed in the sky as the Moon.[85]

While this episode certainly shows Set as an aggressive and violent being with homosexual attributes, it is not the whole story. In other legends, Set is still violent sexually but in heterosexual as well as homosexual situations. It could be argued that Set represents desire or sexuality *per se*. While Isis may be a symbol of love, especially maternal love, she is not usually identified in terms of pure sexuality. Set, on the other hand, seems to embody lust unrestrained.

If we understand Set to represent raw sexuality we can realize Set's place in the Egyptian cosmos. Set is power, at its most primal and basic ("uncivilized") human level. Unrestrained, it results in rape and pedophilia among other depravations. Restrained, it can be a potent source of protection and occult power. But this power lives in a wild and uninhabited place, outside of society, a wasteland of invisible winds and unseen beasts. Society uses this power when the need arises; at other times, it wants it to go away, to disappear— which is as good a description of modern humanity's relationship to sexuality as any.

It could be argued that our reaction to the concept of sexuality is based upon its more controversial aspects. From teen pregnancy and pedophilia to rape, adultery, abortion, pornography, prostitution, sexually-transmitted diseases, and even gay marriage ... sexuality to the modern mind (West and East) is a minefield of dangerous associations. Crowley himself has the reputation of being a polymorphously perverse libertine who engaged in virtually every form of sexual expression during the course of his lifetime and who had many multiple male and female sexual partners covering the entire spectrum of human society, from street corner prostitutes to celebrities, artists's models, poets, actresses, and wealthy matrons. This was Set, the Dark Lord and God of the Midnight Sky and the circumpolar stars of True North in eternal struggle with Horus,

---

85 This episode is discussed in some detail in H. Te Velde, op. cit., pp.32–80.

the Lord of the Sun, the East, and the ecliptic. Crowley, like Jacob before him, wrestled with an Angel on the Ladder leading up to heaven, only in Crowley's case it was the Egyptian god that the Golden Dawn had taught him to fear and distrust, a god that represented the very sexuality that Crowley championed as being the vehicle for attaining the True Mysteries. It was the god of the Black Mass, and the witches's sabbat.

It was this type of sexual expression that so horrified H. P. Lovecraft to the extent that he never actually wrote about sexuality except in terms of disgust at the "orgiastic rites" of those worshipping the Ancient Ones. Lovecraft instinctively understood that extreme or at least non-traditional forms of sexuality were somehow linked to magic, occult power, and contact with supramundane entities. Lovecraft's instincts thus are linked to Crowley's magic and revelations to form Grant's Necronomicon Gnosis. Set, as the Lord of sexual transgression—which means any sexual activity outside of lawfully-permitted reproductive sex—is a Tantric Lord as well in the broadest sense of that term. Grant claimed that Set offers access to other dimensions, and that a deep understanding of Tantra—coupled with western magical practice and analysis—would lead the magician to the dark side of the Kabbalistic Tree of Life.

This "Setian" Tantra would re-interpret Set's infamous sexual acts as ritual requirements designed to plunge the operator into a dangerous realm of consciousness below that (or beyond that) of the waking world. These acts would include everything from solitary sexual practices to various types of hetero- and homosexual acts, including oral and anal sex. While Grant has argued that the enigmatic XIth degree of the Ordo Templi Orientis did not involve anal penetration—insisting instead that the *per vas nefandum* (the "unmentionable vessel") requirement in Crowley's allusions to the ritual refers to the vagina of a woman during her menstruation, rather than to the anus, giving new meaning to the term "Scarlet Woman"—there is precedence for believing that many other forms of non-reproductive sex do have relevance for modern tantric practitioners. Shiva copulated extensively with his wife Parvati except that he did not impregnate her in the usual way but ejaculated either in her hand or her mouth. These (and many other) episodes from both Egyptian and Indian religion would seem to indicate that forms of sexuality other than those intended for reproduction are being implied, and to many mainstream religions any sexual act that does not have as its intention the reproduction of the species is, by definition, evil and forbidden.[86] Thus, what we may call "sacred sexuality"—whether the pale and pastel mysticism of right-hand Tantra with its hours of silent and motionless meditation on the Shakti yantra, or the red meat rituals of the Black Mass replete with bodily fluids and loud fornications, and everything in between—is transgressive by its very nature and belongs to the realm of the Dark Lord.

This leads us into another ritual developed by Crowley and based, once again, upon the rites of the Golden Dawn into which he had been initiated and which continued to influence his magical worldview his entire life. This is the Ritual of the Star Sapphire, known as *Liber XXXVI* (or "Book 36).

First appearing in Crowley's *Book of Lies*, this ritual was designed to replace the Golden Dawn's Ritual of the Hexagram. The Golden Dawn had two foundational rituals that everyone was expected to learn and to perform: the first of these being the Ritual of the Pentagram which was used to invoke or banish—depending on the direction the pentagram was drawn—the four "Platonic" elements (earth, air, fire and water) plus "spirit." Each of the five points of the pentagram was assigned to one of these elements. It is the basic circle casting ritual of the Golden Dawn and versions of it have been used widely in occult groups and practice for more than one hundred years. This includes Wiccan groups, whose members often are not aware of the origins of their rite which is sometimes called invoking the Watchtowers (a direct reference to the Golden Dawn ritual, which was itself based on the Angelic Magic of Elizabethan

---

86 See, for instance, the Papal Bull *Humane Vitae*.

magician John Dee and his medium, Edward Kelly—of whom Crowley believed he was the reincarnation).

The other, more complex, ceremony is known as the Ritual of the Hexagram. In this ritual, each of the six points of the hexagram is assigned one of the six visible "planets," with the center of the hexagram representing the sun. Thus, depending on how the hexagram is drawn, one is invoking or banishing the influences of one of the planets.

Crowley replaced both of these rituals with his own, Thelemic, versions. The Pentagram ritual was replaced by the Star Ruby ritual whose original angelic beings—Michael, Raphael, Gabriel and Uriel—were substituted with godforms more appropriate to Thelema: Therion (the "Beast") Nuit, Babalon and Hadit.[87]

However, when it came to the Hexagram ritual, a fundamental change took place, one that may not be particularly obvious at first glance. This was the ritual that attracted the attention of Theodor Reuss, one of the founders of the OTO, who visited Crowley in London and accused him of publishing the secret of the IX° of the Order in his 1912 book *The Book of Lies*, a situation that led to Crowley's receiving the IX° from Reuss on the spot—and the rest, as they say, is history. Crowley had already received the grades up to and including the VII° from Reuss, but had no idea that the higher grades consisted of the sexual secrets that he had published. Crowley, in writing out these sexually-charged texts, was just being Crowley; he claimed that Star Sapphire came to him in the same sort of heightened state of consciousness that brought forth the other Holy Books that we have discussed, above. It was Reuss who revealed to him what has become the biggest "secret" of western occultism, that

---

87 The original text in the *Book of Lies* has, instead, Chaos, Babalon, Eros and Psyche, in line with the Greek motif of the ritual which is entirely in that language, as the Star Sapphire is in Latin. Crowley changed the Star Ruby sacred names to the more overtly Thelemic nomenclature evidently out of a need to bring it more in line with his doctrine. However, Chaos and Babalon seem more appropriate, especially in light of the Creed of the Gnostic Mass, discussed above.

the core of the practices—from alchemy to ceremonial magic—are sexual in nature, and that the iconography of occultism (including Rosicrucianism, alchemy, mysticism and magic) conceal sexual (or, at least, psycho-biological) secrets.

Crowley went on to rewrite many of the OTO rituals, to become head of the Order in the English-speaking countries, and eventually head of the Order itself after the contentious Weida Conference in Germany. Thus, this particular ritual deserves close scrutiny as it was the catalyst that propelled Crowley to the headship of the OTO; it is also, according to Reuss himself, the secret of the IX° in printed form. In addition, and most importantly for this study, it is a ritual that puts Set—the Dark Lord—front and center.

An entire book could be written on the Star Sapphire, as simple as it seems to be, and we will not explore all its implications and ramifications here. What concerns us directly is how Crowley perceived Set in his own Thelemic context.

The ritual begins with the key phrase, "Let the Adept be armed with his Magick Rood (and provided with his Mystic Rose)." This is the phrase the caught the attention of Theodor Reuss. A "Magick Rood" of course is a rod or wand, and specifically refers to the cross on which Christ was crucified, the "Holy Rood." Thus this first sentence tells the adept to be armed with a cross and a rose, which is the symbol of one of the most famous European secret societies, the Rosicrucians (which name means, of course, Rose Cross or Rosey Cross). A rose and cross emblem was also the coat-of-arms of the man who ignited the Reformation, Martin Luther. Thus, we can see this instruction as being, if not wholly innocent, at least bereft of any overtly sexual connotation if taken in the context of seventeenth-century European occult societies.

However, the rest of the ritual puts this initial phrase into a completely different context.

After giving a number of quasi-Masonic gestures—the L.V.X. signs or the N.O.X. signs both of which have their origins in the Golden Dawn—the adept is then instructed to go to the four cardinal directions, beginning with the East and proceeding clockwise to the other quarters, uttering a series of Latin phrases and drawing a hexagram in each direction.

The Latin phrases are instructive. Translated, they are:

Father and Mother, One God, ARARITA.
Mother and Son, One God, ARARITA.
Son and Daughter, One God, ARARITA.
Daughter and Father, One God, ARARITA.

Ararita is the same word that appears in the original Golden Dawn version of the Hexagram ritual, and is an acronym for a Hebrew phrase that means "One is his beginning. One is his individuality. His permutation is One."

At the end, the adept returns to his original position in the center of the circle thus made, and "making the sign of the Rosy Cross" he then repeats the word ARARITA three times, after which he makes:

"… the Sign of Set Triumphant and of Baphomet. Also shall Set appear in the circle. Let him drink of the Sacrament and let him communicate the same."

There are further Latin phrases after this, which translated read:

"All in Two; Two in One; One in none; these are neither Four nor All nor Two nor One nor None."

Followed by:

"Glory be to the Father and the Mother and the Son and the Daughter and the Holy Spirit without and the Holy Spirit within which was, and is, and is to come, for ever and ever, six in one through the seven in one name ARARITA."

The emphasis in these phrases seems to be the reduction of all dualities to a singularity, evidence of Crowley's fascination with the Indian concept of *advaita* or non-duality. Yet, duality is at the heart of the ritual, so it is worthwhile to pause here to contemplate its intention.

In the first place, remember that Crowley himself insisted that he did not realize that this was the IX° secret until Theodor Reuss pointed it out to him, and told him that it was the secret behind all of western occultism. Crowley wrote it as a sexual rite and expanded upon this intention in a later chapter[88] of the *Book of Lies*, but was unaware of what he had stumbled upon. It may be that Crowley felt he was simply re-interpreting the rituals in sexual terms rather than discovering the real basis behind them. But what does Set have to do with any of this? And why is Set "Triumphant"?

If this ritual is interpreted in sexual terms, as was the intention, we are left with the uncomfortable realization that three of the four "pairings" are incestuous in nature: Mother and Son, Son and Daughter, Father and Daughter. Crowley was delicate enough, or pragmatic enough, not to have included "Mother and Daughter" or "Father and Son" most likely since heterosexual couplings would be necessary in a ritual of the IX° in which both male and female fluids are required for the creation of the Sacrament. This Sacrament is to be consumed by the operator and "communicated." The last word comes from the Latin Mass, and indicates that the Sacrament is to be shared, so that those sharing "commune" with the spiritual force invoked. In the Latin Mass this is done with the sacred Elements— the bread and wine that have been transubstantiated into the body and blood of Christ—so that all those who communicate (i.e., take Communion) share in the experience of contact with Jesus, the slain and resurrected God.

In the case of the Star Sapphire, since the ritual is patently sexual, the Sacrament is composed of the male and female sexual fluids

---

88   Chapter LXIX, or "Sixty-Nine."

and is a form of the Gnostic Mass in miniature, as it were. What Grant points out, again and again in his Typhonian Trilogies, is that these are not simply the gross fluids in and of themselves, but have been transformed through correct performance of ritual. They thus contain occult qualities which normal semen and female secretions (whether menstrual blood or the secretions of the mucus membranes of the vagina—which are carriers of special essences known as *kalas* to Tantra and to Grant) normally do not possess. These qualities have nothing to do with the process of physical reproduction; they are obviously not necessary to facilitate the conception of a human child. An essential element of this ritual (and, indeed, of all sexual magic) is contact with other forces, those beyond the physical world, so that all the grosser physical aspects of sexual intercourse (from desire, to arousal, to intercourse, to orgasm, to the fluids that result) must be re-imagined, transformed, and transcended.

As a ritual of transgressive sexuality, it would be appropriate for Set. Set is "triumphant"—according to the Egyptian texts so far deciphered—in situations of murder, rape, sodomy, etc. In Set's defence of Ra's solar barque, his violence is put to good use in service of the pantheon, and he is triumphant there as well: he destroys a serpent god, Apep or Apophis (with whom, paradoxically, he is sometimes identified). In the Star Sapphire ritual, it may be that the transgressive powers of Set are first identified and then employed in an act designed to bring the adept into contact with his Holy Guardian Angel (as Crowley himself seems to suggest in Chapter 69 of the *Book of Lies*—where the subject of the Hexagram is discussed in terms that are patently sexual and obvious, including an explicit reference to the sexual position known as "69" or mutual oral sex).

The Golden Dawn instructions concerning the Hexagram ritual make it clear that this is a ritual of the macrocosm (the seven planets, seven of the ten *sefirot* on the Tree of Life), as opposed to the Pentagram ritual which is a rite of the microcosm (the four elements plus spirit, or the five Indian *tattvas*). We may say, then, that the Hexagram ritual (both the Golden Dawn original and

Crowley's reworking of it in the Star Sapphire) is a ritual of the heavens, the sky, and the Pentagram ritual is of the earth.

Therefore, the invocation of Set Triumphant at the climax of the rite indicates the unlocking of a Gate between this world and the next, a Gate that is not quite the same as that which Osiris would have unlocked. It has nothing to do with death and resurrection, per se, but of opening a portal to the Nightside of the Tree of Life, to what Grant refers to as the Tunnels of Set. Here once again Crowley has demonstrated the true nature of his mythos, moreover in a ritual that was written in a heightened state of consciousness similar to that which gave us the *Book of the Heart Girt with a Serpent*: the book that formed the link between Crowley the magician and Lovecraft the seer. That there is the performance of a sexual act in the center of the ceremony and the consumption of the "Elements" thereafter is only another piece of evidence that Grant's understanding of the Thelemic praxis as representing contact with the Dark Lord is the correct one.

In religion, humans are subservient to God or the Gods, especially in the Abrahamic, monotheistic religions. In Thelema, the emphasis is reversed with all the focus on human potential. There is no religious dogma in magic, as much as it might seem to be implied. Magicians dare to do what religious, pious human beings do not: to actively approach the Thrones of the Gods using whatever means are available, even the most blasphemous. The Gods may be more powerful, and even dangerous, but the properly trained human being can navigate the heavens and the hells with impunity.

Chaos and Babalon—we might say Set and Ishtar, Dumuzi and Inanna, Shiva and Shakti—represent the deepest occult processes that lie beneath the play of Maya, of the Illusory World of Creation. Chaos and Babalon are also the gateways to the Dark Side of Creation, just as human sexuality is a gateway to deeper unconscious processes that function—powerfully—below the horizon of conscious thought, calculation, and conjecture. They are irrational forces, which is the characteristic that alarmed Lovecraft the most: they were immune to sober, scientific understanding just as the immense vastness of deep space lies outside the ability of the human mind to contemplate.

The other Gods—Isis, Osiris, Horus, Thoth, Anubis, the list goes on and on and not only for Egyptian deities but also the Greek, Roman, African, Indian, Chinese and so many other pantheons—are aspects of the basic and fundamental two, of Chaos and Babalon. For convenience, they can be considered refinements of specific aspects, points of view, chemical components, psychobiological qualities—but that is not to denigrate their importance or value to the magician. Any one of these deities is a potent force far in excess of any human capacity to contain completely.

The Typhonian Tradition—according to Grant's thesis—is the most ancient of all religious and occult traditions. Its origin is in the stars, and it lies at the base of all later cults. That would indicate that its gods are the basis for all later gods, its rituals the purer forms of all later rituals. But that would be to deny that human beings are capable of refining those ancient rites from time to time, of fine-tuning the original processes for reasons of self-preservation, if nothing else. For Grant is not entirely optimistic concerning the designs of the ultramundane, extraterrestrial forces of which he writes so eloquently. His works are not only guides through the Tunnels of Set to the Dark Side of the Tree of Life: they are also warnings, warnings as sincere as those of Lovecraft were fanciful.

And in order to understand those forces, it is necessary to see how they were invoked by a plethora of "unspeakable cults" around the world, in rituals secret and at times profane.

CHAPTER THREE

Unspeakable Cults

"But look there," he continued, "there, sandwiched between that nightmare of Huysmans', and Walpole's *Castle of Otranto*— Von Junzt's *Nameless Cults*. There's a book to keep you awake at night!"

"I've read it," said Taverel, "and I'm convinced the man is mad. His work is like the conversation of a maniac—it runs with startling clarity for awhile, then suddenly merges into vagueness and disconnected ramblings."

Conrad shook his head. "Have you ever thought that perhaps it is his very sanity that causes him to write in that fashion? What if he dares not put on paper all he knows? What if his vague suppositions are dark and mysterious hints, keys to the puzzle, to those who know?"

"Bosh!" This from Kirowan. "Are you intimating that any of the nightmare cults referred to by Von Junzt survive to this day—if they ever existed save in the hag-ridden brain of a lunatic poet and philosopher?"

"Not he alone used hidden meanings," answered Conrad.
—Robert E. Howard, "The Children of the Night" (1931)

ROBERT E. HOWARD WAS ONE of the circle of fantasy authors around H. P. Lovecraft sometimes referred to as the Lovecraft Circle. He contributed to what has become known as the "Cthulhu Mythos" by writing stories such as the one excerpted above which referenced Lovecraft's Cthulhu, the Necronomicon, and other motifs. One of his contributions to the Mythos was the fictional *Nameless Cults* by Von Junzt, which became the awkward *Unaussprechlichen Kulten*[89] in Lovecraft's German rescension and from there into "Unspeakable

---

89 Should probably read *Unaussprechliche Kulte*.

Cults." Howard's most famous creation, however, was Conan the Barbarian, the fantasy character made even more famous by the actor Arnold Schwarzenegger. In 1936, at the age of 30, Howard committed suicide. He was not the only member of Lovecraft's inner circle to do so. In 1951 he would be followed by Robert H. Barlow, the noted anthropologist of ancient Mexico, expert in the Nahuatl language, and the literary executor of Lovecraft's estate. He committed suicide in Mexico at the age of 32.

One of the prevailing themes in Grant's work (and especially in that of Lovecraft and his circle of fellow gothic horror writers) is of cults that are either African, Afro-Caribbean, Middle Eastern or Asian. In other words, cults that could be defined as non-Western. While Crowley speaks of these cults in passing, he does not focus on them to the extent that Grant does, and Grant does so because he feels that the practices and beliefs of these cults hold keys towards understanding underlying themes and techniques of occultism in general and Thelema specifically.

Thelema's origins, as described in the previous two chapters, can be found in the interpretation of Egyptian mysteries by the British organizers of the Golden Dawn, the secret society in which Crowley was initiated, and their reevaluation and re-imagination by Crowley himself. Most of the religious references in the Book of the Law are to Egyptian god forms familiar to anyone who had been through the initiatory system of the Golden Dawn.

But there are tantalizing references to other schemes of initiation in *AL,* and while Crowley did immerse himself for awhile in Asian methods of magic and mysticism his focus always remained on those systems that were most familiar to Westerners, and those elements of Asian systems that were already in translation in English. He had virtually no background in African or Afro-Caribbean systems. He was thus limited in his ability to draw the same inferences and conclusions of later occultists who had access to greater resources, either in translation or through direct experience of the non-Western systems.

This is beginning to be rectified, and it is largely to Grant that we owe this expansion of Thelemic ideas, methods, and practices into non-Western systems of initiation, and vice versa.

However, while the intellectual composition of Thelema has been extended greatly through Grant's work, it is through the creative and visionary accomplishments of H. P. Lovecraft that we owe the emotional content, albeit in ways the horror writer never consciously intended.

"Weird fiction seems to vie with works on witchcraft, voodoo and dark magic."
—Robert E. Howard, "The Children of the Night"

It is the contention of this writer, as well as of Kenneth Grant, that Lovecraft in some way—unconsciously, probably—was in touch with, or otherwise aware of, the same spiritual material that informed Crowley's contact in Cairo in 1904. We have seen in the previous chapter how closely events in Lovecraft's "Call of Cthulhu" mirrored Crowley's *Holy Book* revelations. There are other parallels, and other synchronicities, between the two writers and as we proceed with this investigation we will look at some of them. What is compelling about these correspondences is that the one amplifies and explains the other. Grant's genius lay in making those initial connections between the horror writer on the one hand and the Prophet of the New Age on the other. It was a bold contention, for it was in danger of making modern occultism look like some kind of role-playing game, a sword-and-sorcery affair replete with scary monsters and secret books.

Several of the cults most important to Lovecraft's stories are precisely those that intrigue both Crowley and Grant. These include the Haitian religion of Voodoo (also spelled variously *vodou, vodun,* etc.) and the Mesopotamian religion of the Yezidi. "Voodoo" makes its appearance in Lovecraft's "Call of Cthulhu" as well as throughout Grant's published work. Grant's interest in this Afro-Caribbean religion was intensified through his relationship with Michael

Bertiaux (b. 1935) of *La Couleuvre Noire* (the "Black Snake"), an occult order based on Haitian Vodou with ideas and methods derived from the Western mystery traditions as well as Lovecraftian and Thelemic elements.

Syncretisms, Orientalisms

Bertiaux had spent some time in Haiti before embracing his own particular occult path, and became a member of a society—the Ordo Templi Orientis Antiqua or OTOA—allegedly created by a mysterious and possibly non-existent Haitian occultist Lucien-François Jean-Maine (1869?–1960) of whom there is very little hard information. The OTOA was evidently a mixture of quasi-Masonic ritual and initiation and traditional *Vodun*, forming a bridge between European-style ceremonial magic traditions and the Afro-Caribbean *Vodun* cultus. Jean-Maine was allegedly the inheritor of an ancient Haitian occult lineage that numbers among its lineage-holders the venerable Ordre des Elus-Cohen which had a branch in Leogane, Haiti. This is not the place to go into the history of the Elus Cohen (or "Elect Priests"), so suffice it to say that it was a branch of the eighteenth century Martinist order and the branch most closely concerned with ritual magic. Martinism began as a Masonic-type society in pre-revolutionary France but its founder—Martinez de Pasqually—died in Haiti in 1774. Haiti at that time was a French colony. Hence the suggested French Masonic-Haitian *Vodun* connection.

Bertiaux worked and expanded upon the system he inherited, and brought it into line with Thelema by 1972. His *Vodoun Gnostic Workbook* became quite well-known for its imaginative combination of western esotericism, Afro-Caribbean concepts and terminology, and sex magic. Kenneth Grant saw in Bertiaux's work a verification of his belief that the Thelemic magical current had to be all-inclusive if it represented a genuine change of Aeon. That meant that analogues had to be found in African, Latin American and Asian traditions as well as the more familiar European and Middle

Eastern practices. Not only that, but these traditions would also hold keys to the full implementation of the current, based on their knowledge of occult matters and technologies stemming from their own environment, culture, and history and which might be either ignored or missing in western systems. Knowledge, to Grant, is power.

As we mentioned above, Crowley's own knowledge of these practices was thin. This is not to criticize Crowley, for deep understanding of these mystical technologies had always eluded Western observers and there were few who had the requisite background in the languages and rituals of India, Africa, and the indigenous cultures of all continents in the early twentieth century. That would gradually change, and by the beginning of the twenty-first century a growing number of religious studies and anthropology scholars have made tremendous inroads into Chinese, Tibetan, Mongolian, African, and Afro-Caribbean languages and scriptures, both written and oral. Grant's contribution was to make as much use as possible of the growing body of esoteric literature in translation from Asian and African sources in order to elaborate upon Thelemic themes and to create a more powerful ritual machinery for probing the darker side of occultism.

Thus, not only the Haitian religious system known as *Vodun* but also primary source material on Tantric practices make their way into Grant's grand design. These elements were always there in Crowley's writings and even in Liber AL itself, of course. But before Grant the focus primarily had been on the Egyptian, Kabbalistic and to some extent alchemical characteristics of Thelemic ritual and concepts. Bertiaux—and the Tantric expert David Curwen—were able to contribute to Grant's knowledge of non-European occultism in important ways.

Heretofore, the occult or esoteric practices of any culture were basically consistent with that culture and it's religious and magical ideas. This was the case even when there was obvious borrowing, such as within the syncretic faiths (such as Santeria, Vodun, etc.) where there was an admixture of foreign components with an indigenous belief system. The power of magic rests, however, in its antinomian nature: it lives on the outer limits of what is traditional, acceptable, "normal," and legal. While Gnosticism, for instance, can be understood as a kind of Christian esotericism, it borrowed heavily from Egyptian and Platonic sources, sources that would have been anathema to orthodox Christians.

But this type of syncretism was a result of neighboring cultures meeting each other and borrowing from the religious and esoteric practices of the other. What is proposed in Grant's project is nothing less than a borrowing from whatever source, wherever in the world, and whenever it existed. There is no sense of geographic proximity resulting in adulteration of one method or another, but of the deliberate search through the world's religions, esotericisms, mysticisms and magics for methods that can be adapted to the overall agenda of Thelema. While this seems to have been Crowley's original intention—as reflected, for instance, in the tables of correspondences between the world's religions that can be found in *Liber 777*, a project begun by members of the Golden Dawn and greatly expanded by Crowley—it would be Grant who would make this type of deliberate and conscious syncretism a cornerstone of his cult.

Leaders of religions may quarrel with each other over beliefs and dogma; devotees of religions may fight and kill each other over their differences; but mystics understand each other, regardless of their formal affiliation. Mystics are interested in techniques for achieving altered states of consciousness that can lead them to greater and deeper understanding. The attempt by some in Thelemic circles to forge bonds between Tantra, Vodun, Kabbalah, ceremonial magic, and alchemy represents this point of view. This is not—and should not be—an attempt to find justification for one particular dogma over another, or to prop up one particular interpretation over another. It is, instead, a quest for truth in the discovery of workable techniques. Magicians are interested only in what works. Like scientists from both sides during the Cold War, there is curiosity and a willingness to learn from potential enemies as well as from friends.

The danger in this approach lies in the facile comparisons made between different cultures as if their gods and rituals had exact equivalents among those in another completely different culture. There is evidence of this in *Liber 777* and the tables of correspondences which demonstrate the creators were often too quick to make associations between deities that may or may not have much in common. This tendency has been called "universalism" by the post-modern critics who instead emphasize ethnic and cultural originality and uniqueness. Both of these approaches—in their extreme manifestations—are equally erroneous, in my view.

What Grant has done is to cull these different techniques and approaches in order to discover knowledge that cultures other than his own had obtained through the use of methods that might have been neglected in the West due to ignorance or tabu. This is especially true when it comes to occult or esoteric techniques that are sexually-based or based upon a knowledge of human anatomy and physiology that has been put to use by those who perceived a spiritual analogue to physical properties and functions. While a Western bias has been to downgrade the importance of the human body, or to see the human body as a potential source of sin and transgression, the Asian and African viewpoints reflect a respect for the body and an interest in examining biological functions in terms of their spiritual potential, or their potential for attaining higher—or simply altered—states of consciousness.

Thus, sexuality and drugs became the province of non-Western esoteric practices after the rise of Christianity in Europe repressed and suppressed these ideas. While there is much more to Asian and African forms of spirituality and esotericism than sexuality and drugs, these represented the missing pieces in the Western repetoire.

The story of the OTO has the founders traveling to the Middle East to obtain initiations in "sex magic" and related methods. Pascal Beverly Randolph (a major influence on modern Western esotericism) also claimed Middle Eastern initiations, and Aleister Crowley himself traveled through North Africa and India—as well as Ceylon—in search of African and Asian wisdom.

Grant, however, took a more organized approach to the subject and began collecting previously-unknown or untranslated esoteric texts from these cultures as well as building relationships with those who had already been initiated into those traditions. This included Michael Bertiaux and David Curwen, as we shall see. But Grant did not stop there.

Other forms of creative spirituality were not immune to Grant's all-inclusive approach. Art and literature represented, for Grant, additional avenues to explore for greater understanding of the Thelemic project as well as a source of other technologies that could become part of the magician's arsenal.

Thus, the art of Austin Osman Spare (1886–1956) was given as much regard in Grant's cult as the writings of H. P. Lovecraft. While Lovecraft described the "hideous" practices of Asian and African cults in words, Spare canonized them in his art and his magical system. Grotesque human forms engaged in obscure ritual are powerful images in Spare's magical worldview, just as grotesque alien beings hold blind, omnipotent sway over humans in Lovecraft's world. Even more to the point, Spare understood that words—Lovecraft's metier—have intrinsic magical power as well, and could be manipulated in such a way that the physical representation of a word or phrase could acquire occult potency. It was an attempt to use words as art forms, to reduce words to the ideas they represent: to bring them back to their original status as symbols, as hieroglyphics. Spare's system was atavistic: a going-back in time to the period when writing was first being invented, a time when the written word held tremendous magical power and could be interpreted only by the initiates, the priests.

In this, Spare's system was as much a reference to ancient cults as it was an idiosyncratic occult method of his own devising. This was probably what attracted Grant in the first place, for Spare was a unique individual with a non-denominational approach to occultism. There was no formal Kabbalah in Spare's system, no nod to Jewish or Christian contexts. Instead, it was a kind of orientalist fantasy of occultism and acted as a reach beyond texts as such to the deeper layers of consciousness where our fears and our anxieties (and our sexuality) are located ... somewhere in the limbic brain, perhaps, curled around itself at the top of the spinal cord.

One of the iconic forms of this type of "orientalist fantasy" is the emphasis given to the Kurdish cult of the Yezidi. Since Grant devotes an entire chapter to the Yezidi in his *Outer Gateways*, it behooves us to investigate this religion further and to try to separate the wheat from the chaff.

The Cult of the Peacock Angel

> I read of it first in the strange book of Von Junzt, the German eccentric who lived so curiously and died in such grisly and mysterious fashion. It was my fortune to have access to his *Nameless Cults* in the original edition, the so-called Black Book, published in Dusseldorf in 1839, shortly before a hounding doom overtook the author.
> —Robert E. Howard, "The Black Stone"

> ... he thought the ritual was some remnant of Nestorian Christianity tinctured with the Shamanism of Thibet. Most of the people, he conjectured, were of Mongoloid stock, originating somewhere in or near Kurdistan—and Malone could not help recalling that Kurdistan is the land of the Yezidis, last survivors of the Persian devil-worshippers.
> —H. P. Lovecraft, "The Horror at Red Hook"

The Yezidis and the Tibetans. This same comparison would be made by Kenneth Grant decades later, and not in a fictional sense but entirely seriously. While rumors of the Yezidi made their way into European travelogues and archaeological literature in the nineteenth century,[90] it wasn't until the early days of the twentieth

---

90 One of the earliest sources was the famous British archaeologist Austen Henry Layard in his *Nineveh and Its Remains*, London, John Murray, 1849.

century that they became better known and the subject of one book that set the tone for so many future "revelations": Isya Joseph's *Devil Worship: The Sacred Books and Traditions of the Yezidiz*. Published in 1919, Joseph's book contained the first English versions of the *Black Book* and the *Revelation*: two previously secret and unpublished texts said to be the core scriptures of the Yezidi faith and which, according to Joseph, were translated from the Arabic. These texts are referenced in Grant's books and in other occult and esoteric works that touch on the Yezidi cultus.

Recent scholarship, however, has shown that these two texts are most likely the result of a hoax perpetrated by a well-known antiquities dealer and forger of documents and are not actual Yezidi texts.[91] The Yezidi are said to possess what is largely an oral tradition, composed of many disparate elements including—but not limited to—those of Christian, Islamic, Jewish and possibly Gnos-

---

Articles on the Yezidi had appeared in French a few years earlier by M. Boré in his "De la vie religieuse chez les Chaldéens" in two parts, July and August 1843, in the *Annales de Philosophie Chrétienne*. Isya Joseph published some preliminary articles on the Yezidi in the *American Journal of Semitic Languages and Literatures*, in January and April, 1909 in a two-part series entitled "Yezidi Texts." These would be followed by his book *Devil Worship* in 1919. Another book-length treatment of the subject was *The Cult of the Peacock Angel* by R.H.W. Empson, London, Witherby, 1928, appearing a year after Crowley associate William Seabrook's *Adventures in Arabia: Among the Bedouins, Druses, Whirling Dervishes, and Yezidee Devil Worshippers*, 1927; New York, Blue Ribbon, 1930. For a more recent and scholarly source, see John Guest, *The Yezidis: A Study in Survival*, London, Routledge, Kegan and Paul, 1987, and Giulia Sfameni Gasparro, "I Miti Cosmogonici Degli Yezidi" in *Numen*, Vol. XXI, Fasc. 3, pp. 197–227, and Vol. XXII, Fasc. 1, pp. 24–41, Leiden, Brill, 1974. It should be noted that Crowley's identification with Sumer predates the appearance of popular books on the subject by at least ten years.

91 See for instance J.F. Coakley, "Manuscripts for sale: Urmia. 1890–2" in *Journal of Assyrian Academic Studies*, Vol. 20, no.2, 2006 where the trade of one Jeremiah Shamir in Mosul was cited as a source for documents of dubious provenance. See the *Encyclopedia Iranica,* online edition, New York, 1996- entry, "Jelwa, Ketab Al-" for the reasons (mostly linguistic) behind this claim. Also see the above cited book by John Guest for more information on Shamir.

tic and Zoroastrian beliefs and practices. While they do speak of a "Black Book" that was written in heaven, their religion is based less on doctrine and more on the correct observance of ritual. That said, it is also generally agreed that the texts of the published "Black Book" and "Book of Revelation" *do* accurately reflect the basic beliefs of the main Yezidi clans even though they are not genuine Yezidi scriptures.

Grant first mentions the Yezidi at the very outset of his nine-volume series on Thelemic magic, in *The Magical Revival* first published in 1972. It is clear from this book and virtually all his subsequent works that he considered the Yezidi a core influence and an important spiritual tradition with links to Thelema and specifically to Crowley and Aiwaz. However—except for a single chapter in *Outer Gateways*—he repeats himself on the subject without adding any new material or justifying his concentration on the Yezidi. Much of his information is taken either from Joseph's work or from stray remarks by Massey, etc.

The basic ideas are these:

First, the whole attraction of the Yezidi for both Crowley and Grant is the idea that they are devil worshippers. If not for this, they most probably would have been ignored—not only by Crowley and Grant but by a number of nineteenth-century explorers who mention them in travelogues on the Kurdish tribal areas. If there was an ancient sect in the Middle East that had been worshipping the devil since time immemorial, it would be an important element of *fin-de-siecle* orientalist fantasies about the Black Mass, satanism, and witchcraft.

Second, Grant has the idea—an echo of references found in Massey—that the Yezidi are descendants of the ancient Akkadian and Sumerian cultures that represent some of the oldest (if not the oldest) civilizations in the world of which we have any written record, predating even the Egyptians. This fascination with "origins" is one of the hallmarks of the universalist approach to the study of religion and culture, and is also a component of ideas concerning spiritual succession and lineage (i.e., spiritual authority).

The first of these ideas—that the Yezidi are "devil worship-pers"—is connected to the fact that Shaitan is an important element of the Yezidi belief-system. Shaitan—or "Satan"—is the Fallen Angel who rebelled against God when humans were elevated in importance above the angels. To the Yezidi, Satan will be the first of God's creatures to enter heaven as he will be the first to be forgiven. This reverence for Shaitan is reflected in the tabu associated with the sound "sh" with which the word Shaitan begins. Yezidi avoid using that sound as much as possible because of its connection. This has led to the misunderstanding that the Yezidi actually worship Shaitan, or Satan. Yet, another point of view on the subject is that the name Shaitan is so sacred—and therefore unpronounceable by the pious—that another form of address and identification had to be created to take its place in normal conversation. While it seems likely that the Yezidi do worship (or at least reverence) Shaitan, and are aware of his demonic associations, they do not associate Shaitan with evil. Shaitan's "sin" was in refusing to bow down before Man, claiming that he would bend the knee to no other but God as that is what God had commanded from the beginning. So God punished Shaitan for disobeying his second command while honoring him for his commitment to obeying the first command, thus ensuring that Shaitan would be the first creature to be redeemed.

The chief (pronounceable) object of worship among the Yezidi is known as *Melek Ta'us*,[92] the so-called "Peacock Angel," and has become another focus of Grant's work—as he associates the pea-cock with a host of entities and ideas that reinforce his overall con-cept of a Dark Lord. This is a subject we will examine shortly, but some observers have claimed that Melek Ta'us and Shaitan are one and the same. Indeed, the cosmologies and creation stories of the Yezidi tend to support this idea at times, and to contradict it at

---

92 One author has suggested that the word Ta'us comes from Ta'uz, a form of the ancient Babylonian god Tammuz. Empson, op.cit., p. 184. If so, this would further bolster at least a Babylonian (if not Sumerian) connection to the Yezidis.

others. In the absence of a written text, this confusion (at least to outsiders) is inevitable.

The second issue of importance to Grant is the idea that the Yezidi are somehow descendants or survivors of the Sumerians. Grant's equation can be summarized as: Sumer = Yezidi = Satan = Aiwass. In order to address this idea we have to ask: who are the Yezidi, and where did they come from?

This is a controversial area for ethnologists, politicians, anthropologists and historians of religion alike. The Yezidi themselves claim an origin variously in India or in Sumer; to split the difference, there is a claim that they came from India to Sumer, and are descendants of the Sumerians themselves.[93] That they are presently considered a Kurdish clan is based mostly on their language—most Yezidi speak a form of Kurdish known as Kurmanji—and upon the fact that their tribal lands are within Kurdish territory in northern Iraq and are often counterminous with Kurdish lands in other areas in Syria, Armenia, Azerbaijan, etc. This connection may also be due to the fact that the Kurds in general are subject to varying degrees of discrimination and outright genocide (such as under the regime of Saddam Hussein in Iraq) and the Yezidis are easily one of the most discriminated-against clans in the world.

The problem of the origins of the Yezidis as well as the nature of their religious philosophy is compounded by the fact that their leaders seem to say different things to different people, as is evidenced by the wide variety of academic and journalistic sources that

---

93 The theory that the ancient Sumerians might have come to Mesopotamia from India is one of the options being seriously considered by linguists and physical anthropologists. That they were non-Semitic seems to be generally accepted. That their origins are mysterious and shrouded in the eldritch tendrils of the mists of antiquity is also accepted. See for instance Arkadiusz Sołtysiak, "Physical anthropology and the 'Sumerian problem,'" in *Studies in Historical Anthropology*, vol. 4:2004 [2006], pp 145–158 for an overview of the prevailing theories. At any rate, this new theory is consistent with what the Yezidi say about themselves. It is also implied in the Schlangekraft recension of the Necronomicon when it is attested that the symbol of the Sumerian "race" is the *Ar* with "Aryan" as cognate.

all seem to contradict each other on essential points. The lack of a definitive written scripture only adds to the confusion among outside observers. Combine this with the violent upheavals to which the Yezidis have been subjected over hundreds of years and which entailed the loss of land, documents, and the near genocide of their people on religious and political grounds, and it is a wonder that they have survived as long as they have and that their sacred shrine of Lalish—believed by them to be the center of the universe—still stands in northern Iraq, near the Turkish border.

For our purposes, however, there are actually several pieces of circumstantial evidence that indicate the Yezidis are closer to Grant's concept of them than first appear. In the first place, we remember from the previous chapter that the Egyptian god Set was fond of lettuce and that is how he was tricked into consuming the semen of Horus. Oddly, the consumption of lettuce is tabu among the Yezidis. The "exoteric" explanation for this is that the word for lettuce sounds too similar to the name of one of their prophets. But if the name Shaitan is indeed a version of the Egyptian name Set, then the lettuce tabu makes perfect sense.

Another strange coincidence lies in the fact that the Kurdish word for "God" is Khudâ or "Lord."[94] We cannot help but recognize the similarity between Khudâ and Kutu, the Sumerian word for the Biblical city of Gudua or Cutha, which—according to the Schlangekraft recension of the Necronomicon—is the basis for the name of Lovecraft's Cthulhu or "Man of Cutha" or "Man of Kutu": *Kutulu*. Cutha was ruled by the Sumerian god Nergal and was believed to be the gate to the Underworld, which once again supports a Sumerian or Babylonian connection to the Yezidis who do, after all, live in a region that was once part of the Babylonian empire. Indeed, the ancient site of Nineveh[95] is not far from Lalish and the modern Iraqi city of Mosul.

---

94 See, for instance, Empson, op. cit., p. 174-175.
95 Nineveh, discovered by the archaeologist Layard who also wrote of his meeting with the Yezidis, was an ancient city famously cursed by the Biblical

All that said, while there is no proof that the Yezidis are descendants of the Sumerians or even from another migrating tribe from northern India or Persia, their religion and culture is distinct from Islamic, Christian, and Jewish practices and theologies. One of their most revered leaders—Sheikh Adi—was by most accounts a Sufi mystic. While many observers agree that the Yezidi religion is syncretistic—a combination of various elements from other religious practices including most probably Persian Zoroastrianism, in some ways like Santeria and other Afro-Caribbean religions that mixed Roman Catholic iconography and ritual with indigenous African belief systems—the Sufi element is one that probably encouraged the incorporation of antinomian and even transgressive beliefs, such as the idea that the Fallen Angel will be the first to be redeemed along with the Yezidis. It was after all Sufism that was the first Islamic presence in the islands of Java and Sumatra in the fifteenth century (and earlier) and its influence can be seen there today in such practices as visiting graves, reverencing saints, etc. which are also hallmarks of Yezidism but which are not accepted Islamic practice. In fact, Grant himself seems to make the connection between syncretistic forms of religion, expanded consciousness, and contact with supramundane entities when he writes:

> The Amenta of the Egyptians is identical to the Agharta of the Mongols. The latter with their pre-Buddhistic Bön complex, and shamanistic rites with Tantric implicits, produced a weird combination of savage grotesquery and the profound metaphysical adumbrations of the *Sûnyâtavâda*. ... It is therefore in the Eskimo-shamanistic and the Bön impregnated Buddhism of Tibet, Mongolia, Java and Sumatra, that the fundamental

---

prophet Nahum, who called it a "harlot that was beautiful and agreeable and that made use of witchcraft ..." (Nahum 3:4), as good a Biblical description of Crowley's Babalon as any. Nineveh was also the city where Jonah was sent to preach, and from where he subsequently fled to the sea, only to find himself swallowed by a whale. There is today a shrine to Jonah at Nineveh, believed to be his tomb.

tenets of the Madhyamaka—as permeating the Nyingmapa and Drukpa Cults—are relevant to the Necronomicon Gnosis.[96]

Without going into detail on the definitions of the Buddhist terms, the first impression one gets from that passage is that Grant is playing fast and loose with his attributions by linking Amenta (the Egyptian land of the Dead) to Agharta, the fabled underground city believed hidden somewhere in the Himalayas.[97] That there may be a close connection between the indigenous Bön religion of Tibet and Tantric practices is being debated by scholars of the literature; as is the idea that Bön is a survival of an older, shamanistic cult which certainly seems to be the case. Grant's boldness, however, lies more in making the case that Tibetan Buddhism (which is primarily Tantric) is somehow cognate with Egyptian mysteries and the Necronomicon; and that "savage grotesquery" and "profound metaphysical adumbrations" can combine to form a new kind of spiritual methodology. But this is Grant's forte.

Modern western magic is a refusal to accept the position of post-modernism that each culture is unique and owes nothing to other cultures, even when similar ideas, symbols, and rituals are involved. As a magical operator in the modern world, one has to embrace a kind of neo-universalism in which one recognizes the existence of a symbol structure representing an underlying reality behind all observed phenomena. The expert manipulation of these symbols results in changes in phenomena. The magician is thus sensitive to the power and nature of symbols—including symbolic action, symbolic sounds, smells, etc.—and can draw inferences across diverse cultures and times. Just as human biology is

---

96   Kenneth Grant, *Outer Gateways*, p. 92
97   Agharta is frequently confused with Shambhala. Shambhala is a well-known Tibetan Buddhist concept, which became the "Shangri-La" of Hollywood fame. The origin of the word Agharta and the mythology connected with it is ambiguous and possibly a fictional creation of European travelers and mystics. The Theosophists believe it is a kind of polar opposite to Shambhala and the domain of demonic forces.

the same whether one is a native Tibetan or African or European, etc.; and even though there may be many superficial differences and variations in language, food, and so forth; the symbol systems of different cultures may reveal superficial differences as a result of geography, history, and even religion, but the states of consciousness represented by these symbols are identical or nearly so. There would be no syncretic religions if this were not the case, for if each religion was *sui generis* it would be impossible to incorporate alien gods, rites, and beliefs. Of course, this is not the case with religious *dogma* which fundamentally resists attempts at syncretism; but it is the case with religious *praxis*, which is the only form of religion that interests the magician. As noted previously, the magician is not a member of the congregation of any religion: the magician is a priest and an independent spiritual specialist whose interest solely resides in effective methods (rituals) and convenient modes of analysis (symbol systems). Thus the emphasis on cults versus religions, for a cult is a laboratory of ritual and dangerous practice. It may be a matter of opinion as to whether the ritual came before the dogma or vice versa; but it has been demonstrated in the case of religions as disparate as The Church of Jesus Christ of Latter-Day Saints and Scientology that their origins are to be found in magical—that is to say, occult—ritual. The dogmas came later.

Thus when we speak of the Yezidi religion we are struck by the fact that the emphasis seems to be on correct ritual practice rather than doctrine. There is controversy over whether or not the Yezidi have a written sacred text; their scripture seems to reside in the chants, songs, and prayers that are memorized by the faithful and by their ritual specialists. There is also an emphasis on genetic purity: a Yezidi may not marry outside the faith, and there is no possibility of an outsider converting to Yezidism. This association of the body—the blood, the flesh—with religious purity and acceptability is an echo of the occult preoccupations of many different cultures and religious affiliations. It is also a hallmark of cultic practice: the desire to cut off a group from the outside world in order to maintain the group's physical, emotional and spiritual integrity is (among other things) a form of distrust of the "Other" but it is also a way to switch tables by making the mainstream group the "Other."[98]

In the case of the Yezidi, this is taken a step further when they identify themselves with the supreme icon of the Other in the western world: the Fallen Angel, Shaitan. Their relationship to this form of the Dark Lord is complex. On the one hand, Shaitan is an emblem of bad luck that inspires fear. On the other hand, he is the Lord of the Angelic Hosts and is also known as the Lord of Power.[99] This rather schizoid construct is so reminiscent of the way the Egyptians considered Set as to be virtually identical.

To Grant, the peacock symbol is particularly important for he sees in the rainbow-hued spread of feathers a reference to the *kalas*: the spiritual essences secreted by the female partner in Tantric rituals. While it is possible that the Yezidis have their origin in India—as has been claimed—there is no indication at the present time that anything resembling sexual rituals or Tantra is known among them. Yet, the peacock itself is a curious emblem for a Kurdish clan in northern Iraq to worship for peacocks are not native to that country while they are more common in India.

The portals that lead to the inner chambers of Yezidi shrines are usually adorned with carvings of snakes. The snake is shown as rising up from the ground and appears as a vertical decoration on the right-hand side of the entrance. The appearance of a snake in this context further led observers to believe that there was something vaguely satanic about the Yezidis, since the serpent is a symbol of evil and of the Devil in Judaeo-Christian religions. It was the serpent who tempted Eve in the Garden of Eden, leading to the fall of humanity from paradise. In Egypt, of course, it was identified with Apophis, the evil creature intent on devouring the barque of Ra; but in Indian yoga and Tantra, the serpent represents the coiled energy

---

98   As may be observed in the beliefs and practices of the Qumran sect that gave us the Dead Sea Scrolls. The Qumranites set themselves up as the true Jews in opposition to the Jerusalem Temple Jews.

99   Empson, op. cit., p. 183.

at the base of the spine known as Kundalini. The fact that the Yezidi serpent is depicted vertically alongside the entrance to the sacred shrine may be further—circumstantial—evidence of a connection with Indian beliefs, as a vertical serpent would be an obvious reference to the raising of Kundalini which is the goal of Kundalini yoga as it is of some forms of Tantra. However, there is no evidence for the existence of a "Yezidi Tantra."

One of Aleister Crowley's associates during his sojourn in the United States in 1919 was the noted author and adventurer William Seabrook (1884–1945). Fascinated by the occult and foreign locales, Seabrook had written a number of popular books and magazine articles on his travels in Africa, the Middle East and the Caribbean, and even claimed to have eaten human flesh on at least one occasion.[100] Seabrook's works have been criticized by anthropologists who doubt his ability (or his desire) to separate reality from fantasy, but he stands at the crossroads of the topics that so fascinated Kenneth Grant: the Yezidis, witchcraft, and Vodun. In addition, as a friend of Crowley he seems to be excellently positioned as a source for the beliefs and inspirations behind Grant's overall thesis.

When it comes to the Yezidis, Seabrook claims that these "devil worshippers" maintain a network of seven towers across the Middle East, and Central and East Asia:

> Stretching across Asia, from North Manchuria, through Tibet, west through Persia, and ending in the Kurdistan, was a chain of seven towers on isolated mountaintops; and in each one of these towers sat continuously a Priest of Satan, who by "broadcasting" occult vibrations controlled the destinies of the world for evil.[101]

100 William B. Seabrook, *Jungle Ways*, London, George G. Harrap, 1931.
101 William B. Seabrook, *Adventures in Arabia: Among the Bedouins, Druses, Whirling Dervishes, and Yezidee Devil Worshippers*, 1927; New York, Blue Ribbon, 1930.

There is no further evidence for this claim other than Seabrook's own statements, and it is possible that the towers one sees at Kalish and at other Yezidi shrines were the inspiration for this idea. Yezidi sacred architecture is unique: their shrines are in the shape of fluted cones surmounted by a golden ball that is said to represent the sun. At the base of the cone is an opening through which one can see a fire burning. The fire is an eternal flame, tended by the Yezidis, and is thus reminiscent of Zoroastrian practice.

If the Yezidi faith truly represents a survival of Persian Zoroastrianism, then there is some truth to Seabrook's statement that their "towers" extend through Asia, for the Zoroastrians themselves have survived in India and Pakistan where they are known as Parsis. Forced to flee Persia (Iran) rather than convert to Islam in the eighth and ninth centuries CE, the Zoroastrian community found themselves in Pakistan (near Karachi) and in India in the Gujarat region in Mumbai, the former Bombay. There are several fire temples in the Mumbai area where the Zoroastrians—now known as Parsis from the word for "Persian"—have become pillars of the Indian community, well-known for their charitable works. They also practice a form of "sky burial" known as the Towers of Silence.

Because the elements are considered sacred, the Parsis leave their dead on top of these towers as food for vultures. To bury a corpse is considered a defilement of the earth, and to burn a corpse is considered a defilement of fire (which is a sacred symbol in Zoroastrianism). In Mumbai, these towers are located on Malabar Hill in what is now an upscale neighborhood where they have become controversial due to the fact that the vulture population is declining and the presence of certain antibiotics in the dead bodies results in the corpses taking longer and longer to decay. It should be noted that "sky burial" is also a feature of Tibetan religious and cultural practice, where the dead are left in the open air as food for carrion birds.

It is possible that the unique tower architecture of the Yezidis was conflated with the Towers of Silence in Mumbai to give Seabrook the idea that there was a network of Yezidi towers stretching from Kurdistan to Tibet and Manchuria through Persia. Further, there are still Zoroastrians living in Iran, especially in the city of Yazd which boasts a fire temple whose flame has been burning steadily since the fifth century CE. (The similarity in name between Yazd and the Yezidi has been noted by several authors, but there is no consensus of opinion as to where the name Yezid or Yezidi originated or even what it actually means.) However, there is no evidence that there are "Priests of Satan" who sit atop these towers broadcasting "occult vibrations" for evil purposes.

There are, however, certain sites sacred to the Yezidis which have, for Grant, occult significance. Basing his information on Isya Joseph's *The Devil Worshippers* (but without attribution) he mentions five cult zones, one of which is Lalish (the center of the Yezidi religion already mentioned) and another which is called variously Weran Šahr or Goran Šahr:

> ... meaning the 'sunken city', which recalls the sunken city of R'lyeh where Great Cthulhu waits dreaming.... We are now in a position to appreciate Crowley's claim to have continued, in and through Thelema, the major tenets of the Yezidic cult.[102]

As mentioned previously, Crowley believed his supramundane contact and Holy Guardian Angel Aiwaz to have been a god of ancient Sumer.[103] The Yezidis claim a Sumerian ancestry for their people and their religion and, indeed, reverence a form of Shaitan or Set. Further, the official seal of the Yezidi clan depicts not only the peacock of Melek Ta'us,[104] but also cuneiform inscriptions plus the ancient Sumerian cuneiform symbol for "god," the eight-pointed

102 Kenneth Grant, *Outer Gateways*, p. 106.
103 This claim is made by Crowley in several places, as we have seen. In his *Cephaloedium Working* (1920), he is quite clear in the statement that lists his titles: "... whose Holy Angel his Guardian is Aiwaz 93, the God first dawning upon Man in the land of Sumer...."
104 Indeed, as one Yezidi leader said to a journalist at the time of the US-led invasion of Iraq in 2002, Melek Ta'us means "the ancient one." (Patrick Graham,

star,[105] thus showing their insistence on an ancient Mesopotamian origin for their faith. All of this data is consistent with what Grant calls the "Necronomicon gnosis."

The only lengthy examination of the Yezidis in Grant's works appears as a single chapter in *Outer Gateways*: "The Magical Significance of Yezidic Symbolism." In that chapter, Grant associates the Yezidis with a number of other religions, cults, myths, practices, etc. with a heavy reliance upon coincidences in numerology, similar-sounding words, etc., all with a view towards demonstrating that the Yezidis are the inheritors of an ancient magical Typhonian current that erupted in the system of Thelema as preached by Crowley. Crowley himself implies as much, of course, but Grant attempts to "prove" this connection and elaborate upon it. The problem with his approach is that it is based almost entirely on the few scraps of information available on the Yezidis in a handful of outdated and unreliable sources (such as Seabrook), which are then tied into the grand design using the most tenuous of associations. Thus, for Grant, the peacock is a phallic symbol because the eyes on the peacock's feathers represent the "meatus of the phallus, which is why the cock was typical of Yezid"[106] and:

> The eyes in the tail of the peacock, or the meatus in the phallus
> of Yezid are equally connoted, and are resumed in the glyph
> of the Eye in the Triangle which forms part of the emblem of
> the O.T.O. *Kaph* signifies both the palm (of the hand), and the
> *kaf* ape, which typified among other things the open eye or the

"Iraq's 'Devil Worshippers'" in the Canadian *National Post*, December 17, 2002.) This fits perfectly with the terminology used in the Necronomicon Gnosis.

105 A symbol that also appears in the Schlangekraft recension of the Necronomicon many times on the various seals of the planetary forces as well as prominently on the Crown of Anu (p. 112).

106 Grant, *Outer Gateways*, p. 103. According to Grant the word *Yezid* signifies one of the three persons in one "god" of the Yezidi, the other two being Melek Ta'us and Sheikh Adi, the latter of whom many scholars assume was the real creator of the Yezidi clan although this is still hotly contested. Grant's theology here is suspect.

exposed meatus of the circumcised penis in a state of erection, thus denoting the ever wakeful one. [107]

One is tempted to say that sometimes a cigar is just a cigar. However, we begin to realize that virtually everything in the cosmos can be interpreted sexually, or using sexual metaphor, and that this is a hallmark of the "twilight language" used by occultists, alchemists, and mystics as a kind of meta-language for discussing otherwise ineffable—or "unspeakable"—concepts. There is only one process in the universe, and every science, every art, every religion, every field of occult knowledge can be discussed and investigated using the language of that process. Thus, using sexual metaphor, one can describe ecstatic mystical states as well as the transmutation of lead into gold.

Crowley himself makes this point when he writes:

I have myself constructed numerous ceremonies where it is frankly admitted that religious enthusiasm is primarily sexual in character.... I have insisted that sexual excitement is merely a degraded form of divine ecstasy.[108]

This divine ecstasy is still only a means towards an end. Ecstasy can be chemically induced, or brought about by various other means, none of which would necessarily result in spiritual illumination, acquisition of occult powers, etc. Intensive meditation, of the type enjoyed by anchorites and hermits of various disciplines, also results in divine ecstasy, minus the overtly sexual components. The magical path represented by Crowley and by his mentors in the Golden Dawn, however, sees emotional and psychological states as reflective of spiritual qualities that may or may not be perceived as good or evil in and of themselves: these states are only levels of understanding, of types of experience that do not carry moral

---

107 Ibid., p. 104.
108 Aleister Crowley, *Confessions*, Chapter 61, p. 554.

loads but are informational. They are interpreted within a specific cultural context such as the Kabbalistic Tree of Life or any other complete cosmological system that makes a space for all forms of human experience, including the divine and the demonic. In order for Crowley's system to be the complete cosmology that any magical practice demands, it must make room for what Western spiritual experience would consider demonic, satanic, etc. There are, after all, two "Keys of Solomon" in the repetoire of the Golden Dawn: the *Greater Key*, which is concerned with angelic and planetary magic, and the *Lesser Key*, or *Goetia*, which is wholly involved with the raising of demons. Both are necessary. And it is the peculiar characteristic of sexuality that it can be a "Greater Key," an expression of love, respect, fidelity, a means of reproduction and the survival of the species, a symbol of union with the divine ... and a "Lesser Key," an avenue for the manifestation of the darkest desires of a human being, of sadism, masochism, and all the demons of a Krafft-Ebing grimoire:

> Sexual feeling is really the root of all ethics, and no doubt of aestheticism and religion.
>
> The sublimest virtues, even the sacrifice of self, may spring from sexual life, which, however, on account of its sensual power, may easily degenerate into the lowest passion and basest vice.
>
> Love unbridled is a volcano that burns down and lays waste all around it; it is an abyss that devours all honour, substance and health.[109]

Thus at its core sexuality is as pure as atomic energy: it can be used for peaceful purposes, or for creating weapons. The irony lies in the fact that it may sometimes be necessary to have an atomic bomb, i.e., that for the species to survive a means of protection is often required. This is the basis of Tantra, which sees sexuality as

---

109   R. v. Krafft-Ebing, *Psychopathia Sexualis,* New York, Rebman Co., n.d., p. 3.

a metaphor, as the creative process, as a means of uniting with the divine, and as a means of acquiring occult powers. It is also as good a description as any of the double nature of Set in the Egyptian context, and why Set is associated with sexual ritual and magic by Grant.

While many of the rituals of the Yezidi are largely secret to which outsiders are rarely, if ever, invited there is still no evidence that they engage in sexual ceremonies or elaborate, Tantric-style magical procedures. They may satisfy the requirements of Crowley and Grant that they represent a connection with ancient Sumer and with the worship of the Old God, Shaitan or Set, and while such may be romanticized projections by orientalist observers what is to be respected is that they have not abandoned their faith, even under dire oppression by a host of hostile entities. They maintain their ritual purity, their sacred calendar, their beliefs, and their rites in the face of Iraqi, Russian, Muslim and even Kurdish opposition. They refuse to intermarry, or to accept outsiders into their religion, a religion that is identified not only with their beliefs but with their ethnicity as well. It is the mere fact of their existence that has intrigued and excited European and American occultists, for here is a clan whose religion is so far removed from anything else in the region as to appear bizarre to outsiders and who claim an origin in the vanished civilization of Sumer ... and who worship a god that some insist is the Dark Lord himself.

Obeah and Wanga

On November 1st, 1907, there had come to the New Orleans police a frantic summons from the swamp and lagoon country to the south. The squatters there, mostly primitive but good-natured descendants of Lafitte's men, were in the grip of stark terror from an unknown thing which had stolen upon them in the night. It was voodoo, apparently, but voodoo of a more terrible sort than they had ever known. ... There were insane shouts and harrowing screams, soul-chilling chants and dancing devil-

flames; and, the frightened messenger added, the people could
stand it no more.

—H.P. Lovecraft, "The Call of Cthulhu"

Also the mantras and spells; the obeah and the wanga; the work
of the wand and the work of the sword; these he shall learn and
teach. (AL I:37).

When we discuss the Yezidis, we are faced with very little accurate and reliable information and a lot of speculation. When we
come to the Afro-Caribbean aspect of the Necronomicon Gnosis,
we are in a somewhat different position.

While Haitian Vodun (commonly spelled "voodoo") was just
as vulnerable a hundred years ago to wild speculation and hysteria
as the "devil worshipping" Yezidis, we have a greater store of solid
information and documentation about Vodun and other Afro-
Caribbean religions due to the intense interest shown by anthropologists and historians of religion in recent years. In addition, the
presence of African-origin populations in the Caribbean and large
communities of Afro-Caribbean origin in the United States has
made Western access to these cultures easier than it is where the
Yezidi clans are concerned, since the homelands and central shrines
of the latter are scattered largely through the Middle East and Central Asia in war zones and areas hostile to outsiders.

Vodun, Santeria, Palo Mayombe, and Lukumi share some elements in common with the Yezidis. They do not have a written
scripture, per se. They frequently have been confused with devil
worship. And they represent a survival of ancient forms of religious
experience, in this case from Africa: a continent that they share
with Egypt.

They have also been exploited to some extent by non-African
occultists who see in their rituals methodologies of magical practice
and the acquisition of altered states of consciousness that lead to
greater spiritual power and abilities, especially when re-interpreted
within European and American (i.e., non-African) contexts. Prob-

ably the premier exponent of this type of synthesis is Michael Bertiaux, an important source for Grant.

Bertiaux came to the attention of the broader occult community in the United States through his massive, 600+ page *Voudon
Gnostic Workbook* (New York: Magickal Childe, 1998), but prior to
the book's publication he was already a subject of Grant's Typhonian Trilogies. The first mention of Bertiaux and his unique form of
Thelemic-Gnostic-Vodun appears in two chapters of Grant's *Cults
of the Shadow* (1975) which explain Bertiaux's system in terms that
are both Thelemic and Lovecraftian. Indeed, Bertiaux deliberately
uses terminology and ideas from Lovecraft in his occult work, as
well as terms and concepts that are uniquely his own. But Grant's
initial fascination with Bertiaux's work seems to be the fact that
both he and Bertiaux explored the "nightside" of the Tree of Life,
the realm of the Dark Lord. In Bertiaux's case, he connected the
Dark Side of the Tree with some of the Vodun cults and practices
that would be considered "black magic" in contemporary parlance.
This, coupled with the Crowley and Lovecraft references in Bertiaux, ignited a stream of consciousness in Grant that would heavily
influence his later work. Bertiaux acknowledged the importance of
sexual ritual, including Tantra, and associated it with various types
of Afro-Caribbean practice, and all within a Thelemic context. This
was the Obeah and the Wanga, the missing elements from the Thelemic arsenal of occult methods and systems.

Obeah is a form of Afro-Caribbean magic, what is sometimes
called "hoodoo" in the South. The practice as it is known today
has its origins in Jamaica and consists mostly of casting spells as
opposed to the more religious aspects of Haitian Vodun. There is
evidence that the term comes from an Ashanti word—*obayifo*—
meaning "witch" or "wizard" or even "vampire."[110] Thus it has a
negative connotation. Wanga (sometimes spelled *ouanga*) on the

---

110 See Ivor Morrish, *Obeah, Christ, and Rastaman: Jamaica and its religion*,
Cambridge UK, James Clarke & Co., 1982, pp. 22–23. It is referred to as one of
the "blacker arts." (p. 40)

other hand refers specifically to a small bag used to hold charms, sometimes worn around the neck or kept in a safe place, similar to the Native American "medicine bag" except that the latter is usually worn or carried by the medicine man only, whereas the wanga may be prepared for anyone to wear and usually for a specific purpose, such as love, money, health, etc. and dedicated to a specific loa (lwa): one of the Afro-Caribbean gods. However, both obeah and wanga are sometimes used as terms denoting Afro-Caribbean occultism in general. Wanga is sometimes thought to refer specifically to works of "black" or negative magic.[111]

What, then, is the meaning or intent behind the exhortation in the Book of the Law that one should "learn and teach" the "obeah and the wanga"? Why did Aiwaz use these terms and avoid using, for instance, "Voodoo and Santeria"?

The two latter are religions which have internally-consistent cosmologies, pantheons, and rituals. Obeah and wanga are somewhat looser in their definitions, but more importantly, do not refer to religious dogmas *per se* but to the practical side of religion, that is, magic. Obeah and wanga are occult methods used by Afro-Caribbean spiritual specialists and this is what would have been important to the author of the Book of the Law. After all, the infamous Chapter Three makes it clear that all previous *religions* are "black."

However, as we have seen, the consensus of opinion seems to be that both obeah and wanga are "black arts" themselves. That is, they are concerned with what Kabbalists would consider the darker, or nightside, aspect of the Tree of Life and may be associated with the *qlippoth*: the shattered shards of creation that are tantamount to demons. And the connective tissue to all of this is the focus of both Grant and Bertiaux on the sexual aspect of these dark mysteries. This is an obvious direction for occultists who represent the most transgressive of their breed, for the "white" magician is usually thought

---

111   See A. Metraux, *Voodoo in Haiti*, New York, Schocken Books, 1972, p. 285 where the wanga is defined as "the magical weapon par excellence" which has "a property that is harmful to one or more people."

of as being—if not celibate, then—more chaste than the average person, devoting his or her time and energy to good works, speaking with angels, and yearning for union with the divine: leading a life that would be considered conventionally moral and blameless. There is no mixing of the sexes in this type of occultism, or if there is it is within the religiously sanctioned confines of matrimony.

One only has to remember that the congregations in synagogues and mosques are separated by gender; that even Vedic practice in India keeps the sexes apart as much as possible. Christianity can be seen as an exception to this rule, and it is worthwhile to remember that the earliest Christian rituals known to the outside world took the form of the *agape*, or love-feast. These gender-mixed congregations would meet in secret (often in catacombs or cemeteries) due to their persecution by the state and by other religious authorities. Thus, Christianity could be considered the Satanism of its day.

When the genders are brought together in magical rituals, there is always the possibility that a sexual current will run through the group particularly in the heightened (almost romantic) atmosphere of a ceremony that is conducted secretly, in candle-light, with billowing clouds of perfumes and incenses, specially-designed robes in appropriate colors and materials, and so forth. One form of transgression—occult ritual—implies every other form, including the sexual; in addition, the appropriation of spiritual power away or apart from normative, socially-sanctioned priesthoods can be intoxicating.

In the rites of Haitian Vodun, the above conditions are exceeded through the use of a battery of drums and at times other musical instruments. In these rituals the focus is on the human body as the "horse" to be ridden by the gods in a form of divine possession. At such times, the individual person is no longer "present" as an ego or superego in his or her own physical form but has been momentarily dislodged by one of the lwa. The possessed person's body undergoes a subtle—or sometimes not so subtle—transformation as the personality of Erzulie (the goddess of love and passion) or perhaps of Baron Samedi *de la Cimitiere* (the god who controls access to the

Underworld) or any of the many other gods who take over and cause the possessed person to walk and act in accordance with the characteristics of the particular lwa.

Oddly, these things are not discussed in the *Voudon Gnostic Workbook* of Michael Bertiaux. While it does treat of the many varieties of Haitian lwa it does not focus on the rites most commonly associated with Haitian Vodun, such as the rituals that take place in the *peristyle* and *hounfort*. Instead, Bertiaux treats the Haitian material the way that Crowley treats the Egyptian: as data to be incorporated into rituals and spiritual methodologies more familiar to Western European occult practice. In the case of Bertiaux and his Gnostic Vodun, it is a syncretism of a syncretism.

From a post-modernist perspective, of course, this is hideous: an outrage against the original material, an exploitation of an indigenous culture's spirituality. But that is true of all magic. Magic is, by its very nature, a method and not a faith or a dogma. Its practices transcend the cultural because they are concerned with altered states of consciousness and not with adherence to a particular Law or Tradition. This is how it was possible for Jewish mystics such as Shabbtai Z'vi or a Jakob Frank to "convert" to Islam and Christianity, respectively, and still maintain their following and their reputation as advanced adepts. This is how it was possible for an Aleister Crowley to incorporate yoga and quasi-Tantric practices into his Thelema even though he was an Englishman who had received the Book of the Law in Cairo replete with Egyptian gods doing all the talking. In this context, the creative approach to spirituality of a Michael Bertiaux is entirely consistent. There is virtually no form of occultism in the western world that does not incorporate elements of "other" religions and "other" occult practices. The very liminality of occultism implies that "otherness" will be a constant, determining factor in its construction.

While Bertiaux includes material from diverse sources to amplify his version of "voodoo," he is not alone in examining this Afro-Caribbean system through the lens of other cultures and reli-

gions. While a purist may insist on a strict "African" interpretation
of Vodun—denying any syncretism involving other religions (such
as Roman Catholicism) or other mystical or magical systems—
twentieth-century Haitian writers on the subject frequently invoke
Greek, Egyptian and even Jewish terms and concepts as a means
of expanding upon the rituals and the legends that inform it. This
approach is condemned by post-modern anthropologists and academics as inherently colonialist and racist: the projection of white,
western insecurities about race, sexuality, and religion onto a cap-
tive, "savage" population. The fact that some native Haitian authors
on the subject contribute to this approach does not make the controversy any clearer.

An early author who is sometimes cited in the literature is
Arthur C. Holly. Writing in French under the pseudonym Her-Ra-
Ma-El, his books are a melange of Biblical references, Christian
concepts, Afro-centrism, and a minimum of actual information on
Vodun. His *Les daïmons du culte voudo*[112] is the most-referenced, but
usually derisively. However, in a line often quoted, he does insist on
a connection between Haitian Vodun and ancient Egyptian and
Assyrian religion:

> C'est en vain que les procédés hypocrites ou violents ont été
> mis en oeuvre pour envelopper des ténèbres les phases bril-
> lants de l'évolution mentale du Nègre. Il est hors de conteste
> que l'antique civilisation Ethiopio-égypto-assyrienne doit être
> inscrite à son compte.[113]

> ("It is in vain that hypocritical or violent processes have
> been used to shroud in darkness the brilliance of the mental

112 Arthur C. Holly, *Les daïmons du culte voudo*, Port-au-Prince, Imp. Edm.
Chenet, 1918. See also his *Dra-Po: étude ésotérique de Égrégore africain, tradition-
nel, social, et natural de Haiti*, Port-au-Prince, Imp. Nemours Telhomme, 1928.
113 Holly (1918), p. iii.

evolution of the Negro. It is beyond doubt that the ancient
Ethiopian-Egyptian-Assyrian civilizaton must be credited to
his account.")

and

Il nous parait indiscutable que la tradition Voudo descend en
ligne directe: du sacerdoce et des rites usités dans les temples
d'Ethiopie et d'Egypte.[114]

("It seems to us undeniable that the Voudo tradition descends
in direct line from the priesthood and the rites used in the temples of Ethiopia and Egypt.")

Holly called himself a "Haitian esotericist"[115] and this is borne
out by his lengthy and sometimes incomprehensible study of Vodun
through the lens of a kind of Kabbalah in which each letter of the
Latin alphabet possesses mystical meanings, so that an analysis of
any word (including the names of Vodun lwa) can yield a ware-
house full of secondary and tertiary meanings. His emphasis is on
this system rather than on Vodun itself, rendering his book of interest only to those studying early twentieth-century Haitian Francophone occult philosophy.

Indeed, Holly references all the usual suspects: Court de Gébe-
lin, Fabre d'Olivet, Eduard Schuré, and Eliphas Levi (the Abbé
Louis Constant) are all cited in this work, placing it firmly in the
lineage of French esotericism, Theosophy, Freemasonry, and magic.
This is especially the case with Levi, of whom Crowley believed
himself to be the reincarnation. Except, in Holly's view, Africa
and Vodun were the source for all European esotericism, including
Freemasonry:

114   Ibid., p. 506.
115   Ibid., p. xi.

Sur ce point je n'ai personnellement aucun doute. Car DAm-Bha-Lah, la Mère Divine, la Négresse universelle, le COEUR QUI VIVIFIE l'humanité, est seule capable de réaliser la parfaite solidarité, basée sur l'Amour, entre Noirs et Jaunes. Cela, parce que *Dame*, la Grande Négresse du Ciel, est la Patronne des uns; *Lah*, le Grand-Petit Mulâtre du Ciel, le Dieu panthéistique des autres. Donc la Nation haïtienne se tournera—pour l'adoration dans le plus pur sentiment de *fraternité*—vers le Soleil Levant et son Fils Lumineux—c'est-à-dire, en termes maçonniques, vers le GRAND-ORIENT personnifié par la Reine du Midi et son fils Chiram. En effet, le Salut de la Patrie dépend plutôt de la Franc-maçonnerie que l'Eglise. Et le Voudo, c'est la Mère de la Franc-maçonnerie comme on vient de le l'entrevoir dans les pages précédentes.[116]

(On this point I personally have no doubt. For Dam-Bha-Lah, the Divine Mother, the Universal Negress, HEART THAT QUICKENS humanity, is the only one able to achieve perfect solidarity, based on Love, between the Black and Yellow [races]. This is because *Dame*, Great Negress of Heaven, is the Patroness of each; *Lah*, the Grand Little Mulatto of Heaven, is the pantheistic God of the others. So the Haitian Nation will turn—or worship in the purest sense of *brotherhood*—towards the Rising Sun and his Son of Light—that is to say, in Masonic terms, towards the GRAND ORIENT personified by the Queen of the South and her son Hiram. Indeed, the Health of the Country depends rather on Freemasonry than the Church. And Voudo is the Mother of Freemasonry as we have just had a glimpse in the preceding pages.)

Here Holly shows us that he has an esoteric interpretation of the names of the gods of Vodun, dividing *Dambhala* into separate syllables, each of which has its own meaning and relevance. This is

---

116 Ibid., p. 514.

something that Grant himself does, to similar effect, as in the following word analysis from his *Ninth Arch*, the last in the Typhonian
Trilogies series:

> Frater Achad interpreted the thirteen-lettered word MANI-
> FESTATION as concentrating the magical formula of the
> Aeon of Maat whose 'lesser cycle' was to manifest through
> her daughter, Mâ. This is correct so far as it goes, but there is
> more to it. The daughter typifies the Pythoness of Maat as the
> unawakened (i.e. virgin) priestess in her magnetic and oracular
> sleep. The essential formula may be schematized thus:
>
> > *Mâ* = entranced medium, 'lesser cycle' (of the sixteen *kalas*)
> > *ni* = *Amen*, the Hidden God—the Sun behind the sun (Set-
> > Isis/Sothis).
> > *festat* = Cairo, the *locus* of the Double Current: Aiwass/Nu-Isis
> > *ion* = Aeon; the 'Greater Cycle' wherein the *seventeenth kala*
> > is secreted (i.e., the ultimate and *Secret-ion*).[117]

We will note that in both cases there are references to the Sun,
and the Pythoness of Maat may have something in common with
Holly's Dambhala. While Dambhala normally is considered to be a
male deity, his symbol is also the snake. In Holly's paragraph above-
cited, however, Dambhala is female since Holly focuses on the first
syllable of the word, Dam, and sees in it a reference to the French
word for *woman, Dame*. So Dambhala becomes, for him, the Divine
Mother and Universal Negress, as well as the *fons et origo* of Freemasonry.

While Holly is perhaps an unusual and suspect source for
information on Vodun, we have a more professional expert in Milo
Rigaud. Rigaud—born Emile Rigaud—wrote a number of books
on Vodun, heavily illustrated with photographs of ceremonies and
diagrams of the *vévés*: the arcane symbols that attract the lwa to the

---

117 Kenneth Grant, *The Ninth Arch*, London, Starfire, 2002, p. xxv.

rituals. While his books are comprehensive treatments of his sub-ject, he also falls victim to the type of grand theories that obsessed Holly. He links the practice of Vodun to Egypt and to Solo-mon's Temple, among other places, and he quotes Holly approv-ingly in this instance, implying that he agrees with the Egyptian-Ethiopian-Assyrian roots of Vodun and their contribution to west-ern, European esotericism and Freemasonry.[118]

Both Holly and Rigaud are Haitian authors, men who knew their country and its religious culture as well as anyone, but who wrote about it from a Francophone point of view. Creole is the language of the people in Haiti, and French is the language of the government and the intellectual elite. An educated Haitian, inter-ested in religion and spirituality, first would seek for information in French which inevitably would lead to the fields of Martinism, Freemasonry, the various Gnostic churches, and authors like Eliphas Levi and Papus (Dr. Encausse) and many others, all of whom did, indeed, exert an influence over European and American occultism both through their books and through the organizations and secret societies they joined or founded. Holly and Rigaud would have found in these sources confirmation of what they already believed to be true: that their religious culture was part of a continuum of spiritual experience that began in Africa—everywhere in Africa, including Egypt, the Sudan, and Ethiopia—and thus had tendrils extending as far as the salons of Paris and the secret societies of London, Germany, and elsewhere on the continent.

It's the perceived racist attitude towards Vodun that irritates anthropologists, however. They will insist that Vodun is a religion, and while they do not deny the magical aspects of the religion they will condemn any attempt to see in Vodun anything smacking of the titillating or suggestive. The approach of Bertiaux is attacked by experts who claim that he represents a colonialist and racist ste-reotyping of Vodun of the type we find in Lovecraft, for instance.

118 Milo Rigaud, *Secrets of Voodoo*, San Francisco, City Lights, 1969, 1985, pp. 10–11.

By associating Vodun with sexual rituals and contact with supra-mundane entities—what many average observers would call "black magic" in a purely pejorative way (and perhaps as a thinly-veiled racist allusion)—Bertiaux is seen to be contributing to the Hollywood concept of Vodun as "voodoo" with all the weird rites and licentiousness that the term suggests.

There are problems with this analysis, however. It has become fashionable to assert that any interest in indigenous religions by white observers, be they academics and scholars or journalists and authors of popular books on the subject, is suspect. Edward Said implied as much in his ground-breaking book, *Orientalism*,[119] when he castigated western, European attempts at describing Asia as rooted in colonialist and racist attitudes towards Asians, attitudes that were composed of equal parts of fear, disgust and desire. While Said's thesis has been criticized recently,[120] it is still a difficult hurdle for non-indigenous observers to overcome for it is assumed that they are, *ipso facto*, tainted by the same vulnerabilities. This is even more pronounced among those who go overboard in attacking other non-indigenous observers whom they believe to be inappropriately reverent when it comes to religions like Vodun, for they can be accused of manifesting "white guilt" or some similar desire to be absolved of their race's historical crimes against non-white populations. It is truly a no-win situation, but usually is apparent in academic circles where the near-impossibility of staying above the fray is pronounced. Among occultists there are no such anxieties. In the quest for greater and greater occult power all avenues are fair game, and since occultism can be viewed (by some) as largely psychological and emotional, the racial and sexual stereotypes of any "cult" can be mined for their connections to deeper psychological complexes in the operator.

---

119   Edward Said, *Orientalism*, New York, Vintage, 1979.
120   Authors such as Robert Irwin and Bernard Lewis have attacked Said's work on methodological grounds as well as on charges of erroneous data and sweeping generalizations that include every Western scholar and reporter on Middle Eastern and Asian affairs and culture.

Yet there is another problem for the mainstream apologists for Vodun, and that is that there *are* secret societies in Haiti that are responsible for some of the bad press that "voodoo" gets, and which gave us the infamous "zombie powder" among other things. These societies specialize in those elements of Vodun that could be considered magic as differentiated from religion. Wade Davis has written two books[121] on the subject of these societies which were the basis of his ethnobiological fieldwork in Haiti during which time he was actually initiated into one of these groups. The vigorous attempts by some anthropologists to downplay the more sinister aspects of the Haitian religious experience fall apart in the face of this type of scholarship. Of course, a case could be made that the Haitian secret societies—such as Bizango, Zobop, the Secte Rouge, etc.—bear as much relationship to traditional Vodun as the Church of Satan does to the Roman Catholic Church ... but Davis demonstrates that there exists a much closer bond between the secret societies and normative Vodun than one would suppose, and that these secret societies perform much the same function as the "Illuminati" or "Freemasons" are alleged to do in European countries: they are the real "masters" of the country, operating behind the scenes and meting out punishment where necessary to maintain order in the Haitian communities.[122]

Therefore, for our purposes we can acknowledge that what anthropologists call "Vodoun" or "Vodun," etc. represents an assembly of various African religions under one convenient (albeit misleading) umbrella and that as a religion it deserves the same respect as any other; but we must also acknowledge that such things as curses, blood sacrifice, and even zombification also exist as part of the Haitian religious/occult experience just as antinomian secret societies and "satanic" occult groups exist within the normative

---

121 Wade Davis, *The Serpent and the Rainbow*, New York, Warner Books, 1985; *Passage of Darkness: The Ethnobiology of the Haitian Zombie*, Chapel Hill, University of North Carolina Press, 1988.
122 Davis (1988), p. 284.

white European Christian or Jewish religious experience. And it is within the context of the Haitian secret societies, such as the Bizango, that we find the greatest correlation with the ideas discussed by Bertiaux and Grant.

The element of Bertiaux's unique cosmology that interests Grant is the idea that there are *points chauds* or "hot points" (or "power points") in the universe that act as portals into other realms of experience, as "gates" to the "underworld." The adepts who are capable of entering these points at will are sometimes referred to as *voltigeurs* (or "leapers") in the Bertiaux vernacular. These power points are located on the human body as well as at specific areas of the earth and in the cosmos, in perfect microcosm/macrocosm symmetry. It follows that if these points can be located simultaneously in the body as well as in the heavens (for instance) then physical manipulation or stimulation of those points is equivalent to opening the celestial gates, and a Tantric-type process can be pursued that uses the body and its hidden resources as a vehicle for celestial (and infernal) exploration. An essential characteristic of Tantra is the understanding that psycho-biological processes take place which alter consciousness. In rare instances, these processes may take place accidentally—through some form of physical or emotional trauma—but more often they are the result of careful practice and deliberate application of occult methods such as yoga, meditation, pranayama, and other means of interfering with the normal functions of the human body. If the body is a laboratory and a temple combined, then changing any of the body's processes such as control of breathing, of heartbeat, contorting the limbs into uncomfortable positions for long periods of time, or even taking drugs that alter either the physical or the mental activities of the operator will produce a variety of results that are outside the normal range of human experience.

The occultist uses the tools that are available to seek control over the body's autonomic nervous system—the system that regulates such things as breathing, heart rate, peristalsis, etc.—as well as control over the mind's "autonomic" functions, processes that can be located in what the Freudians call the unconscious mind. This is all quite different from the way of the mystic in prayer who wants to unite with the divine through piety and good works. It is a mechanistic approach to consciousness and divinity that horrifies churchmen and the pious, offending them as much as do frank discussions of sexuality. The pious speak of love and marriage; sex is either not mentioned or is couched in euphemism. The magician speaks of everything in terms of the use to be made of it, its pragmatic application to the desired goal.

This is what one finds in Bertiaux as well as in Grant. It should be noted that Grant's information concerning Vodun is purely of the Bertiaux variety. There is no attempt to offer an academic presentation of the material, no citations of scholarly works on Afro-Caribbean religion juxtaposed with citations from the *Voudon Gnostic Workbook* just as there are no discussions of Roman Catholic doctrines or excerpts from the Lutheran prayer book. There is no devotional literature in magic. The interest of Bertiaux, Grant and Crowley is on spiritual techniques and esoteric technology. The cultural contexts of Vodun, Egyptian religion, to a lesser extent the Tantras, and even the Yezidis are ignored or at least unacknowledged in favor of the deconstruction of their respective technologies—the way a gear-head takes apart an automobile engine to see how it is put together. These techniques give rise—mostly through ritual—to otherworldly experiences that they then attempt to describe and analyze for a wider audience, with wildly uneven results. Grant's presentation of the already complicated and sometimes hyperbolic Bertiaux material verges on the incomprehensible, and I contend that it is not meant to be read as linear prose but as a kind of free-association: language reduced (or elevated) to mantra and chant.

Bertiaux, like Grant, is obsessed with the dark side of esotericism. Traditional Kabbalah, alchemy, Freemasonry, Rosicrucianism are all ignored in favor of the more sinister aspects of the spiritual experience, and ways are sought to contact entities that are believed to exist in other dimensions, entities that are nevertheless understood to be capable of interacting with our own. These are alien beings in every sense of the term: they are not beautiful in any conventional sense: no angels with harps, no long-bearded prophets. These are the monstrous shapes imagined by Lovecraft and other horror writers of his generation; except that for Bertiaux and Grant they are not figments of imagination and thus "not real," but have an independent existence of their own. In the Bertiaux and Grant cosmology, Lovecraft did not invent these creatures: he saw them in his dreams, which are a time-honored method of communicating with the unconscious mind (in a modern sense) or with the spirit world (in a more ancient context). The gods of Vodun may have begun the same way as Great Cthulhu and Nyarlathotep; and the methods of contacting the one may be used to contact the other, and with similar—even measureable—results. What began in a dream may be contacted in a dream, or at least in a trance. The altered states so representative of spirit possession in Haiti—and recognized as such by Lovecraft in "The Call of Cthulhu"—are a way of re-dreaming the original dream, of going "back to Guinee": to an African homeland that exists nowhere on earth, yet everywhere on earth. The *points chauds* are elements of an occult Matrix, places where one strand of the spider's web crosses another. Taken together, they form a membrane over the cranium of the magical operator like the touch screen on a computer monitor. It is where Bertiaux's "voodoo" meets Grant's Tantra that the intellectual and conceptual explosion takes place that leads the Typhonian Order into the realm of the Dark Lord.

In Pursuit of Gold

It was most likely observing the meetings of David Curwen and Aleister Crowley that provided Kenneth Grant with the impetus he needed to realize that Indian Tantra held the key to the mysteries of the OTO as well as to all of western occultism itself. While Grant usually quotes discredited texts on the Yezidis and on Vodun, in the realm of Indian religion and magic he is on somewhat surer ground even as he makes at times reckless use of the texts. For many western occultists, drawn to magic through the works of Crowley or of the other magicians who came out of the Golden Dawn environment, Grant's books were the first that introduced them to Tantra and to the potentiality of this rather messy yet strikingly powerful tradition: "messy" in the sense that no one can agree on what Tantra is; powerful because it deals with magical processes in remarkably clear language.

Of all the unspeakable cults in Grant's repetoire, Tantra is where his erudition (although subject to serious criticism by actual Tantrikas) and his grasp of the terminology shines through. Grant is a knowledgeable non-initiate when it comes to Tantra, but it must be said that he makes mistakes in nomenclature, definitions, etc. which may be due more to the lack of access to published materials (and his own lack of initiation into a Tantric circle) than to any desire to confuse or bloviate. The value in Grant's description of Tantric rites and concepts lies in the fact that it is the first time for many western occultists that they have been exposed to this material and serves as an inducement to conduct their own, independent research. Further, while Tantrikas may object to Grant's cavalier use of Tantric terms and concepts to further his own investigations of the Dark Lord, it is entirely consistent with Bertiaux's approach to Vodun and Crowley's approach to Egyptology and Yezidism. That is not to absolve these magicians from a responsibility to be accurate insofar as possible, but it does demonstrate the essential *bricolage* tendency of western occultists who strive to reach beyond a Judeao-Christian framework and into other, foreign realms. This is the lure of Babalon, of course: the ultimate "foreigner" and seducer of spiritual aspirants since time immemorial.

David Curwen (1893–1984) was an intimate of Aleister Crowley in the period 1944–1947, until the latter's death in December of that year, and they maintained a deep correspondence on magic, alchemy and especially Tantra. Curwen recently (2006) was "outed" as the author of the very influential alchemical work *In Pursuit of Gold* (1976) written under the pseudonym Lapidus (Latin for "Stone"). *In Pursuit of Gold* was subtitled "Alchemy Today in Theory and Practice" which seems to echo Crowley's own *Magick in Theory and Practice* and to a certain extent these two volumes complement each other as modern takes on these ancient arts.

The relationship between Curwen and Crowley was not always fraternal. Crowley soon began to realize that Curwen—who had studied Tantra in India—was more knowledgeable than he when it came to Indian forms of occultism and, of course, in particular Tantra. Crowley's exposure to Tantra was limited to a few English translations of a handful of Tantric texts, whereas Curwen's experience was much deeper and more profound. When both Curwen and Crowley began to realize Crowley's limitation in that regard, the friendship suffered a little. Crowley had to be the smartest man in the room, at least where occultism was concerned, and Curwen was living proof that there were other mysteries, other revelations to which Crowley had had no previous access.

At the same time, a friendship developed between Kenneth Grant and David Curwen, to the extent that Curwen encouraged Grant to explore Tantra more deeply. This would set Grant on the path for which he would become most famous: the exploration of Thelema and the core secret of the OTO as delineated in the texts and practices of the Tantric adepts of India.

The subject of Tantra is vast, and I have introduced the subject elsewhere,[123] but for the purposes of this investigation we will focus on the type of Tantric groups that are of interest to Grant, the "unspeakable cults" of India.

The first such group is the Sri Vidya sect.

Śrī Vidyā ("Holy Knowledge") can actually be broken down into four separate, but linked, manifestations. Basically, it is form of Goddess worship that has as its goal *advaita*, or non-duality. Therefore it is a Shakta tradition (as differentiated from a Shaivite tradition) in which the source of power, of shakti, is imagined in the Goddess. The particular goddess in the case of Sri Vidya is known as *Lalitā*

123 Levenda, *Tantric Temples: Eros and Magic in Java*, Lake Worth: Ibis Press, 2011.

Tripurasundarī. Tripura Sundari means "Beautiful Goddess of the Three Cities," the three cities in this case referring to three different aspects of the goddess as physical, subtle, and supreme. She is usually depicted as a sixteen-year-old girl, and for that reason is sometimes called Ṣoḍaśī or "Sixteen" and *Lalitā* or "she who plays." It should be noted that the number sixteen figures prominently in Grant's number system as the designation for the sixteenth *kala*, the ultimate of the kalas or secretions of the priestess. Her mantra also contains sixteen letters.

The foremost symbol of the Sri Vidya sect is the Sri Meru Cakra, which is a three-dimensional version of the Sri Yantra, usually made of special metals in a sacred alloy that allows the blessings of the Goddess to flow more powerfully. The Sri Yantra is a two-dimensional magical drawing of nine interlocking triangles that represents the unity of male and female—Shiva and Shakti—forces and could thus be seen as a depiction of the essential philosophy of both Tantra and Thelema.

The form of worship known as *Samayachara* takes place in the mind, as even the rituals—*puja*—themselves can be performed mentally if the appropriate ritual objects are not to hand. In this case the Goddess is visualized and the entire ritual is much more personal and interiorized.

In increasing complexity, we then arrive at the form of Sri Vidya known as *Dakshinachara* in which an external form of the Goddess is required: either an idol or the Sri Meru Cakra ... or even a female devotee. It should be noted that in this practice there is no intimate contact between the worshipper and the woman—the *suvasini*—who represents the Goddess although she is a focus for the ritual.

The *Kaulachara* is the one that gets most of the attention, for the external object of devotion is a living woman or a man, or a male and female couple. The famous ritual of the "Five M's"—the *panchamakara*—is part of the Kaulachara repetoire, although not practiced as often or as widely as believed. Since the goal of Sri Vidya is essentially *advaita* and the negation of all duality, the rituals themselves emphasize that there is no difference between the worshipper and the worshipped: that, in effect, everyone and every-thing is the Goddess. Eventually all sense of self—self as a separate entity, apart from the rest of the cosmos—disappears. The use of nudity and sexuality in these rituals, which can be as physical or as virtual as the leader determines, is designed to remove all sense of "otherness" by conquering shame, fear, and carnal desire.

The final, and most controversial, form of Sri Vidya is the *Vamachara* practice. The devotees of Vamachara are the groups that meet in cemeteries and crematory grounds, and which see the Goddess in her terrible and frightening aspect. The idea is to transcend even the grossest, most loathsome aspects of creation, of humanity, of reality. To see the Goddess in the corpses of the cremation ground, to smell Her perfume in the stench of burning flesh, and to hear Her voice in the hideous sounds of an Indian cemetery in the night is the height of spiritual piety. And when the Vamachara circle goes to the extent—as some of them do—to perform *panchatattva* or *panchamakara* (the ritual of the Five M's that includes *maithuna* or sexual contact) in the intimate, overwhelming presence of corpses is to conquer death and to bring all of creation back to a single point: death and the act of conception taking place in the same location, decay and desire obliterating the boundary between this world and the next.

It is no wonder then that Grant would have been fascinated by these practices. He would have seen—as glimpsed through a scrim, at an angle, in shadow—the secrets of the Gnostic Mass and the Star Sapphire ritual exposed and expanded through the intense cer-emonies of the Kaulachara and Vamachara sects. The Tantric texts and rituals would have revealed to Grant the secrets behind the secrets. Shiva and Shakti on thrones in the center of the Kaula circle are analogues of Chaos and Babalon, of what Jung perhaps would call the Shadow and the Anima, and the consumption of the flu-ids in the Gnostic Mass and the Star Sapphire rituals are perfectly comprehensible within the context of the Sri Vidya tradition. In fact, the reasons behind the secrets of the OTO's VIIIth and IXth degrees would be explained and amplified through consulting the

Tantric texts, not only of the Sri Vidya sect but also of a number of other groups from the Kashmiri Shaivites to the Nath Siddhis and, of course, of the Tibetan Tantric tradition with its famous Kalachakra Tantra and the associated scheme of initiations.

Grant would focus on two aspects of the Tantras that he felt were crucial to an understanding of Thelema. The first was the idea of non-duality and the destruction of the ego. This also concerned Crowley, of course, as we have mentioned above, in his pursuit of *samādhi* or the state of actually experiencing non-duality through the identification of subject with object during meditation. Crowley, who was familiar with the *Yoga Sutras of Patanjali* (an English translation of which had appeared in 1914), knew that samadhi was the highest possible state of consciousness that could be achieved while still alive, the only possible higher state being that of the *mahasamādhi* or "great samadhi" that occurs at the time of death.

The second was the concept of the *kāla*.

The best blood is of the moon, monthly ... (AL III:24)

Grant would have been the first western occultist to write openly about this subject, at least the first to enjoy a wide audience among those interested in ceremonial magic and the western occult tradition. The kalas are explained as vaginal secretions, not limited to menstrual blood, which occur during the entire menstrual cycle and which have different occult properties depending on the day they occur. These are not to be understood as the grosser physical form of mucoid secretions or blood, but as their subtler counterparts imbued with qualities that are analogous to the alchemical elements that are involved in the process of spiritual transformation.

The subject of kalas is a complex one, for the production of the kalas depends on the occult capability of the priestess as well as on their manipulation by the priest. There are astrological and astronomical considerations and ritual requirements to ensure the proper condensation of these essences at the right time so that they may be employed for magical ends.

Basically, the word *kāla* indicates a unit of time, most specifically a lunar "digit" or day. Different authorities offer different definitions and identifications of this lunar day. In some cases, it refers to about one-day-and-a-half in solar days, or about 36 hours. In other cases, the authorities insist that each lunar day is equivalent in length to a solar day, only calculated from dusk to dusk rather than from dawn to dawn, etc. Those familiar with Vedic astrology are familiar with this term and with a related term *tithi*, which means the same thing but which is used more often in astrology than in the Tantras.

The important thing to remember here is that the lunar cycle is really the result of the interplay between the moon, the earth and the sun. If we consider the earth to be a vessel for the mingled essences of the sun and moon—a traditional Tantric concept—then the importance of the kala becomes apparent. On different days of the lunar cycle, as the moon gradually waxes from a New Moon to a Full Moon, and then begins to wane again, the quality of moonlight (it's brightness) changes from night to night. The Indian astrologers and Tantrikas imagine this to be the Sun giving the precious Soma to the Moon, drop by drop, until the Moon is full, at which point it begins returning the Soma to the Sun, also drop by drop, until it is depleted; and then the whole cycle begins again. Each lunar day has a specific quality associated with it, as well as a specific deity. It is this concept that is related to the Tantric idea of kalas that Grant writes about so frequently. Each lunar digit or kala has a different quality. When this quality is combined with the individual menstrual cycle of the priestess, then you have a different "tincture" or essence.

Central to Indian religion and especially to Tantra is the concept of *amrita*. Amrita is the combination of the male and female potencies that ensures immortality, and the power to cure illness. It is the source of western ideas about the *elixir vitae* and the Philosopher's Stone. It is the result of an internal process of meditation, yoga, and ritual but also involves alignment with the priest or priestess as well as with the lunar phases themselves. It is an interlocking of the microcosm with the macrocosm—the human body with the stars—in a way that transcends how this is understood by the newcomer to ceremonial magic and alchemy. The sensitivity of the female partner to her menstrual cycle and the corresponding sensitivity of the male partner to the female partner—coupled with: (1) the awareness of both to the external "cycle" of the sun and moon, and (2) the proper performance of rituals that are undertaken with a great deal of personal preparation (particularly in the psycho-biological processes which are subsumed under the control of the autonomic nervous system: in particular breathing, heart rate, etc.)—provides a vehicle for spiritual transformation that would be difficult to surpass. As one identifies oneself with the Goddess through the normal stages of the Sri Vidya puja, but with these other considerations honored, then the goal of advaita or non-duality is obtained through identification of the Goddess with the universe, the universe with the Goddess, and eventually identification of the Self with No-Self: the transcending of opposites and the attainment of samadhi.

In the earlier stages of the process—which can take many years to perfect—the amrita is cultivated, taking care that it does not become a poison instead of a medicine. The Tantras are full of instructions towards this end, although they may at times seem incomprehensible as they are written in the "twilight language" common to all the deeper forms of esotericism both in Asia and in the West. The amrita is the combined essences of the male and female practitioner, as has been described, with the caveat that it is not the grosser elements that are important, for they are only the vehicle for the subtle powers they represent. Only accomplished Tantrikas—or, in the Western context, magicians—are capable of generating these subtle essences. As can be seen, the Gnostic Mass would be capable of this function in only the most advanced case, as well as the Star Sapphire ritual which makes use of the same ideas. But is there really a connection between the Tantras that Grant praises so highly and Thelema? Aside from the obvious similarities, there is other evidence to show that there might be a stronger connection than previously understood.

As Tantric scholar David Gordon White describes in his *The Alchemical Body: Siddha Traditions in Medieval India*:

> In the royal consumption origin myth ... the moon was revived and replenished in its bright fortnight through the offering of a *soma* sacrifice. Soma is the fluid essence of the moon, which, in the sacrificial context, must be bought. With what does King Moon buy back his vital fluids? With a red cow, whose name, *rohini*, is the same as that of the starry woman who was the original cause of his woes.[124]

This is a rich vein of symbolism that could be mined by any Kabbalist with great benefit. As scholar of Judaism Rafael Patai and Kabbalah scholar Moshe Idel have both indicated in their writings, Tantra may very well have been the unseen influence behind European and Middle Eastern forms of alchemy and Kabbalah. In this single myth, we have an indication that there was some cross-fertilization between Jewish mysticism and Tantric alchemy in startling ways.

As Jewish scholars know, a red cow (sometimes called a red heifer, a *parah adumah* פרה אדומה in Hebrew) is required for the purification of anyone who came into contact with a corpse (Numbers, 19:2–19). The cow had to be unblemished, completely red, and had never been yoked or used to perform any work. It would be sacrificed and burned, its ashes placed in a ritual vessel that contains pure "living" water, i.e. from a spring as opposed to collected rain water. Along with the ashes of the red cow, cedar and hyssop are also burned along with the cow, as well as wool that has been dyed red. The resulting water is then sprinkled on a contaminated person using a branch of hyssop.

---

124 David Gordon White, *The Alchemical Body: Siddha Traditions in Medieval India*, Chicago: University of Chicago Press, 1996, p. 36

It is a requirement to have the ashes of a red cow available in the Temple, and for that reason the building of a Third Temple in Jerusalem could not take place until such a red cow had been found that would be a suitable candidate for this ritual requirement. There is no logical argument for this requirement, no reference to other sources that would provide a context for this rather bizarre ritual, and for that reason Talmudic scholars consider it to be a divine mandate. But the connection between a red cow, ritual purity, and living water seems to have a precedent in ancient India and the above citation offers a way towards understanding this rather arcane stipulation.

The word *rohinī* is the key. It does not mean "red cow" specifically but simply "the red one." It is the name of a Goddess, the "starry woman" of the citation, and is assigned to one of the *nakshatras*—the rohini nakshatra—which is the star Aldebaran,[125] found in the constellation Taurus, or the Bull. Rohini is the wife of Chandra, a lunar deity who is identified with Soma. The symbols for Rohini/Aldebaran are the Temple and the Chariot.

Thus we have a Red Goddess, a Red Cow, the waters of purification and Soma, and the Temple. The Moon must buy a red cow and offer it in exchange for Soma, which seems to be a myth cognate to the idea of a red cow being burned and its ashes used to create purifying water. Add to that the symbolic connection to Aldebaran and the Temple and you seem to have a perfect explanation for the Jewish requirement.

Further, the fact that the symbol of the Chariot is also included takes us into another, deeper realm entirely. The "descent to the Chariot" is a practice known in the Jewish mystical practice of the Merkavah מרכבה ("chariot") also known as Hekhalot היכלות ("palace") mysticism. The aim of the practice is to ascend seven levels, or chariots, or palaces, to finally appear before the Throne of God. I have made the case elsewhere that this ancient mystical practice was the inspiration for the degree rituals of the Golden Dawn,

---

125 In astronomical literature, Aldebaran is identified as the star alpha Taurus.

which then became the basis for Aleister Crowley's A∴A∴ degree structure.[126]

There is more evidence that this may be correct. In that in various world mythologies Aldebaran is usually connected to the constellation of the Pleiades, the "Seven Sisters," in the same way that the asterism of the Big Dipper consists of seven stars that are called "the Chariot" in Middle Eastern (and Chinese) cultures. They surround the Pole Star which forms the Throne of God in this system, because it is unmoving and eternal, the axis around which the world turns.

This entire complex of ideas is reprised in the Thelemic idea of the Scarlet Woman, Babalon, as the partner of Therion and whose relationship with the Beast provides the Soma, the life-giving elixir.

To continue the astronomical theme one step further, the brightest supernova explosion ever recorded in human history took place in the year 1006 CE. It occurred on April 30 of that year, which is—as the Necronomicon tells us—the "day the Great Bear hangs from its tail in the sky," i.e., the day the Gate between this world and the next is opened. On the same day, the volcanic eruption of Mount Merapi on the Indonesian island of Java destroyed an entire civilization and buried the spectacular monument Borobudur. It lay under volcanic ash and vegetation for centuries before being rediscovered and eventually reconsecrated by the Dalai Lama—recognized as a temple of Vajrayana, i.e. Tantric, Buddhism.

The supernova occurred in a constellation known to the ancients as *Therion*. The Beast.

These ancient cults—of the Yezidi, of the Afro-Caribbean religions and their secret societies, and of the Tantrikas—are carriers of specific information that modern cultists find indispensable for an understanding of their own traditions, rites, and practices. But

---

126 See the author's *Stairway to Heaven* for a more detailed defense of this theory.

these practices are dangerous. They involve trafficking with the contents of the unconscious mind through manipulation of psycho-biological processes that are still little-understood and recognized even less. To writers like Grant and Lovecraft, they are analogous to trafficking with supramundane entities ... not "analogous" in the way the word is normally used, but perhaps better understood in the sense of "analogue" as opposed to "digital." To Grant and Lovecraft, plumbing the depths of the unconscious mind is not metaphorically similar to plumbing the depths of deep space, they are different ways of expressing the same thing. The practices may be analogues of each other to the non-initiate, but they meet in the rituals and practices of the adept, of the initiate.

> The most ancient mysteries were of a physical, not a metaphysical nature. There was an esoteric and an exoteric version of them, corresponding to the written and the oral Law of the Jews. But, contrary to what is usually supposed, the metaphysical was the exoteric version, not *vice versa*.... The secret, oral, or hidden wisdom embodied in the gloss [to the seventeenth chapter of the Egyptian Book of the Dead], refers to the physical origins of the abstract concepts which appear in the text; spiritual matters are experienced in terms of physical, more precisely of physiological, phenomena.[127]

---

127 Kenneth Grant, *The Magical Revival*, New York: Weiser, 1972. pp. 2–3.

CHAPTER FOUR

THE NECRONOMICON GNOSIS

> Much of the power of Western horror-lore was undoubtedly
> due to the hidden but often suspected presence of a hideous cult
> of nocturnal worshippers whose strange customs ... were rooted
> in the most revolting fertility-rites of immemorial antiquity.
> This secret religion, stealthily handed down amongst peasants
> for thousands of years despite the outward reign of the Druidic,
> Graeco-Roman, and Christian faiths in the regions involved,
> was marked by wild "Witches' Sabbaths" in lonely woods and
> atop distant hills or Walpurgis-Night and Hallowe'en ...
>
> —H. P. Lovecraft[128]

> The deathless Chinamen said that there were double meanings
> in the Necronomicon ...
>
> —H. P. Lovecraft[129]

HIDEOUS CULT, NOCTURNAL WORSHIPPERS, revolting fertility rites
... double meanings. It is this last that gives us pause because it so
eloquently reveals both Lovecraft's own timidity when it comes to
sexuality and religion as well as the basis for the Thelemic, Necronomicon and Egyptian currents upon which Grant expounds
throughout all nine volumes of his Typhonian Trilogies.

Fertility rites.

One could make the case that Tantra is essentially the survival of some more ancient fertility cult operative throughout the
sub-continent, perhaps before the Aryan invasions, and that our
concepts of lingam and yoni, amrita, and Shiva and Shakti all
derive from this practice "of immemorial antiquity." After all, some

---

128 H.P. Lovecraft, "Supernatural Horror in Literature"
129 H.P. Lovecraft, "The Call of Cthulhu"

Tantric practitioners do indeed meet "nocturnally" in remote places to carry out their "fertility rites."

It is this type of public relations effort, carried out not only by Lovecraft but by the Western media in general, that made Tantra and its associated beliefs and practices seem so exotic and forbidden, pretty much substantiating Edward Said's insistence that virtually all Western approaches to Asia were racist and condescending.

However, in the case of Tantra in particular it was not only the white colonialist class that was appalled by these practices but members of the established Brahmin classes of India as well. Nothing disturbs a member of the social and religious elite quite so much as discovering groups of men and women, together, at night, in a cremation ground, worshipping the gods and possibly even having sex in a ritual setting. The very concept would make a Vedic (and a Catholic) priest's head explode. (There is also, of course, the implied threat to the social order and specifically to the orthodox priesthood represented by independent religious practitioners communicating directly with the gods in an unapproved manner.)

Sexuality is such a central feature of human life everywhere on the planet that to describe any social group or organization that is in any way non-traditional or antinomian is to suggest that it's sexual practices are also bizarre, or strange, or unorthodox. It would be difficult to make the case for an American satanic organization, for instance, that practiced the Black Mass as the core ritual of their faith—and whose members were all celibate (by choice or by doctrine) or scrupulously faithful to their spouses. We associate anti-religions with liberation,[130] because we identify religion with restraint, with rules, with doctrines involving the human passions and the attempt to corral them into socially-acceptable channels. Thus any anti-church worth its salt would incorporate sexual liberation or even sexual "depravity" as part of its repertoire.

---

130 And, conversely, liberation theology with anti-ecclesiastical movements, but that is another story for another time.

The Necronomicon Sigil is a compsite of the three signs
of ARRA (the Sign of our Race), AGGA (the Elder Sign),
and BANDAR (the Sigil of the Watcher).

But Lovecraft went a step further. Since he did not identify any of the existing religions and their gods as the "hideous cults" of which he writes (except from a few choice asides to the Yezidi in the short story "The Horror at Red Hook"), he invented another religious entity entirely. He wanted a cult that was older than anything on earth, older than any historically-verifiable religion, something so old that it would have appeared ancient to the pre-dynastic Egyptians and the Sumerians (arguably the oldest civilization on record). It would be the Ur-cult, the original religion, and its origins would be as mysterious and murky as the origins of the human race itself: the stars.

At the same time, Lovecraft understood that the occult rituals of the West and the East—in particular ceremonial magic for the former and shamanism for the latter—could be employed as means of making contact with these forces: forces that he claimed were still interested in returning to the earth, but who had been prevented from doing so because of certain spells that had been cast that closed the Gate between this world and theirs, and which kept their chief priest—the dread Cthulhu—"dead but dreaming" in his sunken city of R'lyeh ... waiting for the moment when "the stars are right" and his devotees on earth chant the right chants and raise him from his grave to invoke the Old Ones once more. The satanic cults of the world—the devil-worshipping, secretive, murderous, or otherwise unorthodox and antinomian—were survivals of this original cult and were keeping its blasphemous memory alive.

Lovecraft's theme is not as internally consistent as the above paragraph would suggest. Lovecraft himself tinkered with it in his stories, and other contributors added to the legends in their own tales, creating what has been called the Cthulhu Mythos. We will not attempt to delineate all the moving parts of the Mythos here, but only focus on those elements that concern what Grant calls the Necronomicon Mythos, which he sees as one manifestation of the underground current that supplies the fuel for Thelema. This is the most contentious aspect of the Thelema gestalt—for many members of the OTO and allied groups are vehemently opposed to Grant's concept of Thelema, and especially to any addition of elements from the stories of H. P. Lovecraft, which they feel are "fictional" and "imaginary" and thus have no place in their religion. (Atheists will find this attitude rather ironic, no doubt.)

Grant's response to this has been to emphasize the importance of the artistic in religion, and especially in Thelema. There were artists, writers, musicians, dancers, and actors surrounding Crowley for most of his life, becoming involved in Thelema to greater or lesser degrees and contributing to the culture of his movement. Imagination, creativity, and vision are essential aspects of the artistic arsenal, which are elements of the magical environment as well. Inasmuch as Thelema's origins are patently magical, the close association of art and Thelema cannot be denied. Crowley considered himself to be the greatest living poet in the world, among other things. He also painted, organized theatrical troupes such as the Ragged Ragtime Girls, and conducted the Rites of Eleusis as public performance in a theater, the last an indication that he understood the role of ritual as drama and of drama as ritual. He also wrote short stories and novels, such as the revealing *Moonchild,* which incorporates elements of the Golden Dawn, the A∴A∴, ceremonial magic in general, Asian religions, etc. all wrapped up in a Thelemic context but with allusions to world events (thus embroidering upon the paranoid fantasy that all world events are orchestrated by a secret society of satanic magicians). *Moonchild* is a *roman-a-clef,* with many of Crowley's friends and enemies portrayed in ways that would amuse only Crowley and anyone else in on the joke. But the occult and magical aspects of *Moonchild* are the most valuable aspect of the novel. Crowley used the novel as a medium for transmitting occult information. Why, then, would we deny Lovecraft the same capability if not the intention?

Lovecraft's understanding was quite similar. His most influential work, the short story "The Call of Cthulhu," is specific in its depiction of artists as the first people on the planet to become aware that something cosmic was taking place involving the race from the stars and the sinister, slumbering high priest, Cthulhu. Some of this awareness is communicated through dreams, and dream control is a key element of the Grant technique.

Take for example these quotes first from Lovecraft and then from Grant:

> It was from the artists and poets that the pertinent answers came, and I know that panic would have broken loose had they been able to compare notes.... These responses from esthetes told a disturbing tale. From February 28 to April 2 a large proportion of them had dreamed very bizarre things, the intensity of the dreams being immeasurably the stronger during the period of the sculptor's delirium.... and some of the dreamers

confessed acute fear of the gigantic nameless thing visible towards the last.[131]

Certain fugitive elements appear occasionally in the works of poets, painters, mystics, and occultists which may be regarded as genuine magical manifestations in that they demonstrate the power and ability of the artist to evoke elements of an extra-dimensional and alien universe that may be captured only by the most sensitive and delicately adjusted antennae of human consciousness.[132]

The sculptor referred to in the first quotation is young Wilcox, who has been having strange dreams and visions the result of which is art that seems to suggest the existence of alien beings. It is the sculpture left behind by Wilcox that instigates the investigation of the Cthulhu Cult, a search that ranges from Providence, Rhode Island to New Orleans, Louisiana to the South Pacific—with side trips to parts of Asia. At the same time that Wilcox is having his unearthly experience artists from around the world are reporting the same type of experience, sometimes with deadly results as some go insane, or kill themselves.

In the second quotation, Grant shows that he is agreeing with Lovecraft's analysis and explains the phenomenon as representing "genuine magical manifestations." This is a key statement, one that Grant uses to justify his use of the Lovecraft material in his Typhonian mythos. One either agrees at this point, or does not. If one disagrees with Grant, then the rest of the Typhonian material makes no sense at all, and can be considered the ramblings of a paranoid schizophrenic or a visionary artist fallen on hard times ... or hard drugs. But then, if one disagrees with Grant, one is tempted to review all of the Thelemic material in the same light, for Crowley

131   H.P. Lovecraft, "The Call of Cthulhu."
132   Kenneth Grant, *Outside the Circles of Time*, London: Frederick Muller, 1980, p. 14

received the Book of the Law under very arcane (if not actually suspicious) circumstances. Crowley insisted that his revelations were
true, and so his followers take them as truth while the rest of the
world dismisses them as fiction. Lovecraft insisted that his stories
were fiction, and so his fans take them as fiction ... even as Grant
and his followers believe that the Lovecraft short stories are genuine transmissions of Thelemic knowledge.

It is important to understand that Grant places a great deal of
importance on what he calls "dream control" and devotes a chapter
to it in his *Outer Gateways*:

> Dream actions are a clue to the magical condition of the sub-
> liminal self. ... The dream is all we may know, normally, of the
> fourth dimension while we are embodied three-dimensionally.
> But we are not so embodied while dreaming. We are then already
> a step ahead, even although we are still viewing the scene from
> another dimension, an inner dimension, which differs from
> dreamless sleep in that it is not totally formless and void. This
> extra dimension is the Mauve Zone. Surrealists, futurists, cub-
> ists, abstractionists, were groping towards its expression.[133]

Here we have the connection between dream control, the
Mauve Zone (the name Grant gives for the Abyss or for a belt of
dark power encircling the Abyss), and the artist, which is basically a
description of what was taking place in Lovecraft's story. By "artist"
here Grant is not indicating the painter of still-lifes or portraits,
of course, but the avant-garde practitioner of Surrealism and the
other movements that came out of the first World War. Surrealism
in particular is important to the study of magic and esotericism
because it used psychology, automatic writing, the Tarot and other
forms of "discarded religion" in an effort to create works of art that
would act as initiatory powers in their own right, through shocking
an audience or causing them to view the world in a way that was

---

133   Kenneth Grant, *Outer Gateways*, London: SKOOB, 1994, p. 149

not comfortable or "normal." By juxtaposing unrelated elements in a poem, a drawing, or other artform, a dream-like state was experienced in our dimension as if an urgent message was being received from Grant's Mauve Zone.

Thus Grant was able to see in Lovecraft's stories—particularly those of the Cthulhu Mythos—a message from the stars as important (or, at least, as relevant) as that received by Crowley. Possibly Lovecraft resisted the message because he loathed the messenger: the creepy, hideous beings that Grant calls "Typhonian Teratomas"[134]: monstrous offspring created by the intercourse between humans and alien forms of life and the source of Lovecraft's vision of "revolting fertility rites of immemorial antiquity." In stories like "The Dunwich Horror," Lovecraft suggests the possibility that humans and alien beings could mate and produce children who would then be hideously ugly and possessed of strange abilities. The idea that humans could somehow mate with gods, demons, and other beings is a staple of much European and Middle Eastern religion and legend. The Greek and Roman myths are full of such tales, and in the Babylonian Talmud and in various Kabbalistic and other texts we have references to Lilith, the Queen of the Night, sometimes as the first spouse of Adam and the demons as her children with the evil spirit Samael.[135] Most famously in the West, the story of the sons of God and the "daughters of men" (Genesis 6:4) seems to tell a similar story of unholy intercourse between two different beings, one human and one not-quite-human.

Lovecraft was a lover of science and an atheist; he claimed more than once in his voluminous correspondence that his stories were pure fantasy, with no relationship to anything real, but perhaps motivated by his intellectual horror of the vast expanses of space that seem to dwarf all human aspiration and potential. He also had

---

134 Kenneth Grant, *Nightside of Eden*, London: SKOOB, 1994, Chapter Six "Typhonian Teratomas."
135 This is possibly a reference to the ancient Babylonian concept of the *lilitu*: demons of the night.

a definite fear and loathing of other races, races he saw as degenerate forms of human life, monstrous throwbacks or deviations along the evolutionary path. While we can regard his native racism with pity or contempt, we can also see beyond it to realize that it is consistent with his fiction. In Lovecraft's tales nothing good can come of the mating of humans with the Old Ones. The genetic anomalies that result would throw the world open to the ravages of these uncaring, oblivious, and insane beings from planets so far from ours that they would be invisible to even the strongest of telescopes.

Mating with the gods, in other words, opens the Gate.

> "The thing has gone for ever," Armitage said. "It has been split up into what it was originally made of, and can never exist again. It was an impossibility in a normal world. Only the least fraction was really matter in any sense we know. It was like its father—and most of it has gone back to him in some vague realm of dimension outside our material universe; some vague abyss out of which only the most accursed rites of human blasphemy could ever have called him for a moment on the hills. ... You needn't ask how Wilbur called it out of the air. He didn't call it out. *It was his twin brother, but it looked more like the father than he did.*"[136]

In the above quotation from Lovecraft, we learn of the magician Wilbur Whateley and his dark rites conducted on an altar in a circle of standing stones, and the summoning forth of a murderous entity from "some vague abyss," i.e., analogous to Grant's Mauve Zone. Wilbur and the monster were twins, because their human mother—Lavinia Whateley, "a somewhat deformed, unattractive albino woman of 35"—had mated with a mysterious, unknown supramundane entity, their father. Lavinia's own father was a wizard of some repute, which explains how she came into contact with the alien being in the first place. And Wilbur Whately, her son? He

---

136 H.P. Lovecraft, "The Dunwich Horror."

was born on February 2, 1913, the date known as Candlemas to the Christian world and as Imbolc or Oimelc to the pagan world: one of the cross-quarter days that are so important to the pre-Christian calendar, coming as they do halfway between the quarter days (i.e., the solstices and equinoxes that are sacred to the solar cult because they represent stages in the sun's progress through the zodiac). The cross-quarter days are the places "between," and it is this "inbetweenness" that attracts the attention of both Lovecraft and Grant.

Further, the choice of February 2 is illustrative of another aspect to Lovecraft's work: his deliberate use of symbols. To the pagan, pre-Christian world that day was called Imbolc, an Old Irish word that means "in the belly," a reference to pregnancy. It is a suggestive date to use for the birthing of a monster, sired by a pre-Christian ancient God or Devil.

As an aside we should note that Lovecraft is always careful to use precise dates in his stories. There is no poetic ambiguity there, no referencing of the month but not the year as one finds in most stories and novels. Lovecraft always insists on specificity in his chronologies, and it is this aspect of his work that makes it so valuable to those looking for connections to real-world events especially as it seems Lovecraft is deliberately trying to tell us something. Because of this characteristic we were able to identify Crowley's fevered writing of some of the Thelemic *Holy Books* at a time when Lovecraft claimed there were orgiastic rites to Cthulhu taking place in New Orleans ... inspired by an Unholy Book: the *Necronomicon*.

The month of February, 1913 was an important one in the art world for it signalled the public appearance in New York City of Surrealist works by Marcel Duchamp. Surrealism is singled out by Grant to be one of the artforms most influenced by occult or magical currents. Only a few days earlier, in January of 1913, Kafka would put down the pen on his unfinished novel *Amerika* forever. But it was during 1913 that Crowley would write the Gnostic Mass, which we have discussed previously, as well as his famous *Hymn to Pan*.

The previous year was when Theodor Reuss visited Crowley in

London and accused him of printing the IXth degree secret of the OTO in his *Book of Lies*, specifically the chapter devoted to the Star Sapphire ritual. He then admitted Crowley to the IXth degree of the OTO, as mentioned previously, and then Crowley was put in charge of the OTO operations in the British Isles.

So, when "Wilbur Whateley" was born, Crowley was embarking on the game-changing actions that would make him the leader of one of the most famous Western secret societies of the twentieth century. As we have seen above, Crowley believed that the Egyptian gods Horus and Set were "twins": that they personified the double wand of power, as they represented the union of Lower and Upper Egypt respectively. Horus was the "good" god, and Set was the Evil One. Thus, perhaps Wilbur Whateley was the "good" twin and his brother—the monstrous thing they had to destroy—was the Evil One, the Set to Wilbur's Horus.

While these associations may seem fanciful, we need only remember how definitive were Lovecraft's stories when matched against corresponding dates and events in Thelema. In order to understand the Necronomicon Gnosis it is necessary to grasp some of the essential elements as transcribed by Lovecraft (and those of his circle) and then to "port" them over to Thelemic elements and note their correspondence. If Lovecraft received many of his ideas through his dreams, as he often admitted in writing to friends, then his process was consistent with Grant's dream control theory and practice. What is startling is that the dreams of Lovecraft would so neatly correspond to the inspirations received by Crowley.

They were both dreaming the same dream.

The reader will remember that the frenzied orgy taking place in the swamps outside New Orleans in Lovecraft's "The Call of Cthulhu" occurred on the same day that Crowley was writing several of what would be known as the "Holy Books." However, there are other coincidences that bear inspection.

For instance, in "The Call of Cthulhu" the young sculptor

Wilcox visits Professor George Angell during the period February 28 to April 2, 1925. This is the time when other artists, mediums and sensitives are experiencing similar visions around the world. Lovecraft has selected this period with care, for there was an earthquake on February 28, 1925 that affected the northeastern United States and Canada. This same earthquake is used by Lovecraft as a device that enables a sunken city beneath the waves of the Pacific Ocean to rise to the surface. While the earthquake in question did not occur in the Pacific, it was obviously the inspiration for the earthquake in the story.

It is compelling to realize that this is a phenomenon that actually has occurred and within recent history. The famous earthquake and tsunami of December 26, 2004, that took more than 200,000 lives in Asia from Indonesia and Thailand to India, also had the effect of raising an entire undersea temple off the eastern coast of India.

This was the fabled Mahabalipuram Temple of the Seven Pagodas, built in the 8th century CE. Only one of the seven "pagodas" had survived into the modern age, the so-called "Shore Temple" believed to be one of the original seven. Just before the tsunami struck, local residents saw the ocean pull away from the coastline as if being inhaled by something far out to sea. As the ocean rolled away, the sunken temple complex was revealed, showing the missing pagodas, only to be swallowed again when the roiling sea water returned. It was as if the sunken city of R'lyeh had materialized out of nowhere as an homage to Lovecraft. That it was an Indian temple seemed to indicate a resonance between the Necronomicon Gnosis and the Tantric interpretation by Kenneth Grant.

The period of general weirdness, insanity and troubled dreams depicted in "The Call of Cthulhu" as beginning with the earthquake of February 28 ends on April 2, 1925 which is the day that an important meeting of the Surrealists took place in Paris, a meeting that would decide how the artistic movement would become politically active, and which produced the *Memorandum of the Sur-*

realist Revolution. Lovecraft never refers to this meeting, of course, and it is doubtful whether or not he would have been aware of it at all. However, the bookending of an earthquake on one side and the Surrealist *Memorandum* on the other is perfectly consistent with Lovecraft's storyline. The shattering effect of the earthquake that shakes the sunken city where Cthulhu lies dead but dreaming, causing him to awaken from his ancient slumber, and the "certain state of fury"[137] that informed the Surrealist movement as these avant-garde artists struggled with altered states of consciousness and altered political states ... all of this becomes part of the Love-craftian *zeitgeist*. The earthquake awakens Cthulhu, and the art-ists—the most avant-garde, the most sensitive to occultism, depth psychology, and automatic writing—assemble in a "certain state of fury" to decide how artistic transgression and political transgression can work together to cause the destruction of civilization as they knew it. The dreams of the Surrealists bled over into the dreams of the Communists, and these dreams were seeded by the high priest of the Old Ones who needs social unrest and dislocation to give his followers the space to perform the orgia necessary to open the channels, the Gates, to the Underworld.

Kenneth Grant may be characterized as the analyst interpreting these dreams, not for the sake of the dreamers but for those of us who struggle to understand the dream content and how it may be relevant to a study of magic and religion in the 21st century. Grant reveals how the Lovecraft material expands upon the data received by Crowley with virtually no reference to the Golden Dawn-type atmosphere of the latter. Lovecraft is seeing what Crowley sees, only he sees it from the perspective of an outsider, someone for whom the symbol-set of the fin-de-siecle British secret society has no meaning and provides no context; and for whom the initiatory structure of the Golden Dawn is not available to protect him from

---

137 From the *Memorandum of The Surrealist Revolution*, 1925.

the experience. Instead, Lovecraft sees it raw, unfiltered. And that is what frightens him.

The basic features of the Necronomicon Gnosis may be reduced to a few convenient elements. The first is Cthulhu himself.

Lovecraft refers to Cthulhu as the high priest of the Old Ones and thus may not be an Old One himself. At least, he is not one of the ancient Gods but is a priest of those Gods. The physical description of Cthulhu shows that he is not human by any stretch of the imagination, with his octopus-like head replete with tentacles. One is reminded of the Egyptian gods who are often depicted as beings with humanoid bodies but with animal heads. What Lovecraft is implying in his stories is that those are the *actual* physical characteristics of the gods and not some sophisticated symbolic interpretation. Conversely, we could say that—if applying the Egyptian standards to Lovecraft's Cthulhu—that Cthulhu does not really have an octopus head but that it is Lovecraft's way of implying octopus-like characteristics.

The Schlangekraft recension of the Necronomicon—i.e., the "Simonomicon"—translates the name Cthulhu as Kutulu: a Sumerian neologism meaning "Man of the Underworld." He is, according to this interpretation, a psychopomp, a guide to the Other World, to the Mauve Zone. He is a liminal figure standing at the crossroads of this world and the next. The word *kutu* has a double meaning: it refers not only to the Underworld but to a specific city in ancient Sumer, Cutha or Gudua. The city itself was considered to be the location of an entrance to the Underworld and, as mentioned previously, it was the home city of the Qureish, the tribe to which the Prophet Muhammad belonged and which was in charge of the Ka'aba when it was a pagan shrine to the Moon God, Hubal.

There is a thus a rich vein of symbolism to be mined in the word Cthulhu. As the editor of the Necronomicon, Simon, points out the word may also be a subtle play on the term cthonic, a word used in anthropology and religious studies to mean "underground" or "under the earth" when referencing gods and spirits that are believed to dwell below the surface of the earth. The pronounciation of the word cthonic in the Oxford English Dictionary is precisely "ka-tonic" and may have also given Lovecraft the pun necessary for his famous Miskatonic University: the fictional location where the dreaded Necronomicon itself is kept under lock and key in the rare book room.

At some point in the far distant past the Old Ones were in control of this planet. When they left, Cthulhu remained behind as their lone contact and high priest but he was defeated in some manner and entombed—either beneath the earth or beneath the waves, in the sunken city of R'lyeh—and remains in that state until he can be awakened by his human followers on earth, when the "stars are right." In his present state he is "dead but dreaming," like a vampire in the coffin; except a vampire may come alive at the setting of the sun, every day, but Cthulhu can only come alive when the stars are right, i.e., when the constellations themselves are aligned in such a way as to provide a channel for the Old Ones to return. There is assumed to be a sort of ritual mechanism in which human followers of the Old Ones can perform an appropriate ceremony *at an appropriate time* and this will serve to awaken Cthulhu so he can begin his ritual for summoning the Old Ones back to earth. The right ceremony at the right time opens the Gate between this world and the next.

While it seems melodramatic and outlandish in Lovecraft's stories, this is exactly what the medieval European magicians believed. The timing of the ritual was extremely important in order for the angels and demons to be properly evoked. In Grant's own system, timing is just as important for the sexually-based rituals of his modified Tantra. The *kalas*—a word that suggests the Sanskrit term for "time" as in *Kalacakra* or "Wheel of Time"—are essences secreted by a woman on different days of her menstrual cycle. It was most likely the lunar phases in the heavens and the menstrual cycle on earth that first suggested the measurement of time and periodicity to pre-historic civilizations. The alignment of the lunar cycle with the menstrual cycle is an essential element of Grant's Tantra; alignments of the planetary cycles are themselves essential to the successful practice of ceremonial magic.

To Lovecraft, the proper alignment of the stars is never described fully. It is a secret science, known only to the worshippers of Cthulhu and the Old Ones. They alone possess the knowledge of how the stars would appear when they were "right." Again, there is precedence in Western and Asian astrology.

To most people in the West, astrology is essentially solar astrology. It is based on the passage of the Sun through the zodiacal belt. In India, however, astrology is sidereal: it is based on the actual positions of the planets when viewed against the stars of the zodiac rather than on a constant (solar) calendar date. Thus, people who believe themselves to be a Libran in the West may very well discover to their shock that in India they are said to be Virgoans. This is due to the precession of the equinoxes that was mentioned previously. Thus, when the "stars are right" in Europe they may not be right in India.

Add to this confusion the plethora of indigenous calendars around the world, none of which are exact matches for the others, and you have time-keeping systems that are unique to each culture. Java, for instance, has at least five calendars in use. Their diviners use all five in determining personal characteristics of the newborn, the best days for starting an enterprise, planting crops, etc.

The European magicians had complex tables showing the rulership of each day and each hour within the day, rulerships that changed with the day of the week. Previous to the rather arbitrary assigment of planets to days and hours, however, were the Babylonian systems of astrology that included not only planets and zodiacal constellations but also a whole host of fixed stars as well as comets and other astronomical phenomena. The Babylonian astrologers actually watched the heavens on a constant, unending basis (something which many of our contemporary astrologers would be uininterested or incapable of doing, spoiled as they are by computerized calculations and real-time simulations of the heavens). They did not view the astral positions as purely symbolic but kept an eye on the skies alert to any new message, any new prediction. Thus, an Ur-cult such as the one we have been suggesting would use an "astrology" that was rather more astronomy than astrology, although partaking of elements of each.

That this Ur-astrology is also concerned with biological functions is one of the missing links in the Lovecraftian ouevre. He hints at it, talks around it with his references to "orgies" and his discussion of poor Lavinia Whately and her demonic offspring. When the stars are right, it's not only the time when Cthulhu can be roused from his subterranean slumber but it's also the time when 35-year-old albino women can be impregnated by invisible alien monsters *as long as the correct rituals are performed.* An essential aspect of the Cthulhu Mythos is that a knowledgeable cult of experienced sorcerers are indispensable to the opening (and especially the closing) of the Gate. Lavinia did not conceive a monstrous creature by accident, after some adolescent fumbling in a hayloft at the Whateley farm. She conceived during a ritual that enabled her father, old Wizard Whateley, to charge the essences (the kalas) appropriately so that— as the Gate opened at the proper time—Lavinia's ovum would have been subtly altered to enable the alien seed to take root.[138]

None of this is described as such in "The Dunwich Horror," of course. It takes a little reading between the lines. Knowing what we know now of how these Typhonian Teratomas are created it is a simple task to go back and re-read Lovecraft with greater understanding of the process and of what was said and most important what was not said or described, but implied. That human sexuality is a means of breaching the boundaries between this world and the next is a staple of Tantra. It was virtually unknown in the West until comparatively recently with the publication of some translated

---

138 That this might have been a veiled or even unconscious allusion on Lovecraft's part to incest has not escaped the author, of course. Yet, as we have seen, allusions to incest are integral to the Star Sapphire Ritual that Crowley wrote under intense spiritual stress and these two eruptions of incest symbolism may be related to the subject under discussion.

Tantric texts in the nineteenth century. But this was common knowledge to the cultists around Cthulhu in Lovecraft's stories.

> Yog-Sothoth knows the gate. Yog-Sothoth is the gate. Yog-Sothoth is the key and guardian of the gate. Past, present, future, all are one in Yog-Sothoth. He knows where the Old Ones broke through of old, and where They shall break through again. He knows where They have trod earth's fields, and where They still tread them, and why no one can behold Them as They tread.
>
> —H. P. Lovecraft, "The Dunwich Horror"

It was Yog-Sothoth who impregnated Lavinia Whateley, who then gave birth to Wilbur Whateley and his monstrous, unnamed twin brother. Yog-Sothoth as the Gate is thus perfectly understandable in the context we have been examining. It is through this unnatural intercourse and its subsequent conception that a Gate has been opened between this world and the next, and a Magical Child created who lives in both.

Grant illuminates this concept when he writes of the assumption of god-forms, a practice that is essential to Thelemic ritual in general. His approach also helps us to understand the nature of Cthulhu, the octopus-headed beast of the statue we discover in "The Call of Cthulhu."

He writes:

> The magical theories which underlie the formula of the assumption of god-forms are of vital importance to an understanding of Crowley's later refinement and rehabilitation of them. The masquerading as animal-headed deities … was done with intent to assimilate the superhuman powers possessed by certain animals.
>
> This formula, which was used by sorcerers of the ancient world, had a profound effect upon the psychology of the operator. Because man evolved from the beasts, he possesses—deeply

buried in his subconscious—the memories of superhuman powers he once possessed. … Any required atavism could be evoked by assumption of the appropriate god-form. … Crowley interprets the formula as a magical unification of larval consciousness, characteristic of pre-human phases of life, with the ultimate product of an exalted and illumined human will … through the instrumentality of psycho-sexual magic. The Sphinx is the most celebrated image of this concept. … the meeting of beast and god through the mediumship of man.[139]

In Lovecraft's stories, these are always considered hideous creations. The Old Ones are gods in their own right, otherwise why do they need a High Priest—Cthulhu—and bands of clandestine worshippers throughout the world to worship and summon them? The offspring of Lavinia Whately then is just such a "meeting of beast and god through the mediumship of man." And, of course, it was accompanied by "psycho-sexual rites" performed by her wizard father on her tortured mind, her virgin flesh: the incestuous element of the Star Sapphire ritual taken to its heinous, albeit logical, conclusion.

The same process is used—can be used—for widely different ends and by operators of widely different capabilities; but it should be obvious that if such a thing as the Sphinx (for instance) actually existed as a living thing, it would be shunned as an abomination, the ancient Egyptian version of a "Typhonian Teratoma." Is Cthulhu, then, the product of just such a union? The "animal-headed" masks used by magicians to connect to their atavisms represent stages of human evolution, as per Grant. If so, then the cephalopod-headed creature known as Cthulhu represents a much earlier stage, something predating the arrival of quadripeds and mammals in general. Cthulhu represents that stage in evolution when life was still in its relative infancy: slime-dwelling, ooze-feasting creatures from the ocean's depths. To connect with Cthulhu, then, is to approach the

---

139   Kenneth Grant, *Aleister Crowley and the Hidden God*, pp. 15-16.

oldest part of the human brain: the reptilian or serpent brain, sitting atop the spinal column, that controls basic "fight or flight" responses as well as ritual, and which is in charge of our sexual responses as well. This has nothing to do with the higher states of love and affection, or of romance and seduction. Rather, this is pure reproductive imperative, pure lust, the seat of the "darkest" passions, those that we—as social beings—attempt (often vainly and with horrendous consequences) to repress, suppress, or flatly deny. It is the realm of what Swiss psychiatrist Carl G. Jung called "the Shadow," an unconscious element of the personality that is linked to the same animal instincts we have described,[140] and which is the repository of a person's darkest desires as well as the source of human creativity[141].

> If that abyss and what it held were real, there is no hope. Then, all too truly, there lies upon this world of man a mocking and incredible shadow out of time.[142]

It is unnameable, by virtue of the fact that this area of human consciousness existed before there were "individuals": it is the aspect of consciousness that becomes most pronounced in mob violence, gang rape, and mass hysteria.

> Violence carried to the pitch of frenzy, either masochistic or the reverse. This unseals primal atavisms, the resurgence of which leads directly to the most ancient (i.e. the original) state of consciousness which, being pure, is cosmic, unlimited.[143]

It is the basic building block of survival (fight or flight) and as such it existed before the ego, before the super-ego, before humans

---

140   C. G. Jung, "Answer to Job" in his *Collected Works*, Volume 11, *Psychology and Religion: West and East*.

141   C. G. Jung, *Memories, Dreams, Reflections*, 1983, London, p. 262.

142   H.P. Lovecraft, "The Shadow Out of Time."

143   Kenneth Grant, *Aleister Crowley and the Hidden God*, pp. 97–98. In this section he references violence as only one way among many to arouse Kundalini.

became conscious of themselves as separate, individual entities with their own souls, their own spirituality, their own potentialities as kings and queens. The physical aspect of the Shadow—the reptilian brain—is believed to be at least 500 million years old[144]: certainly a Lovecraftian time span.[145] There is nothing thoughtful or intellectual about this characteristic. There is no reasoning with it. There can only be control ... or lack of control. And since logic and reason have no place in the "serpent brain," until the advent of depth psychology the only means available for controlling its desires and managing its appetites (other than prison or drugs) were in the realm of ritual in which these unholy or unlawful needs found a safe and manageable channel for expression. Otherwise the world would have long since been filled with Typhonian Teratomas as inbreeding and incest would have degenerated the gene pool and resulted in widespread physical and mental deformities.

This part of the brain also controls the autonomic functions, such as heart-rate, breath-rate, peristalis, etc. which are not normally controlled by the conscious mind but which occur automatically, even while we sleep. It is the target of such practices as yoga and Chinese alchemy which seek to exert control over the unconscious mind through manipulation of the autonomic functions. Thus *pranayama*—one of Crowley's required practices—is the conscious control of breathing, which in turn is the gateway to conscious control of the heart-beat and from there to all the other autonomic functions. It is, of course, an extremely dangerous practice for those who have not been initiated into its secrets by someone who knows what they are doing.

---

144   See the pioneering work of Paul MacLean—the discoverer of the reptilian brain—in this regard.

145   See, for instance, this from Lovecraft's "The Shadow Out of Time": "According to these scraps of information, the basis of the fear was a horrible elder race of half polypous, utterly alien entities which had come through space from immeasurably distant universes and had dominated the earth and three other solar planets about six hundred million years ago." Thus, our reptilian brains and this "horrible elder race" are contemporaneous, if not consanguinous!

The Necronomicon Gnosis involves the deliberate investigation of this dark realm in its entirety, the realm where death and sexuality (the Freudian "death instinct" and "pleasure principle") are so inextricably intertwined that it is impossible (from the outside) to tell them apart, but which provides the engine for all successful Thelemic ritual. For Thelema is a doctrine that rejects repression in all its forms and provides outlets—some socially-acceptable, some not—for the exploration and expression of this "dark matter."

It should be emphasized, however, that Thelema does not provide an excuse for indulging in these antinomian practices willy-nilly, like some kind of occult-oriented swingers club. The only way in which to (productively) access this darker realm, the "Nightside" of Eden, is through the exercise of the Will. The individual—the result of millenia of human evolution—must be in conscious control of its own serpent brain. This is the meeting of beast and god through the mediumship of man spoken of above, the antipodes of human consciousness. The purpose is to assimilate the darker and forbidden aspects of one's consciousness into the higher form of experience, of evolution, so that it may serve as the power-house for greater attainments. In order to do this, the rituals themselves must be accurately timed. There is no better method of controlling the darker impulses than by refusing to allow them expression until "the stars are right."

When the Stars are Right

> The Pennacook myths, which were the most consistent and picturesque, taught that the Winged Ones came from the Great Bear in the sky, and had mines in our earthly hills whence they took a kind of stone they could not get on any other world. They did not live here, said the myths, but merely maintained outposts and flew back with vast cargoes of stone to their own stars in the north.
>
> —H. P. Lovecraft[146]

146 H. P. Lovecraft, "The Whisperer in the Darkness"

One of the critical pieces of information concerning the correct position of the "stars"—i.e., when they are "right"—has to do with the Great Bear constellation, referenced above in Lovecraft's story "The Whisperer in the Darkness." A further note is at the end of that same paragraph when "their own stars in the north" are referenced. Simon has made much of this in his *Gates of the Necronomicon*, and I have focused on the Great Bear constellation myself in *Stairway to Heaven* in an attempt to demonstrate its universality among mystery cults in different parts of the world, including shamanism, Mithraism and even some ceremonial forms of Daoism. I believe that this constellation is a key to understanding the ancient cults of which Lovecraft writes and in this it seems Kenneth Grant concurs.

> All Circle-craft is based either upon the original (stellar) circle
> of the Great Bear, Goddess of the Seven Stars; or the Moon
> and her thirteenfold annual cycle; or on the later and final solar
> circle of the Twelve Celestial houses of the sun (zodiac).[147]

The Great Bear is a circumpolar constellation: that is, it never sets below the horizon but rotates endlessly about a point in the absolute north above the earth, represented in our time by the Pole Star. In other words, these are the "stars in the north" to which Lovecraft alludes in his story. Navigators have used the position of the Great Bear constellation—or its smaller asterism, the Big Dipper—to tell time and direction when no landmarks or other astronomical phenomena are available or visible, such as in the middle of the ocean at night. Remembering how critical time and the measurement of time is to the correct performance of rituals intended to evoke planetary and other forces, we can begin to appreciate the relevance of this constellation to mystery religions the world over. Grant associates the Great Bear with the Goddess of the Seven Stars, i.e. with Babalon herself. In the Schlangekraft

---

147   Kenneth Grant, *Aleister Crowley and the Hidden God*, p. 122

recension of the Necronomicon, it specifically states that the Gate may be opened when "the Great Bear hangs from its tail in the sky." Of course, the Great Bear hangs from its tail in the sky once every day as it rotates around the Pole Star (it is actually the earth doing the rotating, as every schoolchild knows). But at night, when the constellation may be visible, it hangs from its tail (making a straight line from the Pole Star) at midnight on April 30.[148] As we have noted before, this is a date with great relevance, for it is another of the cross-quarter days mentioned above. Known as Walpurgisnacht to readers of Bram Stoker's *Dracula*, it is also known as Beltane or even just as May Eve to pagans and Wiccans. The European equivalent of the American Halloween, it is a day when witches gather for their Great Sabbat atop mountain peaks and commune with the Devil ... with the Dark Lord.

It also has some uncanny correspondences with American and world history. For instance, April 30, 1492 was the day Christopher Columbus received his commission to set sail for the East Indies, a voyage that culminated in the "discovery" of America on October 12, 1492—coincidentally Aleister Crowley's birthday.

April 30, 1789 was the day George Washington took the oath of office of President of the United States, on Wall Street in New York City. The monument that bears his name in Washington, D.C. is precisely 555 feet high: 555 is the number of the word Necronomicon.

April 30, 1945 is the day when it was alleged that Adolf Hitler committed suicide in the Berlin bunker.

April 30, 1975 is the day when Saigon fell to the North Vietnamese army, signalling the end of the Vietnam War.

April 30, 1978 is the day the Democratic Republic of Afghanistan was proclaimed, with disastrous consequences.

And on and on.

---

148 Due to the precession of the equinoxes, the hour has shifted slightly from year to year. See Simon's *Gates of the Necronomicon* for specific dates and times.

Into the north window of my chamber glows the Pole Star with uncanny light ... The Pole Star, evil and monstrous, leers down from the black vault, winking hideously like an insane watching eye which strives to convey some strange message, yet recalls nothing save that it once had a message to convey.

—H. P. Lovecraft, "Polaris" (1918)

Lovecraft's conscious employment of the Great Bear and Polaris in his stories may be an indication that he was aware of the role these astronomical entities play in the cults he describes with such terror. Frater Achad—whose strange insistence on a contemporaneous Aeon of Maat we have already described—had this to say about the same constellation:

The first boy and his mother were called Sut-Typhon.

Sut means "The Opener," and this may be taken in the physiological as well as the astrological sense. The Child was the opener in the sense of being born of the un-mated Mother. The Sun is the Opener of the Day, while Sut as the Star-god was considered the Opener of the Year with the rising of Sothis, and on his rising was the Great Bear cycle founded.[149]

While Achad links the Great Bear with Set in his writings, Grant does the same in the Typhonian trilogies:

Celestial, not terrestrial, lineage was the matter of contention. In the course of ages, the ancestors of the Terrestrial Typhonians came to be typified by the Great Bear constellation connected with vastly ancient myths inspired by dim memories of the earliest colonisers of earth, and descended from Typhonian star systems.[150]

---

149   Frater Achad, *The Egyptian Revival*, p. 2. It should be noted that "Sut" is Achad's rendering of "Set," the Dark Lord.

150   Kenneth Grant, *Outer Gateways*, p. 35

Thus we can see that Grant believes that the earliest coloniz-ers of earth came from a region we identify with the Great Bear constellation which is consistent with the Lovecraft short story ref-erenced above, "The Whisperer in the Darkness," in which alien beings from the Great Bear constellation began coming to earth in aeons past and concerned themselves with mining a specific ore from our planet. Grant is referring in this work to the idea that the type of "lineage" typified by such popular authors as Dan Brown in his *DaVinci Code* and in other works—fiction and non-fiction—that have come out of the *Holy Blood, Holy Grail* genre does *not* refer to an earthly bloodline but to a celestial one (not necessarily a "heav-enly" or "divine" bloodline, but one that comes from off-planet). This is a type of lineage that transcends genetics as we understand it and manifests as occult currents through the ages, much in the way that apostolic succession is a "lineage" within the Catholic and Orthodox churches except that, in this case, the lineage to which Grant refers has its origins not on earth or within earthly organi-zations but in the stars. It is this type of lineage that makes itself known in the works of both Crowley and Lovecraft as we have seen: works produced by these two men, unknown to each other, yet displaying an uncanny pattern of coincidence and agreement. It is what prompted Grant to speak of a Thelemic current as well as a Necronomicon and an Egyptian current, and to identify them as three separate strands of the same lineage.

The Lovecraftian idea that these ancient, extraterrestrial beings came to the earth in order to mine a specific stone has deep reso-nance with a whole host of concepts connected with alchemy, sexu-ality, and Tantra, and it is a theme that Lovecraft has explored in more than one short story.

Aside from the oeuvre published under his own name, Love-craft is known to have helped other authors with their stories, in some cases rewriting them entirely but permitting them to be pub-lished as original works by the same authors. One particular story reinforces the Grant thesis that Crowley's mysterious "Tulu" and Lovecraft's Cthulhu are one and the same.

This is the story entitled "The Mound" and attributed as the work of Zealia Bishop. It was written in the period 1929–1930 and appears in the collection of Lovecraft's "other" works, *The Horror in the Museum*, edited by Lovecraft scholar S. T. Joshi. In this story we have references to "ingots of magnetic Tulu-metal"[151] and the "sacred and magnetic Tulu-metal."[152] This story also has a reference to a sunken city, referred to in a Mexican dialect as *Relex*. Anyone familiar with how the Spanish "x" is pronounced will immediately realize that this word is pronounced "Rel-eh" with a hard "h," thus giving us a form of *R'lyeh*.

In this story we have again the theme of mining specific metals, in this case Tulu metal, which is magnetic and therefore of a north-south polarity consistent with the Necronomicon Gnosis and its emphasis on the north-south axis versus the solar east-west axis. It should be pointed out once again that the word "Tulu" is specific to both Lovecraft and to Crowley: it is a point of tangence between the two authors that reflects a deeper connection than we normally attribute to the horror writer and the prophet of the New Age.

Mircea Eliade, the famous historian of religion at the University of Chicago, wrote concerning sacred stones in his *The Forge and the Crucible*:

> It is not very long since the kings of Malaya kept a sacred block of iron which was part of their regalia and surrounded it with an extraordinary veneration mingled with superstitious terror. … It was not a question of fetishism or of the worship of an object in itself or for its own sake; it was not a matter of superstition but a sacred respect for a strange object outside their own familiar world, an object coming from elsewhere and hence a sign or token of the 'beyond,' a near-image of the transcendental.[153]

---

151 Zealia Bishop, "The Mound" in The Horror In The Museum, edited by S.T. Joshi, Arkham House Publishers, Sauk City,WI, 1989, p. 135.
152 Ibid., p. 151
153 Mircea Eliade, *The Forge and the Crucible*, p. 27. The author can attest that blocks of sacred stone—surrounded by iron fences to keep the profane at a

Eliade equates the practice of mining with a whole host of concepts related to alchemical transformation. The miner was an initiate of the dark mysteries: by working in the caves and hidden places of the earth he was in constant contact with the spirits that dwelled in the underworld. He was also privy to the secret processes whereby a stone could become gold. He knew where objects were buried and hidden. His day turned into night as he descended into the bowels of the earth, below any visible horizon and thus out of reach of the sun and the stars.

The cult of Mithra conducted its mysterious initiations in caves, in the place of mines and buried treasure, away from the light of the sun. For this reason (and several others), I believe that the Mithraists were not worshipping the Sun god and that the sacred Bull that was slain by Mithra was not an emblem of the zodiacal sign Taurus but of the constellation known as the Great Bear. I develop this theory more carefully in *Stairway to Heaven*, but basically I identify nocturnal worship with stellar worship, especially in the case of cults and religions that had no other reason to meet in secret since they were not being suppressed or engaging in antinomian practices.

There was an ancient understanding that there was an analogue between the bowels of the earth and the embryonic stages of gestation. The earth gave birth to gold and other precious metals through a long process of metallurgical gestation. The alchemist understood these processes and knew how to hurry them along, to "induce labor" one might say so that the earth gave up its treasures more quickly. The natural process of human evolution may, one day, result in a being of higher intelligence and spiritual illumination; but it is the work of the magician to "induce labor" in the initiate, to hurry along the natural process of spiritual evolution so that it takes place (at least for the individual) in a single lifetime.

This has relevance for the discussion of the reptilian brain, above; for just as human beings evolved over the long term from

---

distance—are still in evidence in the Archipelago.

watery creatures to amphibious mammals to mammals and finally to homo sapiens, so the human embryo goes through a similar process of living in an aqueous solution until it "crawls out onto dry land," i.e., is born into the world as an air-breathing creature, crawling on all fours and eventually walking upright. In this sense, every magician and every alchemist is an embryo going through the same process as the human embryo, as the metals in the earth, as the entire human race itself. But it must begin by probing the reptilian brain and discovering its contents and neutralizing them, making them servants of the Will. And what better representative of the reptilian brain and the danger and loathesomeness that it conceals than the hideous form of the High Priest of the Great Old Ones, Cthulhu himself?

The Necronomicon Gnosis recognizes that some of the steps along the way were evolutionary dead-ends, at least from the point of view of homo sapiens. While some creatures did not survive and became extinct on our world, the Gnosis insists that not all of them died out permanently but that their scars remain on our DNA, dormant, "dead but dreaming" of the day when they will be "turned on" by environmental or other factors and rise with a roar from the bowels of our own, individual R'lyehs.

The Sunken City

In his house at R'lyeh dead Cthulhu waits dreaming.
—H. P. Lovecraft

Until you make the unconscious conscious, it will direct your life and you will call it fate.
—C. G. Jung

Lovecraft's core story, "The Call of Cthulhu," is the repository of all the basic themes and motifs that appear in his later tales. It reflects his basic preoccupations with ancient races, mysterious cults, non-Euclidean geometry, and the power of dreams. It also introduces us to Cthulhu, the high priest of the Great Old Ones, and the sunken city of R'lyeh where Cthulhu lies dead, but dreaming.

The idea of a sunken or buried civilization is something that has been with us for thousands of years. Plato famously referred to the vanished civilization of Atlantis; and rumors of a Lemuria and a Mu—more sunken civilizations—became prevalent in the late nineteenth and early twentieth centuries. Then there was the Hollow Earth theory and the claim that Admiral Byrd had seen the entrance to this "inner earth" through a hole in the vicinity of the North Pole. So the sunken city meme has been a staple of fantasy history for quite some time.

Lovecraft's genius lay in reinterpreting these stories from a darker point of view. Lovecraft's sunken city of R'lyeh is where the Great Old Ones were defeated by some quirk of space or time, and where Cthulhu lies buried in his house-like tomb beneath the waves. This ancient city is older than Atlantis or any of its other mythical counterparts. It was built—using geometry that was all "wrong"—by the race from the stars, a race that used to own the planet Earth in aeons past and which is on the verge of returning when the "stars are right."

If we analyze this story from the point of view of depth psychology, we can see a certain level of consistency with modern ideas concerning the unconscious and the danger of repressing unconscious feelings and especially the knowledge that lies buried in the deep, forgotten corners of the human mind. In this approach, R'lyeh becomes the unconscious itself, and Cthulhu is the Shadow that waits to be discovered: the potentially dangerous, violent, evil aspect of human nature. An aspect that communicates with us the same way Cthulhu communicates with his followers: in dreams.

Freud famously claimed that dreams were the "royal road to the unconscious," and Lovecraft might have agreed. To the gothic horror writer, dreams were certainly the royal road to R'lyeh, to the dead but dreaming High Priest, Cthulhu. He writes that Cthulhu is in communication with his human followers through a kind of telepathy that manifests in their dreams. This is what triggered the creation of the Cthulhu sculpture by young Wilcox and which sets in motion "The Call of Cthulhu." We learn that this "call" is indeed the dream-stream sent by Cthulhu from deep within the sunken city, from deep within what Jung called the "collective unconscious."

It may be a truism that what demands to be known in our dreams is not some beautiful image of heaven or some pleasing, loving memory—but something more sinister, something uglier that needed to be "put down," that needed to be suppressed in order that the rest of the personality could survive in the real world. The only persons who deliberately evoked those nightmares to visible appearance were the mystics, the magicians, and the shamans. I have written at some length in other works about the shamanistic initiations, and of course Mircea Eliade has discussed this at some length in his seminal work on the subject, Shamanism. This type of initiation involves a direct confrontation with the suppressed psychic material that involves the death, dismemberment, and re-integration of the individual psyche. For someone who has come through this type of experience the dread Cthulhu could hold no fears.

It may also be a truism that this suppressed material is connected with sexual issues. It may involve sexual trauma of the individual at a very young age, or physical or emotional abuse of some kind by an older person. While the exact identity and nature of the trauma will be different from person to person, the Minotaur in the Labyrinth is the same: the different types of abuse reflect different pathways in the Labyrinth, but they all lead to the same Monster at the center. Lovecraft called this Monster by a name he heard or invented or dreamed: Cthulhu.

As described in the Schlangekraft recension of the *Necronomicon*, the ancient Sumerians had just such a sunken city in their myth cycles. The gate to this underworld palace was through the city of Gudua, the city that became Cutha and Kutu. Cthulhu is Kutu-lu, the Man of the Underworld. He is a hybrid creature, as envisioned by Lovecraft, something crustacean or squid-like. As a High Priest of the Old Ones, he is the liminal figure between humanity and the ancient race from the stars. He lives in the Underworld, in R'lyeh, and can be summoned by those who hear his call through their fevered dreams.

In "The Call of Cthulhu" Lovecraft reveals that the rituals required to summon the Great Old Ones involve orgies by people who are of mixed races, the implication being that they are not white Europeans but Arabs, Africans, and Asians ... all races of which Lovecraft was deeply suspicious and fearful. This conflation of unbridled sexuality and exotic races and ethnicities is a common theme in colonialist literature and was a feature in the castigation of the practice of Tantra in India by the British colonizers. Again, Lovecraft has touched on a deep current of occult tradition and methodology in his fantasies, understanding that contact may be made with the darker aspects of the human mind through avenues provided by sexuality. He was not alone in this, of course. The French Decadent poets and authors also made that connection, and the stories of the Black Mass with its worship of Satan combined with sexual orgies are representative of this idea. It was Lovecraft, however, who extended this concept even further by associating the sexual orgies with the worship—not of Satan, or of any human-created or human-inspired boogeyman—but of the most ancient, primordial and non-human race that once controlled the planet and which was on the verge of returning again to reclaim it. Lovecraft wanted to go deeper, darker, into more dangerous territory. He understood that there were levels to human consciousness that could not be plumbed by spiritual dilettantes, and that the rituals employed by sorcerers and magicians had implications far beyond what these individuals believed to be possible ... or desirable. To evoke Cthulhu or any of the Great Old Ones was to invite disaster (from the original meaning of the word, dis-aster or "evil star") and destruction for the entire planet. It was to cause a mental or nervous breakdown for the entire human race.

At the center of this complex of ideas rests the unholy book itself, the Necronomicon. To Lovecraft, this book contains the spells used by members of the Cthulhu cult and instructions on

how to keep the Gate between Us and Them—the ultimate "liminality"—closed forever. The spells are in a language that is unknown,
containing diagrams that seem meaningless yet somehow unnerv-
ing in their weird geometry. It is a repository of bits and pieces of
ancient knowledge—like our dreams, like our own unconscious—
and to read it is to become entranced, to enter a dream state while
awake, to fear oneself going insane. It is a book of Death, as its
name implies, a collection of antique ceremonies and smatterings
of images from our collective past. It offers a symbol set that speaks
directly to the unconscious, to Cthulhu, in the language Cthulhu
uses for communicating to us in our dreams. Instead of Freud's
famous *Interpretation of Dreams* it is a book of dreams that interprets us. It is our collective dreamworld as humans, fragmentary
and filled with lacunae as it may be, a satanic semiotics that offers a
two-lane pathway to our darkest memories as a race of humans and
of our contact—at some distant, immemorial past—with another
race of being, a contact that was perhaps not quite so pleasant as
we may wish to believe. It enables us to interpret and decipher our
dreams (the messages from Cthulhu) but also provides a means for
communicating *back*. As Grant understood, the Necronomicon is
also a manual not only of dream interpretation (a la Freud) but of
dream *control*.

It's how we communicate with the denizens of the sunken city,
whether we call it R'lyeh or the collective unconscious. And it uses
the fiber optic cable of the serpent brain to transfer its bits and …
"bites."

CHAPTER FIVE

SONS OF GOD, DAUGHTERS OF MEN ...
AND WILBUR WHATELEY

... Sophia's focus on her desire and passion to "know" the Father resulted in an amorphous nasty miscarriage.[154]

It was in the township of Dunwich ... that Wilbur Whateley was born at 5 a.m. on Sunday, the second of February, 1913. This date was recalled because it was Candlemas, which people in Dunwich curiously observe under another name ... Less worthy of notice was the fact that the mother was one of the decadent Whateleys, a somewhat deformed, unattractive albino woman of 35, living with an aged and half-insane father about whom the most frightful tales of wizardry had been whispered in his youth. Lavinia Whateley had no known husband ...[155]

The incursion of extra-terrestrial influences into the human life-wave, unconsciously or consciously attracted to the individual embryo, would be a means of incarnating such mutants. The intense magical operations which Crowley performed (especially those which occurred between 1920 and 1924) could, and probably did, engender strange and "unearthly" children.[156]

THE SUBJECT OF THIS CHAPTER concerns the most controversial and perhaps most titillating aspect of the Grant ouevre: his focus on sexuality within the context of magic. We have touched on it briefly

---

154   April D. DeConick, "Conceiving Spirits: The Mystery of Valentinian Sex," in Wouter J. Hanegraaf and Jeffrey J. Kripal, *Hidden Intercourse: Eros and Sexuality in the History of Western Esotericism*, Fordham University, New York, 2011, pp. 23–48. The reference is to the Aeon Sophia, as described in Chapter One of the present work.
155   H.P. Lovecraft, "The Dunwich Horror."
156   Kenneth Grant, *Aleister Crowley and the Hidden God*, p. 52.

here and there in the pages that precede this one, but the author would like to dwell a bit more deeply on this issue since it is so critical towards an understanding of Grant's Typhonian Tradition and many readers possibly would find it difficult to reconcile such material with Lovecraft's known reluctance to discuss sexuality at all in his own work.

In order to do justice to this difficult subject, we will be reverting from time to time to Gnostic texts and interpretations since it may come as a surprise to some readers that the early Gnostics were very concerned with human sexuality and its place in the universe. There were probably as many different versions of "spiritual sexuality" among the Gnostics as there were Gnostic sects. Our sources for this material are unfortunately restricted to Christian commentators who were notoriously hostile to Gnosticism and whose data is thus suspect, as well as the surviving Gnostic fragments themselves such as the Nag Hammadi scrolls. What we will find in this discussion is a justification for much of what passes for "sacred sexuality" in the Thelemic framework, but also an elaboration of Lovecraft's own fears—perhaps unconscious—concerning the potential disasters of "liberated" sexuality and especially of intercourse—carnal and otherwise—with discarnate entities, gods, demons, and ... others.

We will also have recourse to Tantra, as Grant relies more heavily on Tantra than on Gnosticism for an understanding of the inner workings of magic and the relevance of sexual practices to Thelema. Like the Gnostics before them, Thelemites are concerned with sexuality as a form of worship and/or magical power. In this they are no different from the Tantrikas of India, Nepal and Tibet and indeed they share many ideas and concepts in common. To Grant, this was a genuine revelation and he saw a broader context for Thelema in the occult practices of Asia and Africa as well as within the framework of the Necronomicon Gnosis which is not bashful about confronting the nastier bits of occult praxis.

The Celibate and the Hedonist

One of the antipodes in this study concerns the weird polarity of H. P. Lovecraft and Aleister Crowley. The former was notoriously sexually ambivalent, virtually asexual. He lived most of his life as a celibate, married for only two years and even then did not live with his wife for much of that time. The latter was notorious in an entirely different way: Crowley had sex with anyone and it seems anything within reach. Male or female, young or old, of whatever race, whatever degree of physical health or actual physical deformity (like poor Lavinia Whateley, above, who would have made a perfect partner for the English magician, but who had to settle for her "half-insane" wizard of a father).

Their approach to magic was similarly opposite. Crowley enthusiastically engaged in sexual magic for the purpose of creating spiritual offspring who would carry out his various tasks. Lovecraft found such behavior revolting, but in his stories there is a tacit acknowledgement that the system worked, just not in the way Crowley would have anticipated. To Lovecraft, human sexual intercourse with gods, aliens, demons, etc. could only result in hideous monsters out to destroy all of humanity. To Crowley, such intercourse would produce servants who would be more capable than the human version, "You can't get good help nowadays" being the operative principle.

In Lovecraft's stories there are no "good" magicians except for those who become battlefield trained in order to undo some other magician's work, to close the Gate and to send Wilbur Whateley's twin back to where it came, etc. To Lovecraft the person, magic was superstition and at least one cause of humanity's distress, so his position was relatively consistent: no matter how you looked at it, either as a believer or as an atheist, magic was bad. At best it was a waste of time, at worst it was an unholy practice designed to enslave humanity.

Thus, in Lovecraft and Crowley we have two oppposing points of view and two very different personalities. We especially have two very different approaches to sexuality, as well. Then how were these two men somehow "picking up" some identical information?

We can say that Lovecraft was a natural sensitive—as are many true artists—and that regardless of his ideology he was nevertheless in tune with the occult currents of the day. In this he was different from Crowley in that Crowley's art was always in service to his ideology; his novels are occult *romans-a-clef*, his poetry is designed to be used as keys to his magical worldview. Crowley used his novel *Moonchild* to attack and ridicule those he despised, such as Arthur Edward Waite and MacGregor Mathers. Lovecraft used his stories to praise and recognize his friends, such as Clark Ashton Smith.

In fact, Lovecraft *had* friends: a wide circle of friends with whom he pretty much stayed in contact for most of his life, usually through his voluminous correspondence but also in visits out of the State of Rhode Island where he lived to New York City, Florida, and other parts of the country. Crowley, on the other hand, alienated many of his friends over time and those who stuck by him were few and far between. It's hard to be chummy with the Prophet of a New Age.

So for all of Lovecraft's sexual timidity he had more consistent social contacts than the man who would engage in any form of sexual intercourse with just about anyone. They were opposite poles, indeed, and their common interests kept them on the same axis. Both Lovecraft and Crowley wrote of contact with extra-mundane forces, of ancient races, lost temples, bizarre occult practices, and strange, devil-worshipping cults. It is in the tension between their two, diametrically-opposed, points of view that we find the most valuable information and inspired insights.

Lovecraft's most notable discussion of how magic might be used to create hideous beings when coupled with sexual practices is in his famous short story "The Dunwich Horror" which was made into a film back in 1970. It concerns the "half-insane" old wizard Whateley and the unnameable rites he performed on his deformed, albino daughter Lavinia. There were two genetic Whateley lines, the decayed and the undecayed lines according to Lovecraft and, of course, Old Whateley belonged to the decayed line. Thus there was the implication that this particular genetic strain was already tainted and the pattern of abnormal births was an indication either that something was amiss with the wizardry since long ago, or that the genetic abnormalities were somehow necessary to the effectiveness of the rites.

> Wanted: Dwarfs, Hunchbacks, Tattooed Women, Harrison Fisher Girls, Freaks of all sorts, Coloured women, only if exceptionally ugly or deformed, to pose for artist. Apply by letter with a photograph.[157]

Crowley was not averse to having sexual relations with women of different racial and ethnic backgrounds, as well as with women who were physically different in some obvious way. He was also not averse to having homosexual relations, and often as the "bottom" or receiving partner in acts of anal sex. There is no indication that Crowley received much in the way of sexual satisfaction from these acts, and his *Confessions* and other writings tend to support the view that he approached virtually all sexuality from a magical standpoint which was inextricable from a psychological one. As it is almost certain that Lovecraft did not enjoy sexuality (at least, not enough to seek out sexual opportunities with any degree of passion or determination) we might say that these two men shared a common approach. Neither Crowley nor Lovecraft engaged in sexual activity with the primary intention of obtaining sexual satisfaction or gratification. For Crowley, sexual activity was subordinate to the demands of the Great Work: it was ritual and a pragmatic utilization of his psycho-biological apparatus, a method to be used to plumb the depths of his psyche as well as to make contact with other forces in the universe. For Lovecraft it just wasn't an issue at all. For

157 A newspaper advertisement by Aleister Crowley in the New York press. Many miss the humor of the inclusion of "Harrison Fisher girls" in the list of "Freaks of all sorts."

both men, it could be claimed that sexuality was not about physical satisfaction or even need. It was about something else entirely.

Hideous Marriage

> The conflicts now raging in the world are due to the birth-pangs
> of the Aeon of Horus. Sexual methods of establishing contact
> with entities more evolved than man will be perfected and there
> are already signs of their development.[158]

As mentioned previously, there are several similarities that can be noted between the sexual mysticism of Thelema and the Gnostic conception of sexuality and marriage as represented by the Valentinians. We have already seen that the Aeons of Valentinian Gnosticism have their parallels to the Thelemic Aeons. In the case of human sexuality, there are even deeper connections and they can be used as a prism through which to understand Grant's preoccupation with Tantra as a means of reinterpreting Thelemic magic.

The Christian commentator Clement of Alexandria (c. 150–c. 215 CE) wrote extensively on Gnosticism in order to refute it. The Valentinians, alone among the various Gnostic sects, attract his approval because of their positive view towards marriage as the attempt to bring down the divine emanations. The Valentinians—according to Clement—saw human marriage as the earthly representation of the syzygies: the male-female pairs that were the first emanations of the Father and which eventually resulted in the Creation as we know it.

But some of Clement's objections to other Gnostic groups are very revealing.

Clement contrasts the Valentinians with the Carpocrations, who he thinks participated in licentious sexual acts because they believed that by doing so they were imitating the primordial

---

158   Kenneth Grant, *Aleister Crowley and the Hidden God*, pp. 150–151.

powers who had intercourse with one another in order to create the universe.[159]

This is as good a brief explanation of Tantra as any.

Instead, as Gnostic scholar April D. DeConick tells us, Clement was interested in a specific form of human sexual expression that would result in divine offspring:

> Human marriage was procreative, but one form of it produced more perfect offspring than the other. The higher form of marriage included some sort of consciousness-raising during sexual relations to insure that the children would resemble God. Physical intercourse was not driven by lust, but was a matter of the will or intention.[160]

In other words, the Crowleyan imperative "love under will." To make this point more precisely, Clement writes that Christians should:

> … do nothing from lust (*epithumia*). Our will is to be directed towards that which is necessary. For we are children not of lust but of will (*thelematos*).[161]

Thus, Clement of Alexandria insists that Christians are children of Thelema!

According to Clement, human sexual intercourse that was not directed towards the divine—sexual relations that were the result of the lustful feelings of the partners—produced "defective" offspring.[162] Lovecraft would take this idea much further, for he raises the possibility of sexual relations between humans and non-human

---

159   April D. DeConick, op. cit., p. 36.
160   Ibid., p. 40
161   Ibid., p. 36
162   Ibid., p. 40

creatures that result in "defective" offspring, to say the least. Love-craft also identifies what he sees as defective races, ethnicities and bloodlines representing genetic groups that are more prone to wor-ship or summon the dark forces from beyond the stars. This is obvi-ous in such stories as "The Horror At Red Hook," and "The Dun-wich Horror," and certainly is implied in "The Call of Cthulhu."

But the Valentinian Gnostics—according to Clement and amplified by DeConick—believed in spiritual intercourse:

> Through contemplative sexual practices, the Valentinians hoped to conceive children whose souls would contain an elect or mor-ally-inclined "seed" of the Spirit. Sacred marriage was essential for giving birth to such children, who in turn would bring about the redemption of the fallen Sophia and the psyche.[163]

This belief is quite similar to that of the Kabbalists of the Mid-dle Ages who held that it was the duty of pious Jews to engage in sexual intercourse on the Sabbath in order to help the "shards"—the broken pieces of the *sephirot*, the result of an oddly-failed attempt at the Creation—reunite and redeem themselves and by extension the whole world so that the Shekinah herself can reunite with her Bridegroom. These shards are known as the *qlippot*, and Crowley devoted one rather strange document to their study, *Liber 231*. It attracted the attention of Kenneth Grant in the Typhonian Trilo-gies because it seemed to offer a kind of blueprint to the Tunnels of Set: the darkside of the Kabbalistic Tree of Life and the pathways that connect its various power zones, a subject to which we will return in the next chapter.

While sacred marriage is a staple of alchemical literature and appears in the theological adumbrations of the Church of Jesus Christ of Latter-Day Saints (Mormons), it is not as emphasized in traditional ceremonial magic. The iconic figure of the ceremonial magician is of a man who either works alone, or with several (male)

---

163   Ibid., p. 23.

assistants. This is evidenced by the grimoires themselves, which contain formulas for evoking the right spirits or demons to make a woman fall in love, or to seduce a woman, etc.—thus leading one to speculate that the average ceremonial magician was probably the medieval version of a geek: lacking in social graces and silently lusting after the girl next door. Probably the best example of this meme is that of Goethe's *Faust*: the magician who similarly lusts after a woman, the beloved Gretchen, and who uses the Devil's powers to obtain her.

This was not Crowley's problem, obviously. By the time Crowley had appeared on the scene the field of ceremonial magic had undergone quite an overhaul. Beginning with the romantic notions of Eliphas Levi and extending to the Golden Dawn, magic was being redefined as a spiritual practice equivalent to a Western version of yoga and Tantra, with a complex and internally-consistent worldview. Crowley extended this impulse to make of magic an all-encompassing spiritual movement, fueled by the revelations contained in the Book of the Law.

In addition, such intellectual luminaries as Carl G. Jung would elevate the study of alchemy to a serious field of psychological importance, and Gershom Scholem would bring Kabbalah and Jewish mysticism into the mainstream of academic research and analysis. Mircea Eliade introduced the world to shamanism, and his brilliant student Ioan Couliano would focus his knowledge of many languages both ancient and modern on medieval spiritual texts and ascent literature. The influence of these academic writers on the field of magic cannot be over-emphasized, even as they criticized occult authors such as A. E. Waite and Aleister Crowley by name.[164]

The theory and practice of magic was undergoing a sea-change, buffeted by forces both within and without, a process that continues to this day (especially with the outstanding work on Western

---

164 Gershom Scholem himself, in his Introduction to *Major Trends in Jewish Mysticism* (1941) cites Crowley's writings on the Kabbalah as one reason why he felt motivated to write his ground-breaking study.

esotericism coming out of the Amsterdam school led by Wouter Hanegraaf, and that of the late and much-lamented Nicholas Goodrick-Clarke of England). But the aspect of modern magic that received the most attention—and the most confusion—was the constant references to sex as an element of the process. This began with Crowley, as far as can be determined.

While the African-American mystic Paschal Beverly Randolph was undoubtedly a major influence where the sexual aspect of occultism and spirituality was concerned, through his writings and his connections to the Hermetic Brotherhood of Light and eventually to the Ordo Templi Orientis, sacred sexuality was still very much a dark little secret among the Western occultists until Crowley began publicizing it rather openly. The Golden Dawn had its rituals based on the Rosicrucian allegories, and used both male and female participants in its ceremonies (unusual for a secret society at the time), but Crowley took the whole thing much further. As we have noted previously, the Golden Dawn provided much of the theoretical and ritual framework for Crowley's system and, indeed, his A∴A∴ is a refinement of the Golden Dawn degree structure with the additional three degrees at the top of the Tree of Life. Thus it would seem that a mystique of sexuality had no real place in a system that was so perfectly symmetrical to begin with but the OTO changed all of that for Crowley.

There is no doubt that the Book of the Law contains many passionate verses and lusty exhortations, written long before Crowley made the acquaintance of the OTO. This rather startling text might have made Crowley more receptive to the later instructions on sexual magic received from that German order. However Crowley's approach was not informed by a specific program of theory and practice; instead, he tried to incorporate sexual techniques within the context of the Golden Dawn system of magic he inherited and this was not always fruitful. He used various forms of sexual experimentation for every kind of purpose, from charging talismans to attract money or knowledge to using sexual intercourse to attain altered states of consciousness. He was aware that sexual fluids were important, but had to invent ways to use them.

By the time he met David Curwen, who had considerably more knowledge in this area than he, Crowley was already quite old and only a few years from death. Kenneth Grant, however, did not let the opportunity pass to learn from someone more knowledgeable in Tantra and began to understand the realm of possibilities that this new data represented. It is the combination of ceremonial magic, Crowley's own Thelemic denomination, Tantra, Afro-Caribbean magic, the art of Austin Osman Spare and the Surrealists, and the over-arching worldview of H. P. Lovecraft that informs the entire Typhonian Tradition. These quanta seem unrelated and arbitrarily chosen, but in Grant's hands they become indispensable elements of a symphony of occult praxis. The deeper one looks into any of these disparate traditions the more one finds important commonalities.

The Valentinian Gnostics believed that they could create divine offspring through some process of "consciousness-raising" as DeConick puts it. Obviously the reverse would also be true: by a different form of "consciousness-raising" one could create demon children. By fine-tuning the process, one could also create "offspring" that would have whatever characteristics were specified by the ritual. This means that the act of sexual intercourse would take place within a magical context. Clement of Alexandria believed that sex acts that resulted from pure lust would produce children that were somehow "defective"; how much more so children that were produced from acts of sexual intercourse that were specifically designed to attract demonic or otherworldly forces.

The Gnostic marriage was undoubtedly a spiritual one, the act of intercourse elevated to a higher plane; but it was nevertheless a ritual act. It was not motivated by pure lust or emotional or sexual attraction between partners. Oddly, this is the same approach that needs to be taken regardless of whether or not the purpose is to create divine offspring or demonic ones: the concentration of the sexual partners must be focused on the spiritual or magical goal and not on the satisfaction of sexual desire. This is a requirement that effectively eliminates most dilettantes who become involved in the practice of magic because they seek excitement or arcane thrills.

The sexual rituals described by Grant in his Typhonian Trilogies are never explained in full, but there is enough detail to enable the educated or dedicated reader to fill in the blanks. The Gnostic Marriage example of a High Priest or King mating with a High Priestess or Queen becomes the template onto which a series of variations is mapped. In order to deconstruct the Tantric rituals employed by Grant and by the members of his Nu-Isis Lodge it becomes necessary to deconstruct the sex act itself, to reduce it to its various psycho-biological components. The grosser physical aspects of the sex act—the bodily fluids especially—are understood to be place-holders for their more ethereal counterparts.

None of this is helpful, however, if the individual participants are not themselves completely prepared for the ritual. This means that the operators must be demonstrably well-trained in various yogic-type exercises, from pranayama and asana and the basic forms of yogic meditation up to and including the ability to raise Kundalini. While it is not necessary for the participants to be adepts at Kundalini yoga, it is required that they have some basic ability in this regard otherwise the rituals are empty gestures with no force behind them. The ability to meld mental concentration with physical, psycho-sexual response is the key towards successful completion of this type of ritual. It is a balancing act between the body's normal processes and reactions and the exertion of mental control over the same processes, made more difficult because the same requirement is demanded of the partner. In the case of a male and female operator both must be capable of at least the basic level of mental and physical control; it is not useful that only one member of the couple have this ability unless the goal of the ritual is to "vampirize" the power of the less-advanced partner.

As mentioned earlier, one of the essential aspects of the type of training required for Tantric-type operations is the ability to take conscious control of the autonomic nervous system, represented by the reptilian or serpent brain. In Tantric terms, however, this is considered raising the serpent from the base of the spine—the Goddess Kundalini—until it reaches the brain where it meets the Lord Shiva and the alchemical wedding or Gnostic marriage takes place. There are inherent dangers in this type of practice, whether you use Western or Asian terminology to describe it, and the image of the serpent—one of the most venomous creatures on earth but also the one that sheds its skin and becomes a symbol of transformation—is instructive in this regard. It was the serpent who told Eve to eat of the fruit of the forbidden tree, to become "as gods." Yet it was the Gnostics who believed that the serpent in the Garden of Eden was actually the True God, and that the Creator of the world was a demi-urge, a lesser being who intended to enslave Adam and Eve for his own purposes. In this complicated mixture of images and myths we can discern the outlines of sublime truths.

Human sexuality has always been the touchstone for a whole host of tabus in virtually every culture. Society—whether as secular or sacred government or both—has arrogated to itself control over the sexual impulses of its members. Certain types of sexual activity are approved, others are condemned. This is as true in pre-literate societies as in literate and so-called "advanced" civilizations. As in all things, the magician takes back this control—albeit usually secretly—and denies himself or herself nothing in the pursuit of knowledge and personal perfection. In other words, in this scenario, society becomes the demi-urge and the magician is Eve listening to the Serpent. If it is ever discovered that the magicians have listened to the Serpent, society would banish them from its borders: arrested, imprisoned, burned at the stake or hanged. Traffic with the Devil—the Serpent, the Dark Lord—includes not only rituals and beliefs that are contrary to that of the Church or State, but which also involves sexual activity that has been proscribed. This is as true in medieval India with the rise of Tantric sects (in particular the

Kaula circles and the practices of Vama Marg Tantra) as it was in the Europe of the Middle Ages.

Control of the human body and its products—especially its off-spring—has been a focus of modern societies. Sexuality that does not result in the conception of children often has been banned, such as homosexuality, masturbation, sodomy, etc. Further, the children must be conceived within a legally-acceptable environment, i.e., the parents of the children in question must be legally bound in the eyes of the State so that the children are legal inheritors of any property. Bloodlines and real estate are inextricably linked in this way, and marriage is just a means of providing the right documentation to ensure a smooth transition from one property owner (the parent) to the next (the child).

In the degree structure of the OTO, however, sexual practices are given spiritual analogues. It has been popularly—and somewhat erroneously—understood that the VIIIth degree of the OTO concerns auto-erotic practices (what the cynics refer to as "magical masturbation"), the IXth degree refers to hetero-sexual intercourse, and the XIth degree concerns homosexual intercourse. Thus the VIIIth degree and the XIth degree would automatically be considered tabu by the established Church and State for the reasons mentioned above. They represent the intentions of the magicians to ignore the strictures of society in order to grasp more fully the potentiality of sexuality in general, and to extend the knowledge and power of the individual magician through an understanding of the capabilities of the human body and the human psyche.

The IXth degree represents more specifically what we have been referring to as the Gnostic Marriage or the Alchemical Wedding. While it is nominally a degree concerned with heterosexual inter-course (if viewed purely clinically) it has ramifications far beyond what New Age Tantra practitioners would imagine.

As Grant claims:

The obloquy attached to the Yezidi as devil worshippers arose from the notion of congress between human and non-human entities; the angelic Being is the issue of a hideous marriage.[165]

And not only among the Yezidi. The union of male and female Tantrikas in the rites of the Kaula circle, for instance, is not a union of human partners. The union cannot take place until each of the two participants has become identified with a god and goddess, respectively. That means that the individual male must be consciously united with his deity, and at that point see the female partner as a goddess; the same is true for the female partner who must be in the same state of exalted trance, identifying herself with the deity perceived by the male and perceiving the male as a god. Thus the two individuals performing the *maithuna*—the sexual embrace, if the physical act is required by the ritual or by the guru in charge—are no longer human, and the "hideous marriage" may result in angelic offspring.

Ideas about the mating of humans with non-humans are quite ancient and we find examples of this concept in Sumerian and Babylonian religion (specifically in the case of the *lillitu*), in Greek and Roman mythology, and more recently in the fears associated with succubi and incubi in the Middle Ages. According to Saint Thomas Aquinas in his *Summa Theologica*, succubi and incubi were male and female demons respectively (or a single, genderless demon who could take on either gender depending on the circumstances), who stole semen from a sleeping male and then impregnated a sleeping female with it. Nocturnal emissions were believed to be evidence of the activities of the succubus; unmarried women who became pregnant were believed to be victims of the incubus.

Gods could also assume human or animal form and have sexual relations with humans, as in the tales from Greek mythology involving Zeus and his many incarnations for the purpose of seducing

165   Kenneth Grant, *Outer Gateways*, p. 105.

women. The offspring from these unions were always remarkable, and became gods, goddesses and semi-divine beings in their own right. All things being equal, it would be logical to assume that the offspring of any such union between human and non-human (whether divine or demonic or simply extra-terrestrial) would be remarkable and would partake of characteristics of both parents.

Like Wilbur Whateley:

> The boy was not talkative, yet when he spoke he seemed to reflect some elusive element wholly unpossessed by Dunwich and its denizens. The strangeness did not reside in what he said, or even in the simple idioms he used; but seemed vaguely linked with his intonation or with the internal organs that produced the spoken sounds. … He was, however, exceedingly ugly despite his appearance of brilliancy; there being something almost goatish or animalistic about his thick lips, large-pored, yellowish skin, coarse crinkly hair, and oddly elongated ears.[166]

(This was the human twin. The other twin was somewhat … less attractive.)

A look at the illustrations in most grimoires and books on demonology will reveal that the horrific images to be found therein seem to be those of what appear to be deformed human beings: humans with extended limbs, heads of animals, crooked or mis-shapen arms, legs, torsos. It was as if demons were associated with genetic abnormalities, evolutionary dead ends. But according to Grant—and, to a certain extent, Lovecraft—these "dead ends" are, like Cthulhu himself, merely dreaming. They represent sections of human DNA that have lain dormant for millions of years, no longer required for human survival, but which may be switched on in the future as the human environment changes. They may be potenti-

---

166 H. P. Lovecraft. "The Dunwich Horror." It is unfortunate that Lovecraft's apparent racism permits him to use terms that are common among those who denigrate other ethnicities to describe a being that is only half-human.

alities, which is why they have not disappeared from the genetic code and are often overlooked as "junk" DNA, a designation that has been challenged of late. According to Grant, cited below, these genetic anomalies may already be manifesting and may have been switched on through the rituals of Crowley, Jack Parsons, and others beginning in the early-to-mid twentieth century.

Dangerous Liaisons

> There are vocal qualities peculiar to men, and vocal qualities peculiar to beasts; and it is terrible to hear the one when the source should yield the other. Animal fury and orgiastic license here whipped themselves to demoniac heights by howls and squawking ecstasies that tore and reverberated through those nighted woods like pestilential tempests from the gulfs of hell. … Void of clothing, this hybrid spawn were braying, bellowing and writhing about a monstrous ring-shaped bonfire; in the center of which, revealed by occasional rifts in the curtain of flame, stood a great granite monolith …[167]

> The hybrid forms, though monstrous to modern eyes, commemorate man's descent from the stars via a system of totemic symbolism suggested necessarily by the fauna of the terrestrial environment wherein the images were first minted. The beasts indicated, also, another line of evolution which did not have its beginnings on earth.[168]

It's necessary to understand Grant's insistence that the type of hideous creatures of which Lovecraft writes so hauntingly only appear that way to the uninitiated "modern" eye. It follows that the methods employed to create these hybrids would also seem "monstrous" to modern eyes, involving non-traditional forms of sexual

---

167   H.P. Lovecraft, "The Call of Cthulhu."
168   Kenneth Grant, *Outer Gateways*, p. 34

intercourse with non-traditional sexual partners in non-traditional contexts.

The practices assumed under the umbrella designation of Tantra represent much that is non-traditional, and much that involves intercourse with non-human beings. I have written at length about Tantra elsewhere,[169] but for now we can concentrate on those rituals and concepts that preoccupy Grant in the Typhonian Trilogies, for these are the rituals that have attracted so much interest and criticism.

Throughout the Trilogies, Grant makes constant reference to Vama Marg or "left hand" Tantric rituals, to the bodily fluids excreted by both the male and female practitioners, and to the importance of the menstrual cycle to the correct performance of the rituals. He hints that these sexual rituals open gates to other dimensions, other pathways on the Tree of Life. He also emphasizes the need for the participants to be adepts of a certain level: mastery of the practices required by Crowley in his A∴A∴ is essential, such as pranayama and the other yogic techniques. Otherwise, instead of a ritual capable of causing changes to occur in the environment of the ritual operators all that is left is play-acting.

Additionally, we may add the importance of timing.

Traditionally, any type of ritual in Asian countries takes into account the calendar and the astrological conditions, Auspicious times are chosen for either the beginning of a ritual or for the central act of the ritual. This is the same in Western traditions as well, but the calendar used is normally an arbitrary one that does not take into consideration actual astronomical conditions. At the very least, a lunar calendar is employed by the type of Tantric cults of which Grant writes. As in the Necronomicon, stellar positioning is not a mere gesture but is critical to the success of the operation. This is not astrology *per se*; the heavens are a vast clockwork when viewed from the earth, and the planets have greater and lesser distances from the earth depending on their locations as seen against

---

169   Peter Levenda, *Tantric Temples: Eros and Magic in Java*, 2011.

the backdrop of the Zodiac. The stars themselves rise and set at
certain times and the circumpolar stars (which never rise or set)
revolve around the Pole Star and occupy different positions relative
to an observer on the earth according to the day, hour and season.
Sensitivity to these issues involves the magician in the macrocosm:
it forces the magician to be aware of his or her role and position
within the larger universe (a breathing and living organism from
the point of view of magic, with obvious parallels and analogues to
the human organism; to the Tantrika, the universe is the body of
the Goddess). This sensitivity is translated back into the microcosm
as the ritual progresses, in accord with the ancient Hermetic axiom:
"As above, so below."

As Grant writes:

> It is therefore possible to equate the force-fields (the Kundalini
> in the *chakras*) with planetary and stellar powers.... It is pos-
> sible to draw off stellar or transmundane energy by using the
> human organism as a condenser. This is achieved by tapping
> the appropriate power-zone, after Kundalini has animated and
> magnetized it.[170]

With this in mind, let us take a look at the form of the central
rite in Grant's work.

Tantra in Theory and Practice

The coven of thirteen represents the true *chakra* or Kaula Circle.[171]

The Kaula Circle is legendary among afficionadoes of Tantric traditions. It is the one most referenced when the more exotic
forms of Tantra are mentioned, such as worshipping in cemeteries
or having ritual sexual intercourse in a group. In fact, the word *kaula*

---

170   Kenneth Grant, *Aleister Crowley and the Hidden God*, pp. 97–98.
171   Ibid., p. 87

means a "group" or a "family" or a "clan," and it refers to the group of initiates who are led by a *guru* or teacher. When Lovecraft writes about groups of people having orgies in the swamps outside New Orleans as part of a religious ritual in "The Call of Cthulhu," he could as easily have been referring to popular notions concerning the Kaulas.

The approach of the Kaulas—and related Tantric groups such as the Nath Siddhis—towards the human body, sexuality, and even bodily excretions of all types is a positive one: to the Kaula Tantrika, nothing is disgusting or obscene in-and-of-itself. It is the level of awareness in an unadvanced Tantrika that categorizes something as hideous or ugly. In this type of Tantra, nothing can be considered filthy; it is only our attitude towards certain objects or ideas that makes them seem filthy. Thus, nothing is forbidden: no action, no idea, no substance. However, that does not mean that the Kaula initiate may act freely.

The authority of a guru is necessary for the Kaula circle to function, for the guru has the technical knowledge as well as the experience and the discipline necessary to lead the group. While nothing is ugly or forbidden among the Kaulas, the individual members must go through training and preparation before the most infamous of the Tantric rituals—the *pancatattva* or ritual of the five substances—can be performed.

The Pancatattva is also known as the "ritual of the five M's." One important aspect of the rite is the breaking of the Vedic tabus, one by one, which involves eating and drinking various forbidden substances (such as wine) which all begin with the letter "M" in Sanskrit, leading up to the fifth M which stands for *maithuna* or the "embrace," a euphemism for sexual intercourse.

The Kaula circle may have only one male-female couple engage in maithuna as part of the ritual: two people who have gone through sufficient initiations and ritual preparation to enable them to embody the deities, Shiva and Shakti, or there may be multiple couples depending on the circle and its guru. Shiva and Shakti are the archetypal deities of Tantra, and there are Shiva Tantras and

Shakti Tantras depending on whether the focus is on the male aspect—Shiva—or the female aspect—Shakti. Shakti represents power, and the word is sometimes used as a synonym for the feminine aspect of power such as when a particular god is said to "have his Shakti" or is "provided with his Shakti." The female partner in a Kaula circle will represent Shakti just as the male will represent Shiva. Shiva could be said to represent potential energy and Shakti, kinetic energy or the energy of motion.

The Goddess Kundalini, said to reside at the base of the human spine, may also be referred to as Shakti. When Kundalini is raised correctly it will reach the cranial vault where Shiva is believed to reside in solitude. When Kundalini/Shakti meets Shiva in this "chamber" they are said to be in marital embrace. This can be viewed as the Tantric version of the Alchemical Wedding or the Gnostic Marriage. It even has analogues with the concept of the Shekinah reaching upwards from Malkuth to attain union with the Divine in Kether and thus redeem all of Creation.

But before Kundalini can reach her Beloved Shiva she must pass through seven gates or power-zones kmown as *chakras*, or wheels. (The Kaula Circle is called *Kaula chakra*.) These are found in the body, ranging from the base of the spine or the muladhara chakra, to the groin, the stomach, the heart, the neck, the head (at a spot between and behind the eyes) and finally to the last and seventh chakra which is the "thousand-petalled lotus" at the very top of the head which, when opened, rains down the elixir of life—the *amrita* (a Sanskrit word that means "deathless")—into the body. It would be a mistake to localize these chakras as actual bundles of nerves or other physical attributes, for they are believed to reside in the ethereal, or subtle, body. If one imagines there is a kind of electromagnetic field surrounding the body, then the chakras would be found there rather than in the body itself. However, the result of awakening these chakras is a physical as well as an emotional or psychological sensation.

This idea of the chakras and their individual awakenings is central to the rituals described by Kenneth Grant. He places great emphasis on the necessity for the magician to manipulate the energy passing through the chakras of the priestess, for instance. Each of the seven chakras possesses a different set of atttributes and *siddhis*, or occult powers, and it is up to the Thelemic magician to understand these powers and to be able to "switch on" those required by any specific ritual.

According to Grant's understanding of the ritual, as the chakra in the female magician has been "activated" her entire body undergoes a subtle change. It is thought that the excitation of a specific chakra will trigger the release into the bloodstream of a specific hormone from one of the glands associated with that chakra. This will, in turn, affect the characteristics of her bodily secretions, which are then collected by the magician for use in this—or another—ritual.

How this is done, and the steps to be taken to effect these changes, is the subject addressed in the following pages. While Grant utilizes many Sanskrit and other terms in his descriptions of the magical rituals he and his group employed in London in the 1950s and 1960s, some of what he describes may be unfamiliar to those already schooled in Tantra, even of the Kaula or Nath variety. It is to be understood that Tantric rituals and concepts were incorporated by Grant into a Western-style ceremonial magic system already developed by Kabbalists and those interested in Egyptian religion, etc. He never claimed to be a Tantric adept himself, and he shamelessly used whatever Tantric techniques and ideas came his way in his own form of *bricolage*. Then, as his group progressed even further, Lovecraftian concepts were added to the mix: a step which would, of course, be wholly objectionable to orthodox Tantrikas. Thus, just as Crowley cannot be used as a source for Egyptian religion, Kenneth Grant cannot be referenced as a source for Tantra. However, his contribution to the field of Western magic and particularly Thelema is not appreciated until one realizes that Grant did more to explain Tantric principles and rituals than any other Western occultist to that point, and to show how important they were towards a deeper understanding of Thelema. Today, we have an embarrassment of riches where translations of Tantric texts are concerned, and many knowledgeable scholars in the field who are excellent sources for more solid information. Grant, however, gives us Tantra within the context of Thelema and Western ceremonial magic—something the academics are not, as yet, able to do with any degree of authority.

One further note on the chakras:

The alert reader will have noticed that there are seven chakras (traditionally; some texts and practitioners claim fewer or greater as the case may be). These seven are approached, one by one, in an ascent up the human body from the base of the spine to the top of the head. This is obviously analogous to the "stairway to heaven" as represented in the Egyptian Pyramid Texts, Sumerian and Babylonian religion, the ascent literature of Jewish mysticism, shamanistic ascents, the "Walking" ritual of the Necronomicon, etc. It is also analogous to the Chinese system of "walking" on the seven stars of the Big Dipper (part of the Great Bear constellation). These are all cognate ideas that represent something basic and central to the human condition where spiritual evolution and the quest for immortality is concerned. What the concept of Kundalini—and the Grant systems of magic associated with it—offers us is the ability to re-interpret these magical and mystical systems as taking place within the confines of our own, individual bodies.

The seven stars of the Dipper are thus within us as the seven chakras, just as the seven "planets" are present as the chakras, and the seven chariots in *merkavah* mysticism. The genius of Crowley (and later Grant) was in identifying these analogues and realizing that they represented something tangible and real: secret knowledge and a workable technique for attaining that knowledge. And while traditional Kundalini yoga is an internal practice, Crowley and Grant externalized the process so that it became possible to engage in the practice in groups such as the OTO and other occult cells or—as Grant calls them—"power-zones" of dedicated adepts scattered across the earth (like chakras in the body of the priestess). The Gnostic Mass, for instance, is just such an externalization of the process of Kundalini yoga and in the hands of genuine adepts can become a powerful engine of spiritual transformation or, as Love-craft would have it, a terrible device for summoning hideous creatures to visible appearance.

> Only when mind and body are thus in accord, and when the mind concentrates the image or "child" that the body is to bear, is an act of magical creation possible. This child is rarely a human child, but it is physical in the sense that it influences the material plane.[172]

In *Aleister Crowley and the Hidden God*—only the second of the nine volumes that comprise the Typhonian Trilogies—Grant lays out the general program of the ritual, in the chapter entitled "Dream Control by Sexual Magick." While many variations on this ritual appear in his later works, the basic format is the one to be found here.

He first introduces three states of consciousness, the dream state, the dreamless state, and the waking state. Later, he will identify the dream state as being analogous to the Mauve Zone: an intermediary state between that of waking and deep, dreamless sleep. Grant claims that all activity has its origin in the dream state, whether the activity is conscious and willed or instinctual and reactive. The dream state is the plane on which both mental and astral activity takes place. It is also, remember, the state in which—according to Lovecraft—the High Priest Cthulhu communicates with his followers. In the Grant system, this is not a purely fictional device.

Grant credits the German occultist Eugen Grosche ("Frater Saturnus") with having discovered part of the secret of using sexual ritual to induce a trance that would provide an entrance to the same state as that experienced in dreams, with the obvious advantage that one can then control the dream. This is done by the male magician—in this case—making the equivalent of mesmeric passes over a female priestess in a state of sexual excitement with the goal of

---

172   Kenneth Grant, *Aleister Crowley and the Hidden God*, p. 82.

accumulating and then collecting her heavily charged secretions.[173] Grant expanded on this technique considerably, aided by his receipt of important Tantric texts from mysterious sources and through his own study and practice leading the Nu-Isis Lodge.

There are a few Tantric terms it would be wise to introduce at this point since they will come up frequently in discussions of Grant's sexual magic.

The first is *prana*. This means "breath" and is the basis for the term pranayama, which is a form of breath control. As mentioned previously, breathing is one of the bodily functions that occurs automatically: we don't have to remember to breathe, and can breathe in our sleep. But conscious control of breathing is easy, and it is the gateway to control over other the autonomic functions which then gives us a degree of control over the reptilian brain, the part of ourselves that is easily more than 500 million years old and which is the physical pathway to the unconscious mind.

The second important term is *kala*. In Grant's usage the kalas are units of time and refer specifically to the days of the menstrual cycle and to the "essences" that are secreted on each of those days. Each day of the lunar (and menstrual) fortnight has its own kala, and each kala is different from every other in certain ways. There are fourteen or fifteen kalas, depending on how they are defined and divided. The fifteenth kala is sometimes considered the day when the menstrual flow begins, or the day of the heaviest menstrual flow. The association of the lunar calendar with the menstrual cycle

---

173   Kenneth Grant, *Aleister Crowley and the Hidden God*, pp. 84-85. Grosche had fallen away from the German OTO and created his own occult order based on the sexual mysteries at the heart of the OTO, the Brotherhood of Saturn. He also had developed a lifelong enmity with Karl Germer of the OTO. (Germer was also known as "Frater Saturnus.") This unpleasantness led to Grant—who was friendly with Grosche—being ostracized by Germer, with Grant eventually forming his own OTO, etc. The whole sordid tale is unfortunately typical of the way many modern occult societies function, or dysfunction, when it comes to a focus on personalities and not the Work.

and, in particular. with the onset of the menstrual flow gave rise to
the concept of the Goddess Fifteen, which is one way of referring
to Kali, the Bloody Goddess who is often thought of as an avatar of Shakti. The Goddess Fifteen is also analogous to the Scarlet
Woman, for obvious reasons.

However, one form of the word *kala* symbolically represents the
number sixteen, and the sixteenth kala is considered a great secret
and the sum total of the values of the other fifteen. Sixteen is also
the number of vowels (known as the *matrikas* or "little mothers") in
the Sanskrit alphabet and they are used along with the consonants
to form the all-important Sri Cakra (a diagram of many interlocking triangles, very popular in Indian religion and Tantra) to which
Grant also refers—as it is a map of the power-zones with which he
is most concerned. (See page 259.)

There is a lot of confusion over the word kala, for depending on
how it is written, it may refer to a unit of time (as we have seen) but
also the number sixteen, and is related to ideas about the goddess
Kali and even the demon Kali. In a system of transliteration used by
many scholars today, the word *kAla* means "black" and also "death,"
while the word *kalA* means "menstrual discharge," and the word
kala means "semen." *KalA* also means one-sixteenth of the moon's
diameter which thus gives us the kalas as understood by Grant, and
kAla gives us the planet Saturn. While a Sanskrit scholar will be
aware of these differences and not confuse or conflate them, Grant
uses the phonetic similarities between these words the same way he
uses gematria and other word-play in his writings, to show deeper
connections where a scholar would most likely object. (Imagine
equating the words "week" and "weak" because of their homophony,
or "feet" and "feat." To an English-speaking person, such an equivalence is ridiculous, yet there is evidence of this type of cavalier
approach in many of Grant's works, of which equating kAla and
kalA are just one example. To give him credit, he does admit that
this is more in the line of stream-of-consciousness analysis than
a literal Kabbalistic approach.) Yet, even in this short list of possible meanings for the phoneme "kala" we have ideas that are related

in Grant's thesis: black, death, menstrual discharge, semen, a unit of time, and a sixteenth of the moon's diameter, as well as Saturn (planetary representative of the Dark Lord) itself. The appearance of Saturn in this list is interesting because the Greek word for Saturn is *Chronos*, from which we get the word for "time" such as in "chronology." Thus Saturn and time are linked in English, and Saturn and time are linked in Sanskrit as well. Whether this is reason enough to use Grant's method is debatable, however.

There are many variations in the kalas (as vaginal discharges) depending on the relationship between the actual lunar cycle and the menstrual cycle of the priestess. In addition, the secretion of specific hormones from specific glands during the ritual will influence the quality of the kalas. Thus, the body of the priestess is a kind of laboratory and when the priestess has herself attained more advanced levels of initiation then she becomes both a laboratory and a temple: the biological functions have psycho-spiritual analogues which are under (conscious or unconscious) control of the priestess during the rituals; i.e., the priestess may be in a trance at the time of the ritual, and uttering oracular statements all the while, but her training and initiation have given her the ability to respond appropriately—even instinctively—to the magician or priest who is performing it. We will return to the concept of the kalas as we examine the ritual itself.

The next term which comes up frequently in Grant's work is *ojas*. In Sanskrit it means vigor, strength, power, energy, light, and related ideas.[174] Grant uses it in the sense of magical energy, and ojas may be thought of as the natural result of properly charging the kalas during the ritual. The kalas by themselves are considered magically inert until they have been subjected to the ritual attention of the priest. Once they have been successfully charged, they are then carriers of the *ojas*, or magical energy. The normal menstrual cycle

---

174   David Gordon White renders it as "vital fluid." *The Alchemical Body: Siddha Traditions in Medieval India*, University of Chicago Press, Chicago, 1996, 2007. p. 183.

(i.e., the kalas in their normal physical state) is linked to normal human reproduction, but when the kalas have been charged then the possibility of super-human reproduction has been attained.

The term *mudra* is also important in yoga and in Tantra. *Mudra* means "seal" and is a gesture, a sign made with the hands and fingers in different positions (similar to *asanas*, which are positions involving the entire body). These gestures "seal" openings in the subtle body, as well as transmit information to others. Each mudra has a specific characteristic attributed to it, a power inherent in the positioning of the fingers and the palm. We are familiar with Western forms of the mudra, such as holding one's hand with the palm out, signifying "stop," or with both hands held up with empty palms signifying "surrender." In yoga, the mudras have similar associations but all on the spiritual level rather than the secular one. One mudra may mean the union of male and female, for instance, while another mudra indicates the outpouring of blessings. And while the positioning of hands in Western culture carries information only, in yoga and in Tantra the mudras are themselves not only carriers of data but are also carriers of magical power. A mudra performed the right way can be imbued with force by the Tantrika so that it functions much as the magical gestures of fictional sorcerers and magicians. A mudra also forces the practitioner to be acutely aware of the force being generated as the awkward positions of the hands communicate a level of stress back to the initiate which reinforces the original intent. In Grant's work, the *Mahamudra*—or "Great Mudra"—is represented by the Stele of Revealing: the Goddess Nuit arched over the earth which he sees as the Thelemic counterpart to the *Kailasha Prastara*, or the sexual position in which the woman is over the man.[175] This position is analogous to that usually shown in icons of the Goddess Kali who stands upon the corpse-like body of Shiva; this is the depiction of Shakti—of feminine Power—in its most blatant and extreme form, and is also a warning to those who desire to practice the rite we are discussing without

---

175 Kenneth Grant, *Aleister Crowley and the Hidden God*, p. 30.

being fully prepared, for the Shakti can become unmanageable and wild in inexpert hands. This is also the position most effective for the collection of the kalas from the genital outlet of the priestess, a topic to which we will return shortly.

The *asana* is a yogic position which places a degree of stress on the human body, again forcing concentration but also manipulating the body in such a way as to activate certain of its subtle centers, its chakras. Asanas are used in meditation, and are also used in such practices as Kundalini yoga or hatha yoga in which the body is contorted through different levels of difficulty which results in the yogin becoming aware of the inner workings of the body and the interrelationships that exist between different parts of the outer and inner corpus. They also impact the autonomic nervous system, especially when paired with pranayama exercises and the recitation of mantras, and facilitate higher states of spiritual and psycho-sexual awareness.

Prana as already mentioned is usually translated as "breath" but in Tantra there are multiple *pranas*. Normally when speaking of bodily functions the Tantrika is not referring to those with which we are familiar, the visible emblems of these functions, but with their subtler aspects. Thus, prana is not simply "breath" the way we understand it, but subtler aspects of the same. There are at least five "breaths" or five pranas recognized in yoga and Tantra: *prana* is the breath of inhalation, the breath that nourishes life, and enters through the nostrils; *udana* is the exhalation, most noticeable in the act of speech; *samana* is the breath that aids digestion; *apana* is the breath involved in peristalsis and excretion; and finally *vyana* is the breath that moves internally through the body and which stimulates motion and movement of the body through space.

Mantras are syllables or words that have specific associations with deities or spiritual qualities. They can be as short as a single syllable (a *bija* or seed mantra) or as long as a sentence or a verse. Their value lies in the manipulation of sound.

Sound is vibration, and different mantras—because of different combinations of vowels and consonants—vibrate at different rates

when spoken, and these levels can be adjusted through the use of
volume and pitch. They also help to quiet the mind by replacing
chaotic inner voices and random thoughts with a string of seemingly meaningless syllables, thus essentially short-circuiting the language centers of the brain.

Mantras, asanas and mudras, and pranayama all are designed to
counteract the normal functions of the mind and the body. Obviously, occultism is not about reinforcing our basic instincts for survival, but in violating them as much as possible without actually
damaging either the mind or the body, stretching the capabilities
of both in ways that are initially uncomfortable and unnatural but
which in the end open the doors of perception.

We have presented the basic Sanskrit terms and concepts that
are used quite freely by Grant in virtually every volume of the Trilogies. There are many more, as well as references to specific Tantric
texts, but we will not list them all here. Rather, as we come to a relevant citation we will pause to ensure that the reader is completely
informed … or as informed as possible under the circumstances. In
order to read Crowley, one should have a good general education
in Kabbalah, Egyptian religion, and the Golden Dawn system of
initiation; to read Grant, one needs all of that plus a deep background in Indian religion, especially Tantra, some Afro-Caribbean
concepts and terms, and of course the basic reading in Lovecraft's
ouevre. It is a daunting task for the general reader, to be sure, and it
is hoped that this study will facilitate greater understanding of the
writings of this important occult author as well as encourage wider
reading in the topics covered.

The Collection of the Kalas

It should be noted that Grant's preoccupation is with the magical
aspect of Tantra. Even though he does acknowledge its basic theological premises and the Hindu and Buddhist formulas for with-
drawing from the world of illusion to attain the ultimate level of
enlightenment, he is still quite distracted by the practical uses to

which Tantric principles may be applied. This is due at least partly to his Thelemic allegiance, otherwise why not simply become a Tantrika and abandon Thelema (and by extension Western occultism) entirely? Tantra represents a collection of texts, practices, and a peculiar worldview; Thelema on the other hand pretends to be a global spiritual movement with the aim of liberating all peoples in the New Aeon. The pursuit of Tantra is a highly individual one, even though small groups may be involved. The pursuit of Thelema, on the other hand, requires a broader social perspective. Grant, as much as he admires Tantra, still sees it as a tool—among many in the Thelemic workshop. He interprets much of Thelema in Tantric terms and this may be because at times he sees Thelema as a "Tantra for the West," and at other times he senses that both disciplines are discussing the same basic principles and he cannot resist pursuing those links and associations as deeply as possible because the one may help explain the other … or enrich the other through the additional correspondences. In other words, he must find Tantra lacking in something, a something that Thelema can provide.

It is certain that Tantra is Indo-centric. All the terminology and references are to Indian religion, culture and language and require a knowledge of what is popularly known as Hinduism, and Buddhism. This would be ideologically unpalatable to a follower of Thelema who may recognize—intellectually—the contributions of the sub-continent to world religions but who would reject Hindu and Buddhist belief systems.

Thus, Grant's project is to strip away as much of the Indian component of Tantra as he is able and to replace it with Western occult and magical references. (It is a re-interpretation of Tantra, which is why it would be rejected by Tantrikas in Asia and most likely by Tantra scholars in the West.) In order to accomplish this, Grant needs to look at the *technology* of Tantra—the rituals themselves—and peel away the objectionable theology as much as possible. What he is left with should be a system of universal applicability, interpreted within the Thelemic context. And this, of course, is feasible.

In recent years this approach has been made somewhat easier by the works of scholars in Jewish mysticism and alchemy who have speculated that Tantra may very well be the *fons et origo* of the *Sepher ha-Zohar*, for instance, and who use Tantric references to help expand upon Kabbalistic and alchemical themes.

In addition, Tantra has always been a controversial field and even the definition of Tantra eludes most scholars, Asian and Western, so an eccentric British magician's point of view may be as legitimate as anyone else's.

That said, we will now look at how Grant understands the intensely sexual rituals he describes in the Trilogies. We will take as our starting point and template the brief description of those rituals he provides in *Aleister Crowley and the Hidden God*.

This basic form can be characterized as an initiated version of Crowley's Gnostic Mass. It involves a priest and priestess, or a magician and a "witch" (in the popular, not the Wiccan, sense). There may be others in attendance, but the prime operators are a male and a female couple.

The goal of the ritual is the collection of kalas, the magically-charged vaginal secretions of the female partner before they become ojas. We will ignore for the moment the timing issue, as it is a bit complex, but will return to it later on. There is also a appended to this volume a list of the kalas—as lunar digits—and their associated characteristics (probably the first time this has been presented to a Western, occult-oriented readership).

The priestess should be an initiate capable of raising Kundalini. That does not mean that she should be able to raise it perfectly through all six chakras to reside in the seventh, but she should be capable of stimulating the rise of Kundalini to a certain level. The priest may assist in helping her raise it to higher and higher chakras during the ritual, but only as long as there is no danger to the priestess.

The intention of the ritual must be clear from the outset, plainly stated so that all participants are in agreement. This must reflect an act of will from all parties, otherwise the ritual degenerates into a form of "vampirism" with the magician using the priestess for his own ends, or vice versa.

In the Thelemic context we have been discussing, the ritual space must be created according to the understanding of the magician, perhaps using the Star Sapphire or Star Ruby rituals to cast a circle: a sacred space, a *chakra*. The design of the altar and the space may be purely Thelemic, or it may also incorporate Tantric elements such as the Sri Chakra which represents interlocking power-zones based on triangles, the letters of the Sanskrit alphabet, etc. and is a form of the *yoni*—or vulva—of the Goddess.

Perfumes should be chosen with care, to reflect the nature of the ritual.

Lighting should also be carefully designed before hand. It is common in Western ceremonial magic to use candles of a certain number, a certain color, etc. and this may be employed. Or oil lamps may be used instead.

The altar should be provided with a mat or some soft covering for that is where the priestess will be located during the most intense portions of the ritual. The altar should face the north, or the head of the priestess should be in the north, for that is from where the amrita will descend. This is especially so if the ritual is being performed at midnight on the night of the Full Moon, for at that time the Moon is directly overhead (i.e. in the south) and the Sun will be directly opposite, in the north. In the case of Tantra, and the collection of amrita, the Moon is male and the Full Moon is full of the nectar of immortality (the semen of the God Chandra), and the Sun is female, red and pulsing with heat and fire. If it is desired to incorporate Lovecraftian elements in the ritual (as Grant's cultus was known to do) then the appropriate times may be chosen according to the position of the Big Dipper, but always with further reference to the position and the quarter of the Moon.

The deities should be invoked into the priest and priestess, so that they identify with their respective godforms. They may partake of alcohol at this time, both in homage to the original *pancatattva* ritual of the Kaula Circles but also because this was a method

Crowley also used in order to release inhibitions in his assistants. Naturally, only a sip of alcohol should be employed.

The central part of the ritual now takes place, which involves the priestess raising Kundalini. According to Grant, this transpires as she is being sexually aroused by the magician who is performing certain mudras over her body, not necessarily touching her but making passes directly over her erogenous zones (with a wand or with his hands) and raising her to a fever pitch. The goal of this process is to activate Kundalini, to raise it gradually to the higher chakras so that they may be "burned" by the power of the Serpent Goddess and thus release their potencies into the bloodstream of the priestess. These chakras should have been previously opened by the priestess through Kundalini yoga or some other technique, otherwise opening them for the first time this way can be dangerous to her. The magician should bring the priestess to the point of orgasm, but stop just before orgasm is reached. The magician may have sexual intercourse with the priestess if it is considered necessary to bring the priestess to the desired pitch of excitement, but neither priest not priestess should achieve orgasm at this point because it is premature to "ground" or "earth" the energy before it has been fully utilized. (This is in contradistinction to much normative Tantra which requires the orgasms of both parties and even the ejaculation of the male in order for the rite to be "perfect.") It is necessary that there is a flow of secretions from the female genital outlet. These *kalas* will be collected by the magician—either orally, as in cunnilingus, if the intention is to increase the occult power of the magician or to bring him into contact with supramundane forces, etc.; or on a specially constructed talisman of metal or parchment, or on the leaf of a sacred plant, or some other way if the intention is to store it for future use. The magician will then energize them magically so that they become *ojas*.

In an operation described in *Beyond the Mauve Zone*, the magician can also use disks of some metal, placed ove the chakras of the priestess in order to become magnetically charged by the ritual. This occurs as an operation of what Grant calls "stellar magic" and involves the sixth, or *ajna*, chakra. The idea is to charge this chakra—what Grant calls the "sixth power-zone"—so that it magnetically attracts the Fire Snake, causing it to rise from the muladhara chakra up the *sushumna* (the "middle pillar" of the body) to reach the ajna chakra. The metal disks collect the ojas that are generated this way and are then kept in a closed jar for later use, when they may be drenched in the kalas of the priestess to activate them further.

What is the goal of this type of magical ritual? A predictably Lovecraftian one:

> In due course is born a being that is adapted perfectly to existence on a chosen star.[176]

This is an extremely delicate operation. If either the priest or the priestess becomes distracted by lust and by the need to satisfy themselves in orgasm ahead of time then concentration has been lost and the rite loses all its efficacy. The kalas become "earthed" in their usual way, and all that is left is two persons having sexual intercourse. That both participants remain in a heightened state of concentration and focus is critical to the success of the ritual. From the magical point of view, there is nothing particularly powerful in semen and vaginal secretions if they have not been charged previous to being released. The object is not to create a human child (most people can manage that), but something else entirely (as the above quotation from Grant illustrates).

As we have seen, the Valentinians concentrated on the Divine during sex so that they would produce Divine offspring. The method seems strangely similar. Old Whateley was concentrating on incarnating one of the Old Ones on earth. Crowley's quasi-fictional magicians in his most famous novel were pretending to create a Moonchild. Magic is the creation of forms, of illusions, of whole new realities. In Tibetan shamanism, this is known as creating *tulpas*: homunculi designed for specific purposes, as was most

---

176   Kenneth Grant, *Beyond the Mauve Zone*, p. 131.

famously recounted by Alexandra David-Neel. And in Jewish mysticism, we have the Golem.

Thus, what is needed is not two sexually-active people who will have intercourse surrounded by weird diagrams and sandalwood incense. Instead, we need two intelligent and mature—and dedicated—magicians who will push the envelope of sensation as far as it will go, realizing that their sexual energy is more than a metaphor for the primal act of creation—and that it contains power of an incredible nature if taken beyond the normal methods required for human reproduction.

This brings us to the question of initiation. In the Shakta tradition, the female is the more important partner and the emphasis is placed on her secretions. Tantra in this tradition is a very refined, very highly-articulated form of Goddess worship. Women can initiate men into this tradition, which is the reverse of what even Crowley would approve. At the same time, the selection of the appropriate partner was an all-consuming endeavor for Crowley and he went through many women in his quest for the perfect *soror mystica*, or "sister of the mysteries," probably due to his reluctance to take women seriously as advanced adepts. To many Tantrikas, the female kalas are the focus of the rites and the *yoni*—the vulva—is the object of veneration.

The reverse is obviously true for those who favor the Shaivite tradition which elevates the male principle above the female. However, the solution to this problem—as Grant rightly points out[177]—is the fact that Crowley's New Aeon is the Aeon of the Child: the offspring of the two principles of male and female, of Shiva and Shakti. The Child partakes of the combined essences and natures of each and represents a new focus, a new paradigm, for not only magic but for the social order in general. It is, in fact, this Magickal Childe that troubles Lovecraft so much that he castigates the concept as the deformed and dangerous creature conceived by poor Lavinia

---

177   Kenneth Grant, *Aleister Crowley and the Hidden God*, p. 50.

Whateley, but it is nevertheless the focus (expressed or implied) of all New Aeon magical ritual.

Thus, in this case, the kalas are not the only important secretion as the seminal fluid of the magician is also required to effect the "magical birth." This substance is to be charged just as carefully as the kalas in order to be effective, which requires the magician to practice a form of seminal retention and "recirculation." Like the priestess, he must postpone or completely avoid orgasm in order not to "earth" the fluid before it has been charged. He must practice raising Kundalini and sealing the chakras in the same manner as the priestess. In many Tantric traditions it is completely unnecessary (and moreover undesirable) for the male practitioner to achieve orgasm, and especially forbidden for him to ejaculate and thus waste the seminal fluid and its associated subtle essence. Such methods as that known as *karezza* were employed to keep the male Tantrika in a constant state of sexual excitement and arousal during the ritual. If ejaculation did take place, there were methods for limiting the damage.

One to which Grant refers is the practice known as the *vajroli mudra*, which is a way of halting ejaculation in pre- or mid-ejaculation. This involves a great deal of preliminary work in contracting the urethral sphincter (a practice which is also beneficial in curing premature ejaculation). Advanced practitioners are said to be able to use this method to "vacuum" ejaculated semen from the vagina back into the penis where its subtle essence can be drawn up the spine and to the cranial vault as the Kundalini rises. The *Shiva Samhita*—a venerable Tantric text which discusses the vajroli mudra—claims that the loss of semen leads to death and that the Tantrika should never lose his semen under any circumstances. Other Tantric texts are more lenient, but insist that it takes at least a fortnight to replace the semen expended in an act of sexual intercourse and enormous quantities of food to produce even a single gram of the substance. The mention of a fortnight in this regard is due to the lunar association once again, for the Moon is restored—i.e., the semen of the

Moon is replaced—over a fourteen-day period from New Moon to Full Moon.

As David Gordon White points out:

> ... semen is the raw material and fuel of every psychochemical transformation the yogin, alchemist, or Tantric practitioner undergoes, transformations through which a new, superhuman and immortal body is "conceived" out of the husk of the mortal, conditioned, biological body.[178]

To Crowley and his system, the semen is just as important to the creation of the Elixir—the amrita or nectar of immortality—as the female kalas. Indeed, it is the combination of the two that is required and this would seem to be consistent with European alchemical traditions as well. Obviously, in order to produce the magical offspring we have been discussing at length there must be a contribution from both partners, either in the "earthed" physical sense or in the occult, astral sense. As the emphasis in the New Aeon is said to have switched from the pure male-female (Shiva-Shakti) polarity of the old Aeons to their product as a divine offspring, this would seem to make sense and would require the use of such new "grimoires" as the Crowleyan Book of the Law as well as some of the received texts published in Grant's works.

To the magician, the priestess is no longer the priestess. She is a goddess, a Scarlet Woman, a Shakti. To the priestess, the magician is no longer someone she knows in the "real" world, but a god, a Beast, a Shiva. They are drawing down the powers that existed since the Creation—the aptly-named Big Bang—by identifying themselves with the forces that started it all (like Clement's lust-crazed Carpocrations). They are traveling along the 500 million years of their reptilian brains to enter a space and time that is otherwise

---

178   David Gordon White, *The Alchemical Body*, p. 27.

unknowable by living, breathing human beings ... and they are going further and farther than that.

And as they do so, their physical bodies undergo transformative changes. These changes begin with the secretion of glandular substances into the bloodstream so that their breath, their saliva, their perspiration, their seminal and vaginal fluids vibrate with this new life, this new potency.

At the same time, visions are obtained. One of the effects of this type of ritual is that such intensive concentration during a time of sexual arousal leads to a tremendous amount of psychic stress. The body is used to releasing itself in orgasm and ejaculation. If this normal pathway is blocked—"sealed"—through mental control and focus, then the body reacts in such a way that it seeks alternate pathways, thus opening a Gate that is normally closed.

A slight shift of focus will result in a shift of vision, of waking trance. If the goal was to open a Gate, and the focus of both parties is maintained on this goal, then a Gate will open. The power of the unreleased sexual energy will see to it; and the kalas that are secreted at this time will enable the operators to more easily open the Gate at a future time.

It is to increase the psycho-sexual tension that the Necronomicon itself states:

> Know that thou must keep purified for the space of one moon for the Entrance to the first Step, one moon between the First and the Second Step, and again between the Second and the Third, and so on in like manner. Thou must abstain from spilling thy seed in any manner for like period of time, but thou mayest worship at the Temple of ISHTAR, provided thou lose not thine Essence. And this is a great secret.[179]

The reference to the Temple of Ishtar may be an allusion to temple prostitution, and the provision that one not lose their Essence

---

179 *Necronomicon*, p. 37.

should be self-explanatory by now. Prostitutes are not anathema to the Tantrika; far from it. As we already know, Crowley's *soror mystica* was known as the Scarlet Woman or the Whore of Babalon. To the Tantrika, nothing is ugly or hideous or forbidden, thus prostitutes (proscribed by society even as they are secretly tolerated) are as much representatives of the Goddess as any other woman.

The lunar periods are important here, just as they are in Tantric practice. The application is different, of course. The basic theme of the Necronomicon system known as "the Walking" is celestial ascent; at the same time, there is a level of paranoia concerning evil spirits and the evil cults that worship them. Opening the celestial Gates during the Walking is a core element of the process and it shares much in common with the Chinese magical system known as the Pace of Yü which involves proceeding up the seven stars of the Big Dipper, "opening" each of these astral gates along the way. The Walking can be interpreted from the point of view of raising Kundalini up the path of the chakras … and of course the Tantric process can be interpreted in terms of the Walking. It should be remembered that these seemingly different systems are analogues of each other; that the language used to describe one system is essentially the same as the language used to describe the other.

The goal of celestial ascent traditions as well as the raising of Kundalini in yoga and Tantric traditions is the same: to approach a secret or hidden chamber from which immortality can be attained. In celestial ascent literature this is normally viewed as a temple or palace at the top of a ladder of lights—stars or planets—in which God dwells. In the type of ritual traditions we have been discussing this chamber has a physical, microcosmic analogue: the cranial vault.

Within the brain there is a space that is often referred to as the "bridal chamber." It is in the region of the hypothalamus (the Greek word *thalamos* means "bed chamber") located somewhat between—and behind—the eyes, what is popularly known as the "Third Eye." This is the realm of Shiva in Indian tradition: it is where this iconic recluse and hermit waits in silent meditation until he is roused by his wife Parvati or Uma to take part in an extended session of intercourse. It is at the culmination of this sexual embrace that Shiva's semen rains down as *amrita*: the elixir of immortality. This is sometimes described as the crescent Moon overturning and spilling down the seed as a gentle but rejuvenating rain. In Kundalini terms, the Serpent Goddess is raised through the six preliminary chakras to mate with Shiva in an embrace that triggers the opening of the seventh chakra at the crown of the head. In either case, the result is the same: the flow of life-giving nectar begins at the top of the head and continues down through all the subtle pathways—the *nadis*—of the human body. This is the Alchemical Wedding and its result, the nectar of immortality and *elixir vitae*, is the Sixteenth Kala.

While the sexual rite above described seems to focus exclusively on the male as the active partner, this is not really or always the case. The priestess can control the outcome of the ritual through her own powers of concentration and control over the psycho-biological processes taking place in her body. As the magician manipulates her sexual response so that she is near orgasm, she can duplicate what the male Tantrika is able to do in similar circumstances: transfer the complex of sensations (visualized as Kundalini) from the groin level to the brain, i.e., from the *muladhara chakra* to the *ajna chakra* at the level of the Third Eye. This can be done in real physical terms— the way it is taught in Kundalini yoga—or it can be accomplished through visualization alone, which is the safer (although somewhat less powerful) route. The end-result of the ritual—whatever it may be—is visualized as taking place in the cranial vault, in the *ajna chakra* or the thalamus, the "bed chamber," and it is there that the Magickal Childe is conceived. The term Magickal Childe is used here to refer to the desired result of the operation—to charge a talisman, to obtain secret information, etc. etc.—visualized as the offspring of the ritual. Certain Chinese adepts use the same processes to create an immortal body, visualized first in embryonic form extending from the crown of the head (and thus the seventh *chakra*) and then gradually becoming mature.[180]

> Crowley was aware of the possibility of opening the spatial gateways and of admitting an extraterrestrial Current into the human life-wave. In *Moonchild* the incarnation was effected in and through the normal sexual formula, and although the full impact of the moonchild's advent is not described, the reader is left with the impression that, whatever it may have been, it was some sort of a monster in human form endowed with superhuman powers. But no entity incarnating via the usual channels of sex, no physical intrusion of another dimension into the ambience of humanity could possibly exercise power in any but a terrestrial sense. This is because the "power" has been earthed or enfleshed.[181]

The above statement by Grant eloquently sets forth the parameters of the sexo-magical rite, even to the extent of introducing the possibility that a monster with superhuman powers could be incarnated using these techniques. He also reminds us that the usual channels of sex are not capable of introducing the extraterrestrial Current into our own dimension. Control of the body's automatic sexual responses begins with control of the reptilian, or serpent, brain until the entire organism is an instrument to be played by the initiated magician. Once this occurs, according to Grant, the Gates may be opened and the realms beyond the visible, tangible, illusory world can be explored.

And, as Lovecraft warns us, these same Gates, once opened, allow traffic in both directions.

---

180   See the works of Charles Luk for greater detail on this fascinating subject.
181   Kenneth Grant, *Aleister Crowley and the Hidden God*, p.41.

CHAPTER SIX

THE MAUVE ZONE

And I went into the sunset with Her sign, and into the night past accursed and desolate places and cyclopean ruins, and so came at last to the City of Chorazin. And there a great tower of Black Basalt was raised, that was part of a castle whose further battlements reeled over the gulf of stars.

—Jack Parsons, *The Book of Antichrist*

Then, presently, from the blind land behind the mountain, comes one heavy groan, then the sound of a fall, made vile by a titter of malignant tinkling laughter.

There follow ghoulish wailings.

The mystery, the evil darkness of these incoherent cries, sets my teeth on edge with horror. And yet I cannot give up the hope which thrilled me at the Voice. But so keen, so desolate, so deadly, is the pain of my spirit that blank darkness overwhelms me altogether.

—Aleister Crowley, *The Heart of the Master*

It seemed plain to us ... that there were ancient and elaborate alliances between the hidden outer creatures and certain members of the human race. ... There seemed to be an awful, immemorial linkage in several definite stages betwixt man and nameless infinity. The blasphemies which appeared on earth, it was hinted, came from the dark planet Yuggoth, at the rim of the solar system; but this was itself merely the populous outpost of a frightful interstellar race whose ultimate source must lie far outside even the Einsteinian space-time continuum or greatest known cosmos.

—H. P. Lovecraft, "The Whisperer in Darkness"

Does this mean that those from Outside will actually put in
an appearance on earth? If so, then the secret rites hinted at in
grimoires such as the *Necronomicon*, and the Books of Thoth, of
Dzyan, of Enoch, contain the keys to their summoning and we
have for long aeons been blind to their usage.
                            —Kenneth Grant, *Outside the Circles of Time*

I N THE LATER VOLUMES OF the Typhonian Trilogies, Grant reprises
the sexo-magical rituals we have already described and demonstrates
how they can be used to penetrate the veils that conceal from our
sight the vast reaches of deep space and deep time. In fact, he cites
other magicians who—he claims—have already penetrated those
veils and opened a hole in the earth's protective atmosphere allowing the entry of the Old Ones. In other words, they have opened a
Gate.

This dangerous process certainly was begun by Crowley, but later
was amplified by his American follower Jack Parsons. Grant claims
that the atomic explosions of 1945 disturbed the delicate psychic
membrane covering our planet to the extent that other forces began
massing at the rent in the veil and by 1947 began pouring through
in greater and greater numbers. This, of course, was the UFO phenomenon which Grant links directly to the type of magical operations begun by Crowley and continued by his followers. This is a
scenario straight out of H. P. Lovecraft and especially, "The Call of
Cthulhu."

As always throughout this study, we have to remember that
events that take place in the "real" world are mirrors of events that
transpire in the inner, invisible, or secret world and that these two
worlds influence each other in ways that are not obvious to any
but the most dedicated adept ... or most paranoid conspiracy theorist. There is, in fact, little difference between the world view of the
occultist and the nagging fears of the conspiracy theorist; except
that the occultist has a more positive approach to the same material, seeing in the activities of the sinister forces that influence world

events (as well as personal ones) the possibility of reversing the process through an act of will coupled with a knowledge of technique.

It is this realm of the invisible world that occupies us in this
chapter, for it is the backdrop against which all of the theory and
practice takes place. In a sense, we can call this world R'lyeh, to use
Lovecraft's designation for the secret city below the ocean waves
where Cthulhu waits, dead but dreaming.

But to Kenneth Grant, it is the Mauve Zone.

The Sri Chakra

> … the Sri Chakra conceals in its symbolism more than the pos-
> sibility of alien contact, it conceals the keys to doors Outside.[182]

Grant's main focus where Tantra is concerned is the group
of beliefs and practices that come under the general rubric of Sri
Vidya, with its all-important Sri Chakra mandala. Grant claims
that there is a surviving cult of the original Typhonian Tradition
known as the *Anuttara Amnaya*, which just happens to have the
same initials as the secret society founded by Aleister Crowley, the
Astrum Argenteum, or A∴A∴. The Anuttara Amnaya is the repository, again according to Grant, of the true practices of the Sri Vidya
cult which links it to the ancient and all-but-forgotten mysteries of
the Great Old Ones.

Before we go too deeply into the weeds of this concept, it is
perhaps beneficial if we pull back a little and briefly describe the
Sri Vidya cultus and identify the Anuttara Amnaya as best we can.

The word *vidya* has the same root as Veda, and means "knowledge." The word *Sri* is used to mean "divine" or "sacred," so Sri Vidya
means, literally, the sacred knowledge. It is an early form of Tantra,
one which several groups (including the Kaula sect) claim as their
own lineage.

---

182 Kenneth Grant, *Beyond the Mauve Zone*, p. 57.

Sri Vidya is also identified as the worship of Sri Devi, the great Mother Goddess, who in this system manifests as Lakshmi Tripura Sundari, or Lakshmi ("the Playful") of the Three Cities. (The identity of the "three cities" is subject to controversy but may be identified as *sat-cit-ananda*—Existence-Consciousness-Bliss—and in Grant's schema Consciousness is identified as having three states: waking, sleeping and dreaming.) Lakshmi Tripura Sundari is usually depicted as a Red Goddess, a young girl of sixteen years of age dressed completely in red and sitting on a red lotus throne, adorned by a single lunar digit, or kala. In this mode she is called Shodashi ("sixteen" as in "sixteen years old" but also clearly a reference to the Sixteenth Kala) or even simply Bala ("young girl"). Her power is the power of Consciousness itself, or Cit-Shakti. It is Lakshmi Tripura Sundari who is worshipped via the Sri Vidya cult's most famous emblem, the Sri Cakra which is her symbol and which represents the entire cosmos.

The Anuttara Amnaya is one of six "subsidiary" vidyas of the Sri Vidya tradition. The word *amnaya* is related to *agama*, a word that can mean "religion" or a type of special knowledge that is handed down from generation to generation, such as a "sacred tradition." It is often used as a reference to sacred texts in general and to Tantra itself. The word *anuttara* is usually translated as "highest" or "absolute." [183] Thus, Anuttara Amnaya is the Highest Tradition or the Supreme Tantra. It does not refer to a specific group of devotees or sect, but is usually used to identify a specific set of Vidyas within the Sri Vidya tradition, a school of Tantra with its own mandala, teachings, etc. Followers of the Sri Vidya tradition may be initiated (*diksha*) into one or all of the six amnayas, so that the Anuttara Amnaya is really a school within the greater Sri Vidya tradition. Yet, Anuttara Amnaya is also referred to as the "seat" of the God-

---

183 Technically speaking, the prefix "an-" would seem to indicate that *anuttara* (an-uttara) is a negative or comparative term, most likely indicating "not surpassed" or "unsurpassable" rather than a positive term such as "absolute" or "highest," but the sense is more or less the same.

The Sri Yantra or Sri Chakra is an ancient geometric
depiction of the body of the Goddess.

dess Lakshmi Tripura Sundari: subtle, difficult of access, but a path above and beyond all others.

There is, however, a darker aspect to all of this and it involves Shiva in his incarnation as Hatakeswara or Hatakeshvara. In this incarnation, Shiva is the ruler of one of the seven infernal hells or Patala of Indian religion, specifically Vitala. The hells of Patala are inhabited by the Nagas (or serpent gods) as well as by the various Indian demons, such as the Yakshas. Yet, oddly, it is precisely Shiva in his form of Hatakeswara who rules Anuttara Amnaya and guarantees immediate enlightenment to its practitioners. According to the *Hatakeswara Stotra* (a hymn to Hatakeswara), the Lords of Hell pour forth from the mouth of Shiva-Hatakeswara. Thus, in this

manifestation, Shiva is nothing other than the Dark Lord himself
and the ruler of Kenneth Grant's Anuttara Amnaya cult ... and the
Goddess of the Sri Vidya tradition is a form of the Scarlet Woman,
the Goddess Sixteen.

Now for the weeds.

Marmas, Sandhis ... and Qlippot

The Sri Chakra is a map similar in nature—if not design—to the
Kabbalistic Tree of Life and perhaps related more closely to the
Enochian Tablets as employed by the Golden Dawn. It consists of
nine large triangles—four pointing up, five down—superimposed
on each other and thus making a total of 43 triangles and the intersection points (the *marmas* and *sandhis*) between them.[184] Around
these triangles are an eight-petaled lotus, a sixteen-petaled lotus,
and three concentric circles around them. Around that is often
drawn a diagram representing four Gates in the four cardinal directions. The Sri Chakra is an entire cosmological system but it is also
the body of the Goddess in schematic form. Although it is a two-
dimensional figure—a drawing—it also has been made in three-
dimensions: the only one of all the Indian chakras permitted to be
constructed this way.

The characterization of the Sri Chakra as the body of the Goddess is not an idle one. The marmas—the intersection points where
triangles overlap—have their analogues in marmas in the human
body: similar, in fact, to acupuncture points in Chinese medicine.
Ayurvedic medicine is concerned with applying pressure, through
massage, to the appropriate marmas in order to promote healing.

---

184 A *marma* is the point where three lines intersect on the Sri Chakra. There
are traditionally 28 marmas, but some authorities insist on variously 37, 38, 39,
40 or 41 such marmas depending on how they are calculated. The *sandhis* are
the points where two lines intersect. There are traditionally 24 sandhis in the
Sri Chakra. The sum of these numbers—28 + 24—gives us the 52 letters of the
Sanskrit alphabet and thus a kind of Kabbalistic format that could be used to
create (or analyze, or diagram) mantras.

There is even an Indian martial arts technique called *marma adi*, which is a method of killing or disabling a human being by the correct application of pressure—a strike—at one of the twelve "death marmas" on the body (there are 96 healing marmas, and 12 "death" marmas, for a total of 108 marmas in the human body).

To Grant, the marmas on the Sri Chakra and the marmas on the body are reflections of each other. During the ritual we described in the last chapter, the magician is to make passes (or mudras) over the body of the priestess in order to stimulate the activity of specific marmas which in turn affect the chakras. Grant believes that the kalas are brought down from the Mauve Zone into the body of the priestess during the ritual and that the stimulation of the appropriate marmas helps to accomplish this. Then the Kundalini—which Grant has begun calling the Fire Snake—is encouraged to rise through the body of the priestess, sealing the chakras as it proceeds to the cranial vault.

According to Grant in "mystical" Tantra (if such a thing truly exists), the raising of the Fire Snake to the cranial vault is the ultimate goal, for when the Goddess Kundalini and the God Shiva meet the *hierogamos* or sacred marriage is complete. The Tantrika eventually achieves union with the Absolute and attains *advaita*, or non-duality. But in the Kaula Circles that are the primary channel for Sri Vidya, the power that has been raised is drawn back down to the *muladhara chakra* where it is collected by the magician. This is the "magical" approach to Tantra rather than a mystical one and Grant is not bashful about this. He implies that the acquisition of *siddhis*— magical powers—is the goal of his system. He equates the first type of Tantra with the elixir vitae of the alchemists (the amrita), and the second form of Tantra with the Stone of the Wise, the Philosopher's Stone. To a Tantrika, this is an unenlightened approach and one that is usually condemned as unworthy; moreover it is factually incorrect. The Tantras do indeed prescribe the oral consumption of the kalas directly from the genital outlet, the yoni, of the priestess and in fact also generally insist that the elixir is obtained by the mixture of both the kalas—the menstrual discharges—and the semen of the male operator, what is known in the Gnostic Mass as the "cakes of light." The only deviations from this rule concern the ability of the male Tantrika to achieve orgasm without ejaculation, in which the absence of semen is acceptable, or when the male Tantrika is engaged in maithuna—the sexual embrace—with a married woman not his wife, in which case (and according to some Tantras) it is preferable that the Tantrika not ejaculate or not ejaculate in the yoni of his partner. (The Tantras are all over the place where ritual requirements are concerned, and what is and is not desirable or permissable.) What Grant discusses is perfectly comprehensible in terms of the Western magical tradition, with its conscious manipulation and exploitation of mind and body, and that is perhaps where he parts company with normative Tantra. His focus on the raw technology of the system rather than on the philosophy behind it—the Hindu and Buddhist ethical and spiritual traditions—alienates Tantric scholars and Tantrikas. However, it satisfies the need of Western occultists who are not interested in the ethos of the system (who see such considerations as purely theological and thus ideological) but in the psycho-biological apparatus of the human body itself, and how altered states of consciousness and experiences of other realities can be attained through manipulating its inner processes.

In addition, Grant's claim that the kalas are brought down from Beyond to the body of the priestess implies that there is a strong stellar or astral component to what appears to be a psycho-sexual or bio-chemical process. Of course, when the full details of the rite are considered—which includes the lunar phases and other astrological considerations—it becomes obvious that what Grant claims has, in fact, validity. Imagine a solar panel in a land where there is no sun: it doesn't matter that the panel is created perfectly and all its parts are in working order; if there is no sun, there is no power. In the case of what Grant begins to call the Ritual of the Fire Snake, the body of the priestess is the solar panel; the ritual must be timed so that the "sun" is present in the right place at the right time for the panel to provide energy.

This is true of all ceremonial magic, as any glance at the medieval grimoires would certainly reveal. Magical rituals depend as much on correct timing as they do on the preparation of the magician and the occult implements to be employed. It is this emphasis on timing—in Tantra, in Daoist magic, in alchemy, and in Western magic—that reveals the deeper character of occultism in its dependence on the interrelationship between the microcosm and the macrocosm. What casual observers may not realize, however, is that the macrocosm can be just as dangerous as the microcosm. After all, Cthulhu can be summoned only "when the stars are right."

This leads to another element of Grant's thesis: that these marmas or entry points into the Mauve Zone exist in space, exist in the human body, and exist on the earth. Here they are power-zones on the body of the planet, exploited by cults or groups of adepts who are sensitive to their use and initiated into their mysteries. Such marmas represent, as the blurb on the first edition of Grant's *Outside the Circles of Time* states:

> … a network more complex than was ever imagined: a network not unlike H. P. Lovecraft's dark vision of sinister forces lurking at the rim of the universe.

The Sri Chakra, like any perfect cosmological system, must take into account the existence of what the non-initiate may term "evil." Some of the marmas and sandhis provide means of entering areas of existence that are inimical or hostile to normal human consciousness: the realms of the demons, or Nagas. It is, in fact, precisely these regions that most attract the attention of Kenneth Grant.

One of the schemes that can introduce the Western occultist to this concept is that of *Liber 231*, a small treatise by Crowley that is concerned entirely with the realm of the Shells, the *qlippot*. In order to appreciate this text it is necessary to understand that the Tree of Life of the Kabbalists—consisting of ten spheres or *sefirot* joined by twenty-two paths representing the twenty-two letters of the Hebrew alphabet—also has a "dark side."

According to the Golden Dawn system of interpreting the Tree of Life, there is a "space between" the lower seven sefirot and the upper three. This "space between" is referred to as the Abyss. It is sometimes believed to be the realm of another *sefirah*, Daath. In diagrams of the Tree this sphere is often shown with a dotted instead of a solid circle to signify that it is not a "true" sefirah in the scheme of things but a "shadow sphere."

In the seventeenth and eighteenth centuries, Daath was the subject of much speculation and it was Jacob Frank—a messianic figure of the eighteenth century who combined Jewish, Islamic and Christian concepts in his movement—who emphasized the importance of Daath to his own system. To Grant, Daath is the "Outer Gateway" to the Mauve Zone. It is a kind of "anti-sefirah."

In addition to Daath, there are the qlippot which are described in Crowley's *Liber 231*. These are the shells of a shattered sphere from the first Creation (according to one tradition) and they occupy twenty-two "anti-paths" on the Tree of Life. The marmas and sandhis on the Sri Chakra are points, or bindus, on the diagram that are the intersections of lines; the qlippot are paths between the spheres on the Tree of Life, so they more resemble lines than points. But this is a superficial difference. In practice, the qlippot are as much gateways to the Other Side as specific marmas or sandhis.

Liber 231 is one of the Holy Books, which was received, along with the others we have already discussed earlier, that were written by Crowley during a white heat of inspiration at the same time that Lovecraft decided the Rites of Cthulhu were taking place in New Orleans. Crowley does not give any instructions for how the mysterious tables of the 22 qlippot—the 22 "scales of the serpent"—should be used. It was eventually up to Grant and his Lodge to explore the possibilities and to use the tables as a map for penetrating the Mauve Zone. These 22 "demonic" or "qlippothic" paths are the Tunnels of Set that Grant opines lies between the realm of dreams and the realm of dreamless sleep (which latter is itself analogous to the state of non-duality). They are reflexes of the 22 paths on the Tree of Life, shadows of those paths, forming a Shadow Tree of which Daath is the central Gate. His New Isis Lodge worked extensively with the qlippot and specifically with *Liber 231* in an attempt to map its potentialities.

Grant goes further, attempting to link the 22 qlippot with an equal number of kalas. The number of kalas seem to multiply with the systems applied, and this equating of them with the Tunnels of Set may be ill-advised. (A similar problem exists with Crowley's attribution of the *I Jing* trigrams with the sefirot on the Tree of Life; the number systems do not equate and it is a violence to try to force them to fit. There are other, better solutions.) While the kalas are vaginal secretions that can be used as elixirs it is not certain whether these secretions can or should be equated with the qlippot on a one-to-one basis. If the qlippot are pathways—the Tunnels of Set, as Grant calls them—then the kalas may very well be the fuel that enables one to travel them, or the keys to opening their gates.

Grant employs both systems—Tantra and Kabbalah—in his lengthy digressions on the nature of the Mauve Zone and the realm of Darkness where the Old Ones dwell. And it is through ceremonial technologies such as the Ritual of the Fire Snake that contact can be made with this realm by using specific gateways. The Kabbalists would employ the qlippot system and the sphere of the Abyss, Daath, in their approach to what Grant calls the "Nightside of Eden." And the practitioners of the Kaula Circles or the Anuttara Amnaya would employ appropriate marmas and sandhis of the Sri Chakra, in combination with the kalas and the ojas. In either case, a psycho-sexual technique is employed: either the sexual magic of Aleister Crowley, the OTO, or the Hermetic Brotherhood of Light, or the Tantric rituals of the Kaula Circles. Kenneth Grant was able to combine both of these approaches, largely through identifying cognate ideas and methods and by "porting" one system over to the other, incorporating Tantric techniques within a Western, ceremonial framework.

While this approach may seem wholly arbitrary to some, the infusion of genuine Tantric methods within the Thelemic *rituale* produced a spark of new life into the latter. As we can see from

Grant's published work the new insights that were obtained by using Tantric techniques in a Western ceremonial setting were remarkable. And the rush of prose out of Grant's pen due to this combustible mix is alone evidence of how the secret rites of the Nu-Isis Lodge were able to fuel nine non-fiction works on the subject, as well as much fiction and poetry, not counting the contributions of other members of the Grant circle.

And this is as it should be, according to Grant, for it is the Mauve Zone that is the source of all human creativity, imagination, fascination, and obsession. It is represented in the microcosm by a zone that exists between the dream state and the deeper, dreamless state, and is the source of artistic impulses and contact with divine and demonic forces. But these are its positive characteristics. There are negative ones as well, and they are the forces that challenge the magician on an individual basis just as they confront society in general. These are the demonic forces that so frighten the protagonists of the Lovecraft ouevre. And summoning them—or any aspect of the Mauve Zone—can have disastrous consequences.

The French poet Artur Rimbaud famously declared that it was necessary, in order to become a Seer, to engage the complete "derangement of the senses." Our normal sensory state is designed to cope with the visible world, in order to ensure the survival of the body; only the shamans, initiates, magicians and alchemists look beyond maintaining the integrity of the physical body and extending consciousness beyond that of the visible, tangible universe. In order to do this, risks are taken.

The methods used to "derange the senses" or alter perception may include drugs, alcohol, fasting, or other tools that are potentially dangerous to the human organism and counter-intuitive when it comes to discussing the health and survival of the body. It is as if the body's normal systems and processes must be challenged in order that a space be made for the new experiences. This is because our minds and bodies are part of an integrated "psychosomatic" system, and an effect on one will have an impact on the other. This is what Grant calls the "retroversion" of the body's normal processes.

Retroversion is a method he identifies specifically with Set, the
Dark Lord—as Set represents "evil" in the cosmic scheme, or those
things that challenge the status quo.

We have already seen this in our discussion of the necessity of
conscious control over the body's autonomic nervous system and
the reptilian brain. In order to experience altered states of the mind
it is therefore necessary to alter the state of the body.

In the Afro-Caribbean tradition, this altering of the body's
autonomic systems can be effected through the use of drums.
Drums exert a control over the heartbeat of the devotees, which
is one of the autonomic processes. In this situation, the drummers
control the psycho-biological response of an entire group of devotees, and it is within this highly-charged environment that the phenomenon of possession by the gods takes place, often in multiple
devotees. The type of drums used and the rhythms employed will
change the results, invoking specific deities. But the drumming still
takes place within the greater context of the ritual itself, which is
under the control of the priest. These methods—while they can
cause change to occur in and of themselves—must be used within
the ritual structure in order to be effective. Anyone can take drugs
or alcohol, for instance, but although the senses may be deranged as
a result, the long-term effects will not be conducive to the attainment of spiritual illumination or occult capabilities. As we have
already indicated, sexual activity by itself is not capable of producing
the type of spiritual breakthroughs of which the writings of Grant,
Crowley, and the entire field of the Tantras are an indication. What
is necessary is the deliberate structure of the ritual, for that is where
the effect of the Will will be felt and that is what will provide the
channel for the energy raised. As the Crowleyan imperative has it,
"love under will."

There is no guarantee that the experience will be pleasant or
productive. The ritual structure will provide a certain level of opera-
tional security if the ritual participants have been prepared carefully beforehand. This preparation is not only in terms of yogic-
type practices, meditation, etc. but also intellectual study so that

the various moving parts of the ritual are understood and made part of the psyches of the participants. In other words, the various techniques used to insure protection must be internalized so that they are second-nature. The instinctual response of the individuals to perceived danger is what will protect them, since there is no physical weapon that can be used to defeat what is essentially an ethereal or at least non-corporeal threat. The mind will be forced to locate the appropriate defense mechanism—for instance, during a confrontation with an entity from the Mauve Zone that appears hostile or somehow dangerous—and the only weapons at its disposal will be those learned in the preliminary phase of the training.

Even then, however, the effects of such intense ritual workings may be felt for days, weeks, or even years after the fact as the experience is digested and connections to other—unconscious—material is strengthened. That is why such an experienced occultist as Francis Israel Regardie—a one-time secretary to Aleister Crowley and a Golden Dawn and Rosicrucian initiate—strongly recommended that those interested in entering onto a path of occult practice first go through several years of psychological analysis in order to identify as much as possible any deeply hidden problems that would be inadvertently triggered or exacerbated by occult practice.

To Grant, who experienced most of the twentieth century and the first decade of the twenty-first, the enormous changes that took place during that time were an indication that something had gone terribly wrong with the cosmos. Grant believed that the type of changes a magician effects on his own psyche as a result of his occult practice can have an impact on the world at large. This is, after all, the whole basis of magic as a system for manipulating reality and the experience of reality. Grant's thesis is that the present state of affairs is the result of an accumulation of occult operations on the one hand (acting on the ethereal plane, perhaps), and scientific, social, and technological operations on the other operating in the "real" world.

Today we hear of sights and sounds experienced outside the body, in the skies, in the oceans, and deep within the earth. It is as if a cosmic Fire Snake activated the terrestrial power-zones, or reflected into space the chakras awakened by sub-atomic radiations. ... the Earth is beginning to exhibit the catastrophic effects of such artificial stimulations of the Fire Snake.[185]

When Grant writes "as if" he is being coy, for it is clear that he believes this is precisely what happened. One must read Grant carefully with a view towards extrapolating some of the broader statements from the minutiae of sexual rituals and Hebrew, Greek and even English gematria. His clearest paragraphs are those that reveal his certainty that the stories of H. P. Lovecraft, the art of the Surrealists and of Austin Osman Spare, and the modern phenomena of UFOs and abductees, are all in a sense reflections of a real universe beyond our own. His incorporation of Tantra, Kabbalah, magic, and all the rest can be seen as an attempt to reconcile his deeper, inner belief in the reality of the horror fantasies of Lovecraft with a comprehensive worldview that could explain them in some kind of internally-consistent way.

Grant clearly believed that the world was undergoing an invasion from some other dimension or from somewhere Beyond. This invasion was being experienced as the UFO phenomenon, among other things. The eruption of interest in occultism, horror films, alternative religions, etc. indicated to Grant that something was already working its way into our world and that the only ones who could interpret this event were the sensitives. Not limited to magicians or occultists, sensitives include artists, writers, and other people who deal extensively with imagination and creativity: qualities that are associated with the Mauve Zone. In this Grant takes his cue from Lovecraft, of course, but that doesn't make his conclusions any less reasonable.

---

185 Kenneth Grant, *Beyond the Mauve Zone*, p. 70.

In present times, with the massive reawakening in man of the subtle faculties connected with the *Ajna-Vishuddha* complex of chakras, a more sinister element pervades the picture. Man is no longer subject only to his innate tendencies, his organism has undergone changes which render him increasingly susceptible to influences from Outside. ... Whatever 'it' is, or whatever its provenance, it poses serious problems for the magician. Alien intelligence is intimately involved with the movements of the Fire Snake, the energies of which are known to be interactive with the denizens of other dimensions.[186]

At the same time, there are occultists who are deliberately attempting to make contact with these beings from other dimensions, other worlds, through the medium of the Mauve Zone, and they included the membership of his own occult lodge in London. These contacts did not stop when his lodge ceased activity in the 1960s, however, for he writes:

> ... there are today magicians who are forging links with power-zones in unfathomable space and with voids beyond time.[187]

Again, we can clearly recognize the Lovecraftian influence in Grant's vision. Grant specifically links Cthulhu with the Fire Snake, i.e. with Kundalini, as it is asleep in the waters of the deep (which Grant links to the two lowest chakras, the muladhara and svadisthana chakras)[188] and can be raised by the right evocations and when the "stars are right." To support this, he also quotes frequently from the Schlangekraft recension of the Necronomicon.

It is quite possible that the famous Lovecraftian description of Cthulhu as "dead but dreaming" indicates Kundalini which is asleep until it is awakened, but also refers to Grant's three forms of con-

---

186   Ibid., p. 60.
187   Ibid., p. 80.
188   Ibid., p. 58.

sciousness: awake, dreaming, and dreamless sleep. Cthulhu, as "dead but dreaming" seems to refer to a realm between "death"—dreamless sleep—and dreams: in other words, the Mauve Zone. Kundalini is also a Serpent, an amphibious creature that could be linked with Cthulhu. A Serpent in her cave beneath the earth; Cthulhu in his house beneath the sea. Both raised by magicians and occult practice and, when they do, they change our world forever.

This is the point at which Grant makes a rather astonishing claim, among many astonishing claims. He begins a story that sounds like something out of a fantasy magazine yet later insists that it is not metaphor but an account of a real event that occurred "recently" (*Beyond the Mauve Zone* was published in 1999). It contains much that is only comprehensible if the previous material we have discussed is understood.

In this tale, Grant references an Order that exists in the present Indian state of Assam. This Order is Tantric and initiates into the type of Tantra we have been discussing. He links this Order to "stray references" found in the Necronomicon, among other places, and says it represents an oral tradition spanning generations. The Order at some point created or contacted or somehow incarnated an Entity from the realm of what Grant calls "transplutonic Isis": a star not necessarily in our dimension, but one from which Grant's Nu-Isis or New Isis Lodge obtained its heritage and legacy.

The Entity dwelled on the Earth during which time "more and more women gave birth to offspring imbued with the 'child's' alien propensities. ... Many earth-dwellers experience strange dreams and horrendous nightmares in which they glimpse the fantastic force of their own terror."[189] Eventually, our planet became a "far-flung outpost of Nu-Isis."[190]

But that is not the end of the story. Eventually, the Entity spends "many years in Assam studying with a Tantric Adept" after which they both disappear, only to "surface" in a network of tunnels

---

189 Ibid., p. 133–134.
190 Ibid., p. 134.

underneath Kamrup which Grant calls "the terrestrial power-zone of the Fire Snake." The Entity then assumes the identity of an eccentric scientist—I am not making this up—who has an image of Nu-Isis in a cabinet before which burns an eternal flame. The image was of a woman, "suave, metallic, her body cast in vitrified *ojas* ..." and at a particular time the image comes to life and the scientist "cohabited regularly" with this "alien embodiment of the Fire Snake" until an explosion destroyed the scientist's laboratory and "the surrounding terrain was violently upheaved by the impact of a series of elemental disasters."[191] However, all was not lost for a daughter had been born out of the cohabiting of the scientist with the statue—although she seems somewhat unpleasant.

After this, Grant writes that it is not a magical allegory but an account of the "recent astral history of the earth."[192]

Let us take a moment to deconstruct the narrative, for it will yield some fascinating fruits.

In the first place, Assam is considered by some historians to have been the birthplace of Tantra. It is located on the far north-eastern end of India connected to the rest of the sub-continent by a narrow pass throught the mountains. Its ancient name was Kamrup, and it represented an independent kingdom bordering on Tibet. Grant identifies Kamrup as the ancient capital of Assam, but that is not technically true as Kamrup was the name of the entire kingdom (now a district of Assam).

It is the story of the eccentric and reclusive scientist, however, that is intriguing for a number of reasons.

In the 1930s H. P. Lovecraft went to Florida to visit Robert Barlow, a young man who was an aspiring writer. They had developed a friendship through correspondence, and Barlow was thrilled to have his idol come down from Rhode Island to see him in the Sunshine State. After visiting Barlow in De Land, Volusia County,

---

191 Ibid., p. 134–135.
192 Ibid., p. 135

Lovecraft went down to Key West. This first visit was in May—June of 1931. There were several other trips to Florida thereafter.

However, this visit to Key West opens up a number of intriguing possibilities. At that time, there was a strange, eccentric and reclusive scientist living in Key West, moreover someone who had been involved in the occult back in his native Germany, and who had spent time in India studying with gurus before eventually winding up in Australia at the beginning of the First World War. Significantly, he befriended a Sri Lankan monk who was a friend of Crowley's mentor, Alan Bennett.

His story was one of the most bizarre episodes in Florida (or any state's) history. The man was known variously as Count Carl von Cosel, or Carl Tanzler, or Georg Karl Tänzler (1877–1952).

Tanzler was born in Dresden, Germany, and according to a lengthy article he had written for *Fantastic Adventures* magazine, he had paranormal experiences since he was a young man living in his family's castle. He had recurring visions of a lovely woman—a famous ancestor—and another vision of a woman whom he called by various names, including Ayesha. But these were incorporeal women and disappeared as soon as he was aware of them. Fearing he was being haunted, he contacted several important paranormal experts in the region around Dresden.

These included names that are perhaps not as well known today, but were famous in their time. In the list were Carl du Prel (1839–1899), J. K. F. Zöllner (1834–1882) and Carl Kiesewetter (1854–1895) among many others. The problem with Tanzler's list is that most of these men would have been dead by the time he was having his experiences. In fact, du Prel died at the age of sixty and would have been alive at the time Tanzler was having his strange visions, but Zöllner would have died when Tanzler when was only five years old, and Kiesewetter would have died when Tanzler was only eighteen. According to Tanzler's own account he was 20 years old when he asked these venerable gentlemen to assist him in his confusion. So it seems Tanzler was not being completely honest in compiling this list in an article published in September, 1947.

Eventually he left Germany for a tour to Asia, stopping first in Italy where he had another strong vision of this ethereal woman, Ayesha. Then at some point before the outset of World War One Tanzler found himself in India.

In that country, where he claimed he was studying Indian religion, he woke up one day to find himself in a morgue. Evidently something had gone wrong with one of his meditations and the local people thought he had died.

From India, he went to Australia where he was interned during the War even though he had become a naturalized British citizen. While he was in the internment camp, he made the acquaintance of a Sri Lanken monk named Nyanatiloka Thera. This particular monk was a friend of Crowley's mentor Alan Bennett when the latter was known as the Bhikku Ananda Metteya. The two monks lived in the same ashram for a period of time.

From there, Tanzler went back to Germany after the end of the war and was encouraged by his family to emigrate to the United States. He stayed in Germany from 1920–1925, the period that saw the collapse of German society due to their loss of the war, the Depression, and the rise of Nazism with the famous Beer Hall Putsch of 1923. In April, 1926 he arrived in the United States and moved first to Zephyrhills, Florida and then to Key West where he found work as a radiologist in 1927.

On April 22, 1930 he met a young woman, a tuberculosis patient by the name of Maria Elena Milagro de Hoyos. She was a twenty-one-year-old Cuban-American woman and a local beauty. Tanzler recognized her as the woman in the visions he had been having all his life, and fell in love with her. He courted her even though they were both married to other people. He tried various means to cure her of her illness, and claimed to have made good progress. But her family intervened. They did not want her seeing this self-professed medical man, but instead insisted that she return to the hospital and do whatever the regular doctors told her to do.

Maria Hoyos died on October 25, 1931. That should have been the end of the story, but things became increasingly strange after that.

Tanzler built her an elaborate mausoleum in the local cemetery, one to which he alone would have the key. While visiting her constantly he began a series of bizarre medical procedures designed first to keep her from decomposing, and then to raise her from the dead. In fact, as far as Tanzler was concerned, she was not really dead at all.

The story of how he attended to her is told in great detail in the *Fantastic Adventures* article, but suffice it to say that he claimed his ministrations were successful. Maria Elena was able to open her eyes, move her limbs, and speak. Tanzler kept several IVs pumping fluids into her body and removing other fluids and fighting a constant battle with maggots, but in the end he was certain that he was successful in bringing her back to life.

It was only a hurricane—Grant's "elemental disasters"—that disrupted Tanzler's operation. He was forced to take Maria Elena's body out of the mausoleum in the dead of night and bring it to his home—where he built a special cabinet for her (in the shape of an aircraft … Tanzler had been making preparations to fly them both out of Florida as soon as she was "well enough" to make the trip).

Eventually, however, he was discovered by members of the young woman's family. This was in October, 1940. That means almost *ten years after her death*. Tanzler had been living with the corpse in his house and—according to some accounts—"cohabiting" with it—all that time.

He was arrested but the charges were dropped due to the expiration of the statute of limitations for corpse-tampering. Maria Elena's body was buried in an unmarked grave and Tanzler, who could no longer stay in Key West due to the notoriety, moved back to the Zephyrhills area and then eventually wrote the story that appeared in *Fantastic Adventures*.

We have one certain indication, other than Tanzler's own insistence, that he was involved with the occult long these events transpired. He wrote an article about his experience in the Australian internment camp for none other than the *Rosicrucian Digest*, published in March, 1939. This was before his arrest, but years after the death of Maria Elena Milagro ("miracle") de Hoyos. When he finally died in 1952, he was found with a life-size effigy of Ms. de Hoyos.

Some dreams never die.

There are so many coincidences between this story and the one told by Grant in *Beyond the Mauve Zone* that we are forced to consider the possibility that they are one and the same. Add to this the idea that Lovecraft almost certainly knew of this story— it would have appealed to him immensely—and one wonders if it could have inspired his famous story "Herbet West—Re-Animator" (1921–1922) except this tale was written ten years *before* the events in question, while Tanzler was still in Germany. Another case of Lovecraft seeing into the future?

Tanzler does not refer to any German or American occult orders or initiations in his few autobiographical writings. He seems to have belonged to AMORC—the publisher of the Rosicrucian Digest—and he claims to have lived for awhile in India (somewhere in the period from about 1912–1914 or so) and studied yoga and Indian mysticism. His close friendship with one of Alan Bennett's fellow monks is also intriguing, but in the end we do not have much more information than that.

Was Tanzler a member of any occult lodge or secret society? We can't answer that for sure, but his account of how he tended to the corpse of his beloved Maria Elena has all the hallmarks of an occult operation and seems to fit some of the details given by Grant—who may have heard the story from someone else. The interesting detail given in Grant and not in Tanzler is the existence of a "child," a daughter (presumably non-human) born out of this unholy wedlock. Depending on how Tanzler was "cohabiting" with her corpse—if there were Tantric elements involved—Grant could have been revealing some privileged knowledge about the case.

The woman that Tanzler kept seeing he identified at one point as a priestess named Ayesha. Ayesha then materialized in the form of Maria Elena, who then died from tuberculosis before they could be married. Tuberculosis, of course, is the illness most associated with popular ideas about vampirism: the condition of a corpse who has died of TB bears resemblance to ideas about vampires, and as someone wastes away from the disease they exhibit all the symptoms popularly associated with having their blood sucked from their bodies.

There is much to work with here, indeed, and perhaps one day we will come a little closer to understanding what really motivated Tanzler—an otherwise responsible, scientific-minded German, a world-traveler, a man of at least three nationalities (his native German, plus his naturalized British then his naturalized American citizenships), friend of monks and practitioner of Asian mysticism, and even member of a Rosicrucian group.

But what brings it all together is sexual magic.

Sexuality is the key that opens the Gate to the Mauve Zone. That does not necessarily mean that sexual intercourse within a ritual setting is the only way this can be done. Instead, other methods of awakening the Fire Snake may be employed, including purely passive methods such as meditation and yoga, as well as the other means of "deranging the senses" that are available, from drugs to drumming. Systems that involve the autonomic nervous system directly are the easiest—i.e., fastest—way to accomplish this goal, but they are also (obviously) the most dangerous. Tantric experts insist that no self-initiation in Tantra is possible; that one should always seek the help and training of a qualified guru. The problem with this advice, as good as it is, is that so many gurus have been exposed as dangerous themselves, or at least as unreliable and corrupt. Thus, many seekers have fallen back on self-initiation as the

222

22222

only possible way, not realizing that this path may be at least as dangerous as following a false teacher.

The sorcerers that populate Lovecraft's works often work in groups. There was the orgiastic cult in "The Call of Cthulhu," and the devil-worshippers in "The Thing on the Doorstep," as well as the Starry Wisdom cult, and the Dagon worshippers in "The Shadow Over Innsmouth." But there were also solitary practitioners, such as Old Whateley in "The Dunwich Horror." What connected all of these disparate characters was the Tradition itself.

Lovecraft's *weltanschauung* is fairly consistent. There was an ancient race from beyond the stars who visited or populated the Earth at some vastly distant time, but whose devotees still exist in the world, usually intent on bringing back the Old Ones to rule the Earth again. Alternatively, there are ancient texts found by independent sorcerers—texts like the Necronomicon—that provide formulas for evoking these seemingly unpleasant creatures from their extra-dimensional, supramundane homes for reasons that are hard to fathom. No one really knows why Old Whateley wanted to bring down one of these creatures to impregnate his own daughter. No one really explains why these cults in the swamps outside New Orleans would want Cthulhu to awaken from his million-years-slumber. It seems to be understood, if unspoken, that there exists in some human beings a deep desire to experience what is on the other side of the great divide that separates us from true knowledge; that the experience of the occult is addictive; and that contact with beings from "other worlds" may be scientifically impossible or unproveable, but nonetheless real to those who have had that contact—for it changes their lives forever.

Many people have experiences that can be described as paranormal or otherworldly. No matter how much scientific minds try to explain these experiences away using perfectly rational arguments, the emotional content of these experiences remain stronger than the best common-sense explanation. The occultist makes a deliberate attempt to have as many of these experiences as possible, in a controlled environment and under repeatable circumstances.

The approach to these paranormal or otherworldly experiences is a carefully-constructed one. It often has as its purpose the attainment of superior knowledge and ability, or the acquisition of paranormal powers. This has the potential to derange the average person.

The human psycho-biological organism has been trained for survival. Every action must be understood as somehow promoting that need. When actions do not make sense as survival strategies—such as ritual magic, and other processes deemed "retroversions" of the survival instinct—then the organism is stressed. It finds itself forced to come up with a rationale for these actions. If the occultist is not well-trained, then the psyche is vulnerable to the effects of deep-seated psychoses and the mind can find itself obsessed or even a bit more deranged than even Rimbaud would be comfortable experiencing.

While this can occur in an individual—and it does, with more regularity than one might believe—the effects have wider consequences. When an occult ritual goes awry with even the most competent magician—with side effects that Kenneth Grant refers to as "tangential tantrums"[193]—then the results can be felt in the immediate environment. Strange phenomena occur, some banal, others weirdly compelling, experienced by non-occultists as well as those with a vested interest in the outcome of the ritual.

This is the Mauve Zone making itself felt through a rent in the veil that separates it from the "real world," something about which the Schlangekraft recension of the Necronomicon warns us when it insists that we close the Gate lest something creep through when we are unaware. This is also consistent with medieval attitudes towards demonic conjuration, when the correct construction of the magic circle is required and its physical integrity insisted upon. The circle is the Gate the magician uses to venture into the Mauve Zone; it is also the wall that he erects between himself and the entities that live there.

---

193 Kenneth Grant, *Beyond the Mauve Zone*, p. 77 and in Grant's *Hecate's Fountain*.

One of the requirements of both Tantra and magic is that one's partners in the rituals be selected carefully beforehand. There are numerous examples given in the Tantras of the correct type of priestess; the grimoires of magic are rather less clear on the subject, but it is nevertheless an important factor. One can control one's own actions during the ritual; it is much more difficult to do that and to control the actions and reactions of others, whether the priestess in a rite of maithuna, or assistants in a ritual of ceremonial magic.

It was quite likely this particular problem led to one of the most famous—and influential—rituals of modern times. It involved one of Crowley's most brilliant disciples, a man who was literally a rocket scientist. It ended in the destruction of the magician on the one hand and the creation of a new cult on the other.

No discussion of the Mauve Zone would be complete without reference to the example of John Whiteside Parsons (1914–1952): an example of how an occult life can go terribly wrong and yet still contribute so much.

We are used to the example of famous artists and writers being car wrecks as human beings. Edgar Allan Poe is one example, a brilliant author and poet who was an alcoholic and who died in a gutter. Vincent Van Gogh is another, as are any number of modern rock stars. Hemingway committed suicide.

Some of Lovecraft's inner circle can be included, such as the creator of *Conan, the Barbarian*: Robert E. Howard who committed suicide at a young age. And Lovecraft's own literary executor, the brilliant scholar Robert Barlow, committed suicide in Mexico on January 2, 1951 when he was still a young man in his thirties.

The artistic life can have that effect on people. Too close contact with the Mauve Zone, over too long and extended a period of time, is poisonous if it is not controlled. Once that Gate is opened it must be constantly policed, and closed if the threat level rises.

Therefore, in the occult world there are similar lists.

One of the most important names on that list is Jack Parsons.

His story has been told in several places and we won't go into too much detail here. He was a rocket scientist who made an important contribution to the war effort in the 1940s, and was a founding member of the Jet Propulsion Laboratory. Most famously, he has a crater on the Moon named after him: a fact that should be of some importance to those who follow the Kaula path, for Parsons was also a magician and a follower of Aleister Crowley. For a time he ran the only active OTO lodge in the United States, in Pasadena, California. It was probably due to this, and to several unlucky friendships, that he eventually lost his all-important security clearance and subsequently had a hard time finding work. It was the Cold War, and paranoia about crazy California occultists ran about as high as it did for crazy California communists.

In June of 1952, at the age of thirty-eight, Parsons blew himself up in a garage outside his home. Opinions differ as to whether it was an accident, a suicide, or a murder. There is room for all three versions.

But it was in 1946 that everything changed.

Parsons had met a science-fiction author and Naval officer named L. Ron Hubbard as the war came to a close. Parsons had run a kind of salon out of his home for writers and for people interested in the occult. Hubbard had heard of it, and began frequenting the home, meeting Parsons and developing a close relationship with him. Hubbard's background was sketchy. Declassified FBI files on Hubbard tell a story that is somewhat at odds with the official version promoted by Hubbard's creature, the "religion" known as Scientology.

Regardless, from January to March, 1946, Parsons enlisted the assistance of Hubbard in a series of ambitious magical rituals known as the Babalon Working. The goal was to summon or incarnate the Scarlet Woman herself with a view towards creating a "magical child." The inspiration for this manouver was evidently Crowley's novel, *Moonchild*, which we have already referenced. The method was consistent with Crowleyan sex-magical techniques, such as we have been discussing at length in these pages, and the result—at least, according to Grant—was predictable.

At the completion of the first part of the ritual, a red-headed woman—Marjorie Cameron—appeared at Parsons's home, waiting for him as he returned from the ritual in the desert. Parsons took this to be a sign that the ritual had been successful, for the Scarlet Woman is famously a red-head. They soon formed a relationship and married. The next phase of the ritual was to use IXth degree OTO sex magic rituals in order to incarnate a magical child who would be the Thelemic messiah.

A study of this event is instructive for anyone who has managed to follow this report thus far. Everything we have been discussing comes together in the story of Parsons and Hubbard and the Babalon Working, from Thelema to the OTO, sex magic, Babalon, creating magical offspring ... and opening a Gate that perhaps should never have been opened.

Hubbard's agenda in all of this is a mystery, except that in the end he made off with a great deal of Parsons's money in a venture called Allied Enterprises. Hubbard absconded with the funds to Florida (and Parsons's former girlfriend Sara Northrup) where he bought a boat and tried to escape. According to the story as it has been told many times, Parsons chased Hubbard to Florida and when he saw that his former partner making for open waters, he conjured a spirit to raise a tempest and force the ship back to shore ... and that is exactly what happened. Hubbard was detained by the Coast Guard and told by the court to repay the money he had stolen from Parsons.

Within a few short years, Hubbard would write *Dianetics*—the book for which he is best known—and began the creation of what would become Scientology. In the early years of the movement he would often claim to have met Aleister Crowley and to praise him in speeches and talks he gave to his followers. Later, he would drop all references to Crowley and downplay his involvement with the Parsons lodge of the OTO.

One thing, however, seems to be agreed upon by those who study the case, and that is that the rituals performed by Parsons, Hubbard and Marjorie Cameron were effective, but in ways no one had expected or planned. The common analysis has it that the rituals "blew a hole in the space-time continuum" through which ... something ... came in.

The rituals took place from January to March, 1946. Parsons wrote the text that he claimed was the "fourth chapter" of the Book of the Law, *The Book of Babalon*. By June, 1947, the UFO phenomenon had begun with the Kenneth Arnold "flying saucer" sightings, and the Roswell incident the following month. The Dead Sea Scrolls were discovered that year, and the CIA was founded in the Fall.

And on December 1, 1947, the Great Beast himself, Therion, Aleister Crowley the Prophet of the New Aeon, died at his home in England.

Kenneth Grant, who had been studying with Crowley in 1945, was at the Beast's funeral and later worked closely with John Symonds, one of Crowley's literary executors. He became involved with the OTO and by 1955 his Nu Isis Lodge began the intense workings that became the basis for his Typhonian Trilogies. He would focus on sex magic, and on the concept that a Gate could be opened between this world and the next by the experienced or capable magician.

His group worked with fiction—short stories and novels—as magical environments, which was an inspired strategy. What difference is there, after all, between the narrative we find in fiction and that which we find in the myths and legends that make up scriptures and Tantras? If a story works—if it conveys a truth, elicits an emotional response, tells us something we did not know before and allows us to own that something—then it has much the same function as a scriptural text. The first dramas were religious in nature; the first theatrical performances were rituals. It was through this direct experience of working with fiction to provide ritual elements that Grant and his lodge came to realize that inspired fiction was as legitimate a source of occult knowledge and technique as sacred texts.

Science fiction authors have made contributions to science, such as Arthur C. Clarke and his invention of the geosynchronous satellite, among other ideas. Fantasy and horror authors make (unconscious) contributions to occultism and magic by identifying information at deep levels of the human psyche. By focusing on fear and horror, these authors directly address our most hidden nature, which is another way of saying that they open a Gate into the Mauve Zone.

CHAPTER SEVEN

The Dark Lord

… when the world was destroyed by fire on 21st March, 1904, one's attention was inevitably called to the similarity of this card to the Stele of Revealing. … This being the beginning of the New Aeon …

—Aleister Crowley, *The Book of Thoth*

My father died in 1904, but without any message to leave to me, or to my only child … it was this boy who reversed the order of family information …

—H. P. Lovecraft, "The Rats in the Walls"

But why do we think that love is a magician? Because the whole power of magic consists in love. The work of magic is the attraction of one thing by another, due to a certain affinity of natures …

—Marcilio Ficino, *De Amore*, VI, 10

In order to progress beyond a certain point in the Golden Dawn, one had to demonstrate one's ability to conjure a spirit to visible appearance. This had to be witnessed by other initiates in order to pass the test.

Contact with non-human entities is one of the inescapable requirements of magic. There is no magic without this type of supramundane communication. And the most intense form of this contact is sexual.

Those who have been inadvertently or unwillingly involved in this type of encounter speak of it in sexual terms. The UFO abductee experience seems to include various types of (often uncomfortable) sexual encounter with alien beings. In the Middle Ages average men and women complained about incubi and succubi. The

Witches' Sabbat is portrayed as a kind of orgy. Lovecraft's aversion to sexuality may be a reflection of this unconscious understanding that, somehow, sexuality and contact with alien forces are linked.

This is the basis for what we have learned of the Typhonian Tradition.

In a Typhonian Order newsletter published in Miami, Florida in the 1990s we find the bold statement:

The central concern of Magick is communion with discarnate or extraterrestrial Intelligences.[194]

This is characterized by Grant as the "occult policy of the OTO"[195] and it more or less throws down the gauntlet. There is no insistence on lofty spiritual goals or an Asian-inspired quest for non-duality or nirvana. While these are certainly present in Grant's works they are there almost as after-thoughts. After all we have read—and it has been only a drop in the Typhonian bucket—we know that this "policy" of communion with discarnate and extraterrestrial Intelligences involves some form of sexual magic or Tantra.

Why is this specifically Typhonian, then? After all, Crowley's Thelema also involves sexual techniques and is not characterized as Typhonian. Grant is clear on the difference between the two approaches. Grant's magic is stellar-based, while the mainstream of Thelema is solar-based. His emphasis is not so much on Horus as it is on Set, and he is willing to accept input from sources as diverse as Jack Parsons, Frater Achad, and even H. P. Lovecraft. He is reaching for a greater scope for Thelema and believes that this is achievable through the operations of ceremonial magic with sexual or Tantric enhancements conducted as a series of experiments to gather more, and deeper, information about the nature of our universe. This universe is not perceived as the visible solar system and the star systems outside of it alone, but as that universe plus other

---

194 Kenneth Grant, *Beyond the Mauve Zone*, p. 274.
195 Ibid., p. 274.

dimensions, other realities beyond the ones we see or measure with our conscious minds.

Tantra deals with enormous lengths of time, elaborate cosmological systems, and an intense intellectual component—but viewed from within a worldview that states the cosmos was created by means of a sexual act between the gods, and that therefore the entire created universe reflects that sexual polarity. The power that fuels the universe has its analogue in sexual energy. Our bodies contain the source of this energy, the Fire Snake—dead but dreaming—at the base of our spines; and as individual as this seems it is also universal. The Kundalini coiled at the base of my spine is identical to that at the base of yours, and they are both identical to that at the base of the spine of the Universe (the body of the Mother Goddess), which is identical to that at the base of the spines of the gods themselves. It is a machine, a technology, that bridges the gap between science and religion, between mind and body, between reality and the Other.

Sexuality is an ancient metaphor for this power. It crosses cultural, racial and religious lines. Sexual spirituality can be seen in the occult practices of China, India, Southeast Asia, Africa, the Caribbean, the Middle East, and Europe. Fertility rites have been observed among pre-literate societies the world over, and painted on cave walls dating back thousands of years. This is the "apostolic succession" of the Typhonian Tradition.

Using sources as diverse as de Santillana and von Dechend's *Hamlet's Mill,* as well as the more fanciful projects of Zecharia Sitchin and Erich von Danniken, we can see that a stellar—rather than a solar—tradition is the oldest form of occult theory and practice. Reference to the famous Dogon tribe of Mali, in Africa, reveals to us a sacred tradition that is based on stellar, and not solar, considerations and computations that take place in the wilderness. The venerable astrological system of India—Vedic or Jyotish astrology—is sidereal-based and not solar-based. There is a definite Current that involves this tradition, and with it we can begin to re-evaluate some of the history we think we know about such groups as the cult of Mithra—which this author insists was an astral and not a solar cult.

Truly, it is written that "Every man and every woman is a star," not a sun or even a moon. Much of what Crowley wrote is intelligible from a stellar or astral perspective as opposed to a purely "solarphallic" one. Some of Grant's criticisms of Crowley's approach to magic are legitimate; that does not mean that Crowley's Thelema has been somehow devalued in the process. It can only benefit from constructive ideas and the expansion of its theory and practice into new, uncharted territories. Yet, any criticism of Crowley is considered anathema in some quarters, and those with lesser initiations feel unequal to the task of questioning either Crowley himself or his (appointed or unappointed) heirs.

So what is needed is the Dark Lord.

Set is the Opponent, the Adversary (like his Christian avatar, Satan). It is the role of Set to set himself up in opposition to the status quo, to the consensus viewpoint, to traditional beliefs and practices. He is the Other, and as such represents alien concepts and methods. Just as the Elixir Vitae is formed of both the male and female elements, and just as the Aeon of Horus is the Aeon of the Magical Child—the offspring of those elements—so too Set is the polarity required by Horus to balance the new religion and bring it into greater recognition.... And to contribute to the birth of new—non-human— offspring.

In the Catholic Church, there is the role of the Devil's Advocate. This individual is there to question every aspect of the life of a person being considered for canonization as a Saint. While he works for the Church, his job is to try as hard as he can to challenge and defeat those who would support the canonization. Set's role is similar, but much more far-reaching.

Set is the avatar of all such Devil's Advocates. He is, in fact, the Devil himself according to some traditions. He is the Dark Lord, the "dark" at the end of the Tunnels of Set. He represents all that humanity has suppressed, repressed, and oppressed since time immemorial. There is no Aeon of Set, for Set is not relegated to a solar period, an equinoctial precession, or any kind of calendar. He cannot be contained that way. Set's position in the heavens is as the Pole Star or, at least, as the circumpolar asterism we know as the Big Dipper, but which the ancient Egyptians recognized as the Thigh of Set: the all-important device made of magnetic iron—Lovecraft's "Tutulu metal"—that "opened the mouth" of the mummy, of the corpse, of the re-animated God.

Set is polymorphously perverse. He'll have sex with anything. He'd do his mother if he could. He is the symbol of unbridled lust, which is characterized as evil, vulgar, rapacious, etc. by his parents. Sexuality is the first thing societies control and legislate. It is the one power that, if unchecked, can topple governments, impeach presidents, destroy careers. Sex must be tied, like Set, to the prow of the Ship of State or the Ship of Saint Peter ... or just the Ship of Fools.

Set and Shiva hang out. Both are wild men, living in the wilderness. Shiva is the Lord of Destruction, with Brahma (Lord of Creation) and Vishnu (Lord of Preservation) forming a holy Sanskrit Trinity. Set spilled his seed, and so did Shiva.

Set comes from the stars. He is not from around here. Even his token Egyptian animal is unidentifiable. He is an Alien, in every sense of that word. And that means his natural consort is the alien woman, the Strange Woman of the Bible: the Scarlet Woman, the Red-Headed Goddess of the Red Lotus throne.

Set is the Beast. He is *Therion*. Set is that supernova that exploded on April 30, 1006, when his asterism "hung from its tail in the sky" and destroyed a civilization, and buried one of the largest temples in the world under a mountain of volcanic ash not to be seen again for more than eight hundred years.

Set is the reptilian brain. The serpent brain. That ancient legacy from the Great Old Ones, from five hundred million years ago. Fight or flight, it's all the same to Set, but my money's on fight.

Set is the Lord of the Underworld. He is cthonic. He is Kutu-lu. Cthulhu. High Priest of the Great Old Ones. In his underground, underworld, undersea James Bond villain-villa. They feared him in

Egypt. They were terrified of him in Sumer. They searched everywhere for him among the Cathars, the Albigensians, the Templars, the Witches ... and finally found him in the mirrored plates of their own armor.

Set is the key to understanding human existence. He is the key because he is the one Lord we fear the most, and *don't know why*. He is the Ghost in the Machine, the Father of Lies, the King of Demons, the Lord of the Flies. He pub-crawled with Job. He wrestled with Jacob. He hit on Eve while she was naked and Adam wasn't home, the Dog.

He walked up to Jesus and offered him the world.

Like he cared.

Set is the Master of Deception and Dissimulation, but not of Classification. Set does not work for governments and has no desire to serve and protect. Governments have never been very kind to Set, so besides being the Master of Deception he is also the Lord of Leaks.

Set is the Force of Retroversion. He reverses the flow of energy in the universe, the onward march of time, the linear measurement of space. He's the up of the down, the down of the up. The backwards glance. The lateral pass. He's tricky that way.

Most importantly, however, Set has his throne in the deepest, darkest recesses of the human unconscious. And the human unconscious is the gateway to all the other zones of reality that comprise the magician's neighborhood. He's in deep, but that's because we've put him there. If human beings are social animals, and need society to feel safe and comfortable and to sleep their way through existence, then Set needs to be suppressed. And when Set is suppressed, then everything connected to Set is suppressed. And that's how most of us live.

It's not a very magical approach to life.

But it's safe.

Let's look at the 24th Tunnel of Set, that known as Niantiel.

Kenneth Grant describes what was seen on a tour of this Tunnel, this scary back alley on the Tree of Life. And it's not pretty.

It's about a Death Cult whose members "became addicted to necrophilia." The ritual involves sex with a "ritually slain woman dedicated to the deity with whom contact was sought." As we have learned, the occult policy of Grant's Typhonian Order is contact with discarnate Intelligences, and in this case, both the Intelligence and the Vehicle are discarnate. According to Grant, virgins were kept especially "sequestered" for these rituals. Once slain, sex with the corpse was almost immediate as the astral form of the slain woman was sent to a realm between earthly and "post-mortem consciousness." All of this was to enable the magicians to use the freshly-liberated spirit of the victim to travel to the desired realm and communicate what she saw back to the cult.[196]

This is a form of necromancy, and versions of it exist in many cultures. Contact with the dead is tabu in many religions and sexual congress with a corpse is especially heinous.[197] However, the Tantric rites that take place in cremation grounds in India come pretty close to this example. Sexual congress—maithuna—can take place in the presence of a corpse, and not necessarily one that has died recently. To a true Tantrika there would be nothing inherently objectionable about having sex with a corpse as nothing is hideous to the truly enlightened. There are many Tantric ikons that depict Kali, for instance, dripping in blood and skulls, standing on the corpse of Shiva. Foul substances are no longer foul in the realm of the Dark Lord:

> The mediaeval Alchemist perhaps came nearest to the pure
> doctrine with his analysis of substances popularly considered

---

196 Kenneth Grant, *Nightside of Eden*, p. 223.

197 Oddly, however, in the United States necrophilia is not an important criminal act and is treated as a misdemeanor in seven states, including New York.

unclean. He knew that dross was the outer form of the Hidden
God...[198]

And

That which repels, that which disgusts, must thou assimilate in
this Way of Wholeness.[199]

Even Austin Osman Spare, the visionary artist and natural
magician, weighed in on the subject:

Perversion is used merely to overcome moral prejudice or conformity. By persistence, the mind and desire become amoral,
focused, and made entirely acceptive, so the life-force of the Id
is free of inhibitions prior to final control.[200]

In the rituals of the *Kalachakra Tantra*—the form of Vajrayana Buddhism practiced in Tibet by the Dalai Lama into which
he has initiated thousands of people all around the world—there
are instructions for the preservation of urine and faeces in special
jars at various points of the Mandala, as well as those for blood and
semen. (I have already discussed this in *Tantric Temples*.) The moti-
vation is probably the same: to demonstrate that there are no "bad"
substances, no "ugliness" in the world, but that all is a manifestation
of the Goddess, and there is no purpose in prefering one substance
over any other.

After all, even the Bible tells us that "the Stone the builders
rejected was the cornerstone." (Psalm 118:22; Acts 4:11)

This ugly substance, this forbidden act, this rejected Stone ... all
can be understood as relics of the Dark Lord.

---

198   Kenneth Grant, *Aleister Crowley and the Hidden God*, p. 89.
199   Aleister Crowley, *Liber Aleph*, chapter 23.
200   A. O. Spare, *The Zoetic Grimoire of Zos*.

The problem with the scene depicted as having taken place in the Tunnel of Set known as Niantiel is that a woman was slain for the purpose of contacting the Old Ones. Everything else would be permissible to a Tantric Adept, in our world, except murder and human sacrifice.

Except ... except ... it has been known to occur. Human sacrifice was not unknown to the various Tantric sects of India, Tibet, and even Southeast Asia. Tantra is about power, about *shakti*, and there have been Tantric kings who coveted the power represented by the Goddess Kundali and who applied that arcane knowledge to the world of politics and government. Kings have never been squeamish about killing people; add a religious or occult justification and it just makes it easier.

The *kapala*—the human skulls used as sacrificial vessels in the more shamanistic of the Tibetan Buddhist rituals—were sometimes selected from appropriate victims while they were still alive and using them. The requirements for these skulls are complex and specific; there was no way one came across an appropriate skull by accident. It had to be by design. The same for the skulls to be used for the *damaru*, the ritual drums. And the care and preservation of these skulls was also a matter of some concern. The best way to keep the skulls from drying out was to rub them with fat; the best fat was that obtained from the cremation grounds.[201]

We know that human sacrifice, sometimes on a large scale, did exist in various parts of the world. The Aztecs were famous for massive sacrificial events. While we consider ourselves too advanced and civilized today to engage in this type of barbaric behavior, the possibility still exists.

We are entranced by tales of serial killers and we have romanticized them to the point that we have made of them the new Dracula: urbane, intelligent, sophisticated, like Hannibal Lecter. But the

---

201 For more detailed information and sources, please see the author's *Tantric Temples: Eros and Magic in Java*, 2011.

reality of serial killers is quite different, just as the original vampires were believed to be little more than animated corpses.

Don't be seduced by the Dark Lord. His power rests in the things we have hidden from ourselves; and, yes, sexuality is one path that brings us before his throne in the sunken city. But he must be approached with care, and with caution.

Otherwise the Dark Lord will fuck you up.

The Typhonian Tradition is ancient, according to Grant. This is not so unbelievable as it appears. As Ioan Couliano tells us:

> ... witchcraft was still practiced in certain zones of eastern Europe at the end of the nineteenth century as a direct deriva- tive of shamanism. Beliefs recorded in Paleosiberian caves around 1000 BCE were still valid less than a hundred years ago. How can we explain such amazing continuity? ... a simple set of rules would generate similar results in the minds of human beings for a virtually infinite period of time.[202]

This perfectly accords with the writings of Grant who does not insist that his discoveries came from a long line of initiates stretching unbroken back to the Stone Age or beyond. What he does say is that the Typhonian Tradition itself is ancient, and that there have been bodies of adepts at various times in various places who have either kept the Tradition alive, or who have rediscovered it and breathed new life into it. The "simple set of rules" is what counts, and those of the Typhonian Tradition are straightforward and reflect a preoccupation with darkness, danger, and the system- atic and deliberate transgression of social and religious tabus.

But that is a psychological and anthropological perspective on the Tradition, which may satisfy some but which does not tell the whole story. Eventually, psychological and anthropological ideas

---

202 Ioan Couliano, *Out of This World: Otherworldly Journeys from Gilgamesh to Albert Einstein*, Boston, 1991, pp. 8–9.

go out of fashion and change with the times. New ideologies, new trends in intellectual pursuits mean that we keep looking at the same material from the point of view of where we are standing at the time.

The serious pursuit of magic—as of shamanism, of Tantra—requires that your point of view shift to that of the source of the knowledge. It requires that you abandon your safe place. Otherwise you are only standing at the edge of the Abyss and taking quick glances over the side. There is no information in that pose, no initiation possible in a state of suspended animation. You must enter a place where all the cool academic theories no longer obtain, where the comforting "it's all in your head" platitudes and attitudes have no meaning—because your head, your body, your soul and spirit are all fully engaged in ways they never have been before, and it is not what you expected when you bought the ticket.

The above is true about magic in general, but in the case of the Typhonian Tradition it is especially important to understand these challenges. Because it is not a solar tradition but a stellar one that reaches back into the very origins of the human race, the Typhonian magician is working without a net. As in the case with the Necronomicon, normal modes of protection may not obtain. The entities one meets in the Tunnels of Set—as per Grant's trilogies—are not those that were bound by the Seal of Solomon; they are older than Solomon, older than dynastic Egypt, older than Babylon. The only reasonable description we have of the realm and its denizens is what we come across in Lovecraft.

The Typhonian Order focuses on the Lovecraftian entities, especially those of the Cthulhu Mythos. The standard demons and evil spirits of the Judaeo-Christian tradition are unequal to the task of representing the deeper archetypes that are encountered in this high-intensity approach to the magic.

More than that, however, is the stated goal of the Order which is to make contact with discarnate and extraterrestrial Intelligences. This is perfectly in accord with the Lovecraftian tales which are concerned almost exclusively with this type of contact. In fact, by using terms like "discarnate" and "extraterrestrial" the Order is changing the parameters within which traditional ceremonial magic functions.

Magic's nineteenth and twentieth century European and American manifestations were still concerned with the medieval grimoires and their lists of demons and angels. It was a purely sectarian approach that was based on a Judaeo-Christian worldview. Groups like the Golden Dawn reinforced that approach but added Egyptian and other traditions to the mix, thus expanding their reach somewhat.

But the Typhonian Order grew up in the post-World War II era, in the age of atomic weapons, the Cold War, the space race, and UFO sightings. The idea of contact with entities other than human took on different meanings and implications. Magic was no longer limited to a traditional religious environment, but in the mid-late twentieth century took on more contemporary dress. There has been more technological development in the seventy years since the end of World War II than there has been in the previous thousand years, and this has affected the awareness of occultists in the West. What had seemed magical a hundred years ago—communication over vast distances in an instant, machines that can talk and answer questions, images transmitted through space without the use of wires, flying through space across the entire world, etc.—are now commonplace. The siddhis—the magic powers that are the result, or the side effect, of Tantric and magical practice—were now within the reach of everyone on the planet. Magic, then, had to reach further and farther to identify the source of its power and its utility, leading some to ask: Is magic useful? What does it contribute?

The art and science of psychology began to encroach on some aspects of the initiatory process. Add to that the use of hallucinogenic drugs and another secret chamber of esotericism had been breached by technicians and tinkerers and government grants.

Why do magic, then, when you can drop acid? Or undergo a few years of depth analysis? Or go into a trance watching television or listening to your iPod?

There was only one thing left and it was the hallmark of ceremonial magic.

Communication with the Unseen. Traffic with extraterrestrial beings. Dinner dates with the discarnate. As early as the 1950s, Kenneth Grant and his circle realized that the only thing separating magic from science was the ultimate ambition: contact with the Otherworldly. Rather than sitting passively on a couch and recounting one's dreams, Grant said let us become active participants in our dreams. Let us study and employ dream control. Let us revert the normal processes of mind and body until we pass through the Gate into another mode of being entirely.

Let us take back our souls before the scientists and the shrinks wash, rinse, and spin-dry our brains. Let us boldly go where no man, woman, computer nerd, or intelligence officer has gone before. The people running our massive, space-based telescopes are probing the universe in ways never before thought possible; they are looking at the beginning of the universe in the seconds after the Big Bang, and taking snapshots of it to show their kids.

The only alternative left to the magician is to (a) posit the existence of a universe invisible to human eyes (aided or unaided) and (b) go there.

It may be true that one day science will be so advanced that it will be indistinguishable from magic, but that's not the point of orders like the Typhonian which put the human being back in the center of the cosmos. The world has become so enamored of its toys that it sits and waits patiently for the next new development, the next smartphone, the next flat screen TV. The toys have become the center of the universe; the tools are replacing the mind, and as they do they replace the spirit. Technology is replacing pure science.

But magic can be done on the cheap. All it takes is determination, discipline, and practice. It is not for the couch potato or anyone looking for a quick fix. And that is why it is safe from the sweaty palms of the technocrats. For now.

Grant's thesis is the same as Lovecraft's to a certain extent. They both concentrate on contact with extraterrestrial, supermundane creatures. Lovecraft fantasized about it; Grant tried to figure out how it could be done. But Lovecraft was a scientist and an atheist. The concept of sex with aliens frightened and disgusted him. Grant was a magician, and the possibilities of sex with aliens was like something out of *Star Trek*: weird, maybe, but not necessarily a bad thing. Orgiastic rites in the jungles to summon Cthulhu? "I got that," says Grant.

But this is all much more important than that, more important than the author's glib references. It comes down to more than how far magic or science can take the human race. It is about who owns the process.

One of the author's favorite thinkers is Michel Foucault. Now Foucault was a wild man himself. Check out his photographs. Read his books. He was French, but don't hold that against him. Foucault knew that a central focus of the State was control of the human body. Humans are viewed as expendable assets by the State (and, as we know, by the corporations as well). Human beings are to be controlled, manipulated, exploited, but never respected or elevated. Humans are force-fed bad food, bad religion, bad politics, bad economics. They are sent by the millions to fight and die in inexplicable conflicts. They are told what to eat, what to wear, how to behave.

And for the most part, humans do behave. They are desensitized by media, threatened by governments, kept on subsistence diets, and generally lied to by everyone.

But Set, the Dark Lord, is not about behaving.

Thelema was brought to the earth as a means of spiritual liberation, as an announcement that big changes were taking place. It claims to empower the individual, to introduce that individual to his or her true potential to become kings and queens in their own kingdoms. But to some, the solar aspect of the New Aeon looked a little too much like more of the same: hierarchies handing down encyclicals, governing the Minervals, deciding what is and is not kosher. Kissing up to the Ninth Degrees. Nodding sagely when outrageous claims of advanced spiritual attainments were made. The same old song and dance, to some. Not what they signed on for.

Crowley became nervous when disciples started to take his message of spiritual independence seriously and acted on it. Goodbye, Frater Achad. Goodbye, Jack Parsons.

Control of the apparatus became more important as each decade went by. That is the way of all groups, all religious movements. It's what happened to Christianity, which today bears little or no resemblance to the original. Two entire branches of the Church—the Catholics, and the Eastern Orthodox—split over a *single word* in the Creed and have remained separate for the last thousand years. Oh, sure, there was politics involved, too. What's your point?

What Grant envisioned was a far-flung network of Thelemic cells—power-zones as he calls them—each investigating their own aspects of the Mauve Zone on their own but getting whatever help or support the home office can provide. As an international businessman in the last decades of the twentieth century, the author had a far-flung network of power-zones himself: they were called representative offices and they were established in countries around the world. They were largely autonomous, but had to report to me on a regular basis so I could help them to achieve their goals. It's a system that works, rather than having all the sales and marketing people sitting on their collective muladhara chakras in the home office, using the phone and trying to look busy. You need people in the field.

Grant knew this, and he put people in the field. It's just that the field in Grant's case was the Tunnels of Set.

The information these cells came back with was unintelligible for the most part, as one might expect. While in the Tunnels, everything seemed consistent and the experiences were genuine, and the synchronicties multiplied. Out of the Tunnels and trying to make sense of the experiences, the data often was baffling and the import uncertain. It would take years of attention to the minutiae of the experiences to render them at all useful to others involved in the same project. That is where Grant's feverish, extreme form of Kabbalistic analysis came to play.

The words, phrases, numbers, and associations jumble, struggle, leap, and slither from Grant's mind like the rantings of a schizophrenic on the subway. One wonders at times if the pages of the Typhonian Trilogies were written in crayon on the backs of flea market flyers. But Grant was sane. He was a lucid, functioning, and dedicated individual trying desperately to tell us something and realizing—as do all mystics—that normal human language is not equal to the task. So, sure, a lot of his gematria is suspect but then he knew that going in:

> There can be no association of ideas, no correspondences of any kind, between numbers or the ideas which they represent, except in the consciousness of their subject, because no thing exists as an objective reality, ... Numbers can mean to the qabalist precisely what he wishes them to mean within the framework of his magical universe. ... This is the basis of the science of numbers, and the rationale of numerology as a creative art distinct from a merely interpretative gauge of phenomenal probabilities.[203]

Grant calls this "creative gematria." It's the point at which this author has the hardest time with his works, for it implies a breezy lack of concern with any kind of consistency, and is thus relatively useless for demonstrating connections and associations to others. While his philosophical reasoning may be sound from the point of view of *advaita* or non-dualist thinking in which every number is the same as any other number, it is not useful for paying the bills. It may work well on a subjective level as the magician makes his way through unfamiliar psychic territory and uses these number games as a way of leaving breadcrumbs along the trail so he can find his way back, but when it comes time to try to convince the rest of us that these connections exist, then we are back to the crayons and the schizophrenic in the subway car. Reading Grant is often an exercise

203 Kenneth Grant, *Outer Gateways*, p.158–159.

in stripping away the gematria—the pages and pages of it—in order to get to the straight prose, for it is in the straight prose that he makes his most astonishing claims, his most ambitious statements. The creative gematria adds little to the experience and, in fact, can be quite distracting.

There can be no Typhonian Tradition without Lovecraft, and I will tell you why. The stories of H. P. Lovecraft provide the narrative for this form of Thelema. The protagonists and antagonists one finds in his stories can be identified among the initiates of the Orders and their bewildering experiences in the Tunnels of Set. Lovecraft is all about Darkness, and so is the Typhonian Tradition.

But even more to the point, the very name "Typhonian" in Grant's usage implies an ancient Tradition, one that goes back to before "monumental Egypt" as he calls it, before the days of the pyramids and the Sphinx—when Egypt was still really an African country with the combination of African religion and magic that would be distilled in later centuries into the Egyptian forms we know today. Grant's project is to go back to the pre-literate, pre-historic times because there is where the money is buried. He wants to take us back to the ancient civilizations that he opines once existed on the earth, like Atlantis and Lemuria. And he wants us, at the same time, to go to the stars.

And that is Lovecraft's project, as well. Lovecraft wrote about nothing else save this Tradition. The Great Old Ones, the entombed High Priest Cthulhu, and all the other creatures that populate his stories with horror and gore, are all atavisms of those times, and they share one thing in common: they came from the great Vastness of deep space and deep time. None of this penny-ante fooling around with the planetary spirits for Lovecraft (or Grant). Oh, no. That's for the tyros. "*Planets?*" you can hear Grant saying. "We don't need your stinking *planets*! We've got the *stars*, baby!"

This was the original magic, the Ur-magic, the magic that was reserved for the initiates. Any fool can watch the sun and the moon and come up with a ritual form based on the year, the seasons, the rising of the Nile. But it takes time, patience, dedication and an uncommon intelligence to watch the stars at night, every night, for years and years, and build star charts, maps, tables of declination and right ascension, and to measure the distances between these vastly-distant points of light in tiny incremental fractions of numbers. And then to realize that something important is going on up there, something "monumental," and it has a direct effect on what goes on here, on the earth, on the place They visited countless Aeons ago. And to which They might one day return.

The Typhonians.

The very word we use in the modern age for referring to otherworldly ideas, planes, levels is "astral," which means "starry." It is the Starry Wisdom cult of Lovecraft's story "The Haunter of the Dark." We hear talk of the "astral plane" and the "astral body" and rarely stop to consider what that means. It is the astral self that is indestructible, that is capable of doing the kind of time and space traveling that both Grant and Lovecraft describe. And entire cults were built around its cultivation and use.

One of Grant's power-zones, the K'rla Cell, was designed with just that idea in mind. He describes it in *Beyond the Mauve Zone,* and tells of the intention of its members to contact Azathoth and Yog-Sothoth, both Lovecraftian entities, and to use "psychosexual dynamics concealed in the Necronomicon."[204] This group eventually identified the star Betelgeuse as the home of the Elder Gods, and a black hole somewhere in the constellation Sagittarius as the home of the Great Old Ones.

It is this kind of magical practice that allows Grant to write seemingly outrageous statements (for a serious occultist) as the following:

Yog-Sothoth is the zenith of which Tutulu is the nadir, As solstitial points they are balanced by their equinoctial counterparts

---

204 Kenneth Grant, *Beyond the Mauve Zone,* p. 115.

East and West, represented in the Necronomicon cycle by Hastur and Shub Niggurath. The full complex formulates the Great Cross which typifies the crossing over from matter to spirit. This is represented on the Tree of Life by Daäth, and by Death in the Voodoo imagery of Baron Samedhi.[205]

Well, you wanted us to take seriously stories about talking snakes, burning bushes, and Sodom and Gomorrah as the basis for a religious current that has lasted more than five thousand years; why not replace all of that with the Great Old Ones and Shub Niggurath, the "Goat with a Thousand Young"? Grant is saying we need a new narrative, because the old one is not working. The old one is not up to the challenges we will soon face as resources become limited, fanatics get the Bomb, and governments go all Emperor Nero on our ass. At least, with the Necronomicon Gnosis, we look the danger straight in the Eye. We grapple with the unpleasantness, the threats, the tension and stress of knowing that there is some spectacularly ugly catastrophe lurking at the edges of our consciousness as the alien forces of which Grant writes so eloquently mass at the rent in the veil, waiting for the Gate to open … or are already pouring in.

The Book of Revelation, of Apocalypse, where we first encountered the Scarlet Woman and the Beast was written at a time when it seemed civilization was coming to an end, much like the present age. Empires were at stake. Nations were being swallowed whole. The Jewish revolt had failed, and that failure would have consequences for the next two thousand years. And in 33 CE, "God so loved the world that he gave his only-begotten Son."

Well, guess what? It's two thousand years later, and God has changed his mind.

---

205 Kenneth Grant, *Outer Gateways*, p. 12.

The End

> Who knows the end? What has risen may sink, and what has
> sunk may rise. Loathesomeness waits and dreams in the deep,
> and decay spreads over the tottering cities of men.
>
> —H. P. Lovecraft, "The Call of Cthulhu"

> The force is completely blind, depending upon the men and
> women in whom it manifests and who guide it. Obviously, its
> guidance now tends towards catastrophy.
>
> —Jack Parsons, *The Book of Babalon*, 1946

Grant does not want us to worship Cthulhu or any of the Great
Old Ones. That's not the point. But we have to be aware of the
forces that these names and ideas represent because they are real
forces, real ideas. Much of Grant's work involved identifying these
forces, trying to understand them, to place them somewhere within
a context with which we are already familiar—but not in reducing
them to a simple equation of Cthulhu = Set. He knew there was
much more to it than that. Yet, such shorthand coding is useful in
the beginning for it sets the parameters of the problem in a creative
way. When we start with Cthulhu = Set we will eventually wonder
in which ways are they the same, and in which ways are they different. What can Set tell us about Cthulhu, and vice versa? Why is Set
"real" and Cthulhu is not? And is that statement true?

The Typhonian Tradition works at that very point where human
imagination and creativity have provided the world with its great
religions and its great art. They are all, in a sense, works of imagination. They all come from the same place. The direct experience of
the Divine can be horrifying and potentially deadly; the Bible is full
of such stories. So is Lovecraft. So is Grant.

Magicians don't try to build ethical structures around their
experiences and try to tell other people how to live their lives. Well
… they shouldn't, anyway. Crowley's dictum, quoted towards the
beginning of this study, may very well be wrong. The aim of magic

should *not* be religion, at least not as we understand it. Magic is an artform, and you don't create religions based on a painting or a pop song. You just create more magic.

Magic is the "science and art of causing change to occur in conformity with will" according to Crowley. That doesn't sound much like religion. When magicians stop doing magic, they create religions. The context of magical systems that arose out of the Judaeo-Christian tradition was linear: there was a beginning, the Creation, and an end, the Apocalypse. Everyone's eye was on the finish line. Thus there was a beginning and an end to magic, as well.

But the Typhonian Tradition says that there was no beginning—just ancient days—and no end, because the universe is eternal and the yugas and the kalpas repeat themselves endlessly. Time is not linear. What goes around ... well, you know.

The magic of the Typhonian Tradition, therefore, is an ongoing project with no end in sight, which basically means no religion in the foreseable future. And that's probably a good thing. The Dark Lord represents chaos, not stability, not established institutions like churches and states. As humans, we crave stability but we need to get our heads around the chaos first. Because chaos is what's happening. We need to come to terms with the Dark Lord.

In the Necronomicon, the initiatory program is important. The rising on the seven levels of initiation is a requirement before one goes sailing off into deep space. One must be psychologically prepared for what will follow. These seven stages have their analogues in Chinese alchemy and in European alchemy. They are phases of purification and reification (and here purification is meant in a purely technical sense and not in a moral one). In India, one rises one chakra at a time, and it can take years to accomplish the entire program.

But once that is done, it's open season on trafficking with discarnate entities. The Necronomicon Gnosis is perfectly consistent with both the Egyptian and the Thelemic currents, as Grant insists. The literature of each helps to explain the other; the practices of each amplify and extend the other. The psycho-sexual techniques of Tantra can be employed in rituals of the Necronomicon as well as within the Egyptian context, breathing new life into each. Just imagine for a moment equating Cthulhu with Kundalini, which is precisely what Grant suggested. Or equating both with the Egyptian deity Set. That was Grant's intention and it is obvious from his work that he (and his followers) was dedicated to just that.

The Dark Lord, like Kundalini and Cthulhu, lies dead but dreaming. In psycho-sexual terms, at the base of the spine waiting to be "evoked" through the "orgiastic rites" of the followers of Cthulhu. In magical terms, simultaneously deep within the bowels of the earth and at some unimaginable distance in deep space.

Thank God for quantum theory and non-locality.

We have seen that Crowley wrote a series of texts in 1907 that he called the Holy Books, and that these were "received" texts, much like the Book of the Law itself. These writings are the most clearly Lovecraftian of all the pre-Grant Thelemic material, with the possible exception of Jack Parsons and his *Book of the Antichrist*, written in 1948 and a year after the Roswell incident and the Kenneth Arnold UFO sighting … and a year after the death of Crowley himself.

I believe it is fair to say that Crowley did not understand completely the import of the Holy Books. (It has been demonstrated that it took Theodor Reuss to alert him to the fact that one of his rituals, *Liber XXXVI* or the Star Sapphire ritual, was an encoded form of the IXth degree ritual of the OTO.) The Holy Books in general are rather dark, and the language is pure Gothic horror. These are, the author contends, works that more properly belong to the Necronomicon Gnosis aspect of Thelema. Read in that light, their meanings become clearer.

The same can be said of the work of Jack Parsons. He was intent on incarnating the Red Goddess, and equally intent on incarnating the Anti-Christ. He was focused on bringing about the End of Days so that the New Aeon could dawn. Yet, there is something faintly disturbing about the *Book of Antichrist* that recalls some of the accounts we have of alien abductions. In this brief text, he writes of being called by Babalon to continue the work he began with Hubbard in 1946, two years earlier. He then proceeds to describe a strange scene in which he approaches "cyclopean ruins" and a tower of Black Basalt. A robed figure shows him four of his previous lives, one as Simon Magus, then as Gilles de Raiz, Earl Bothwell, and Cagliostro. Then, in a line that almost prefigures what abductees would say, he writes:

> And thereafter I was taken within and saluted the Prince of that place, and thereafter things were done to me of which I may not write …

The brief account of his "Black Pilgrimmage" ends with him taking the Oath of the Abyss, filled with terror and foreboding, after being told, "It is not certain that you will survive …" It is then that he assumes the identity of the Antichrist.

He would die in an explosion less than four years later. He was 38 years old. His mother committed suicide a few hours later upon learning of the death of her son.

This is a Lovecraftian scenario, straight out of "The Dunwich Horror" or any number of his other stories: the magician who is also a scientist, summoning spirits, trafficking with discarnate entities, taking mysterious oaths in fear and trembling, proclaiming himself the Anti-Christ, and then dying in a spectacular ball of fire.

And at some point we have to accept that this is what is happening: that the bizarre themes we find in the purple prose of Gothic fiction have become the operating principle of our world.

Lovecraft wrote that the artists and the sensitives are the first to notice the incoming forces of the Great Old Ones. He could have added magicians to that list and, indeed, there *were* occultists among those who, in "The Call of Cthulhu," responded to the Call. What he failed to realize—as an atheist—is that the occultists can push back.

Those who "push back" in his stories are not occultists, but academics, scholars, intelligent third parties who find the unholy books, figure out the forbidden formulae, and then send the Old Ones back to where they came by closing and sealing the Gate. The Typhonian Tradition, however, is composed of the very type of people Lovecraft's stories demonize: the magicians themselves. They have the unholy books, they know the forbidden formulae. And it is true, they *do* open the Gate.

> That cult would never die till the stars came right again, and the secret priests would take the great Cthulhu from His tomb and revive His subjects and resume His rule of earth. The time would be easy to know, for then mankind would have become as the Great Old Ones; free and wild and beyond good and evil, with laws and morals thrown aside and all men shouting and killing and reveling in joy. Then the liberated Old Ones would teach them new ways to shout and kill and revel and enjoy themselves, and all the earth would flame with a holocaust of ecstasy and freedom. Meanwhile the cult, by appropriate rites, must keep alive the memory of those ancient ways and shadow forth the prophecy of their return.
>
> —H. P. Lovecraft, "The Call of Cthulhu"

KALAS, TITHIS, AND NITYAS

WHILE KENNETH GRANT goes on at great length through all of his books in discussing the *kalas*—the vaginal secretions that are so central to his concept of Tantra and Thelemic magic—he does not enumerate them or describe the individual kalas. For someone who wants to dig deeper into this system, this is a glaring hole in the data. There are some good reasons for this, and one of them is that this is a subject fraught with complexity and a bewildering number of Sanskrit terms and Vedic references, not all of which agree with each other. Another reason might be the advisability of using Vedic astrology in conjunction with the Ritual of the Fire Snake. And Vedic astrology is not well-known in the West (aside from a few popular books on the subject) and it is virtually ignored among the Thelemic magicians of the author's acquaintance (admittedly, very few!). To become reasonably expert in Vedic astrology would require a good knowledge of Sanskrit and tremendous patience with the rather disorganized and confusing array of books on the subject, and this is somewhat lacking among occultists in the West.

So what the author offers here is a list of the kalas with their associations and a discussion of the kalas and the *tithis*: the phases of the Moon which are the same in number as the kalas and which can afford us a better understanding of the whole subject. In addition, the *Nityas* will also be listed: these are the deities associated with the individual phases, or tithis. In this way, it is hoped that the new generation of Typhonian magicians (and those simply interested in the subject) will have access to a more profound understanding of the praxis.

As a side note, there will often be those who object to bringing in Asian concepts and practices into a seemingly purely Western or European discipline. The objection may be from an academic, anti-universalist point of view or simply may be a matter of taste. But the Typhonian Tradition, as the author understands it, is concerned with the pre-dynastic Egyptian traditions and those that are much older even than Sumer or Mohenjo Daro. If we recognize that control over the serpent brain is a key feature of this type of magic, then we also must recognize that this part of the human anatomy developed before the races had become differentiated from each other. What we share is the basic psycho-biological structure of our anatomy. The practices that work in India will also work in Mexico, in Europe, and everywhere else once linguistic and cultural differences have been addressed. It's just that they have been codified better in India and China, which—as many academics now seem to agree—was the source for the Western alchemical tradition, even though they were patently biological (and not strictly or exclusively) mineral.

The Typhonian Tradition, it should be obvious by now, rejects nothing and accepts whatever works.

The Kalas

Quite often, the kalas are identified with the tithis, or the phases of the Moon. However, the phases of the Moon have their own nomenclature (really little more than numbers) while the kalas have more descriptive names.

There are sixteen kalas, of which only fifteen are considered visible. Their names are as follows:

1.	Manada	No translation available, but possibly "measurement"
2.	Pusha	nourishing
3.	Tusthi	contentment
4.	Pusthi	increase
5.	Rati	love
6.	Dhruti	motion

7.	Sasichini	No translation available
8.	Chandrika	moonlight, illumination
9.	Kanta	beautiful, beloved
10.	Jyotsna	moonlight
11.	Shri	auspicious; also a reference to Lakshmi
12.	Priti	pleasure, gratification
13.	Angada	bracelet
14.	Purna	complete, full
15.	Purnamruta	full of amrita
16.	Amrita	the Elixir Vitae

In the above list, the last kala—Amrita—is the invisible one. Readers will recall that amrita is the word signifying the elixir vitae, the soma that descends from the cranial vault (or from a space a little above it) down through the body once union between Kundalini and Shiva has been attained. For this reason, the kala named Amrita is ruled by a Nitya (in this case, a kind of Goddess of the kala) called the Maha Tripura Sundari, i.e., the Goddess of the Sri Chakra. The other Nityas are as follows:

Nityas

1.	Kameshvari	"Lady of Desire" (also the Goddess Parvati)
2.	Bhagamalini	"Flowering Yoni" (also the Goddess Saraswati)
3.	Nityaklinna	"Wet Nitya" or "Always Wet"
4.	Bherunda	"The Goddess of Liquid Gold"
5.	Vahnivasini	"Fire Dweller"
6.	Maha Vajreshvari	"Great Lady of the Thunderbolt" (also Maha Lakshmi)
7.	Shiva Duti (Rudri)	"Shiva Messenger"
8.	Tvarita	"Swift"
9.	Kula Sundari	"Beautiful Woman of the Half Month"

10.	Nitya	"Eternal" or "Constant"
11.	Nila Pataka	"Sapphire Banner"
12.	Vijaya	"Victorious"
13.	Sarvamangala	"All Auspicious"
14.	Jvalamalini	"Garlanded with Flames"
15.	Chidrupa (Chitra)	"Wise" ("Bright")
16.	Maha Tripura Sundari	"The Great Goddess of the Three Cities"

Thus, as we have said, the last Nitya—Maha Tripura Sundari, also known as the Goddess Sixteen—is not visible, and is associated with the kala Amrita.

Tithis

As mentioned, the names of the tithis are really just numbers in Sanskrit, but since one will come across the names again and again in the Tantric and Jyotish literature, the full list is given here:

1. Pratipada
2. Dwitiya (i.e., "second")
3. Tritiya (i.e., "third" etc.)
4. Chaturthi
5. Panchami
6. Shashthi
7. Saptami
8. Ashtami (this is the Half Moon phase)
9. Navami
10. Dashami
11. Ekadashi
12. Dwadashi
13. Trayodashi
14. Chaturdashi
15. Purnima (for the Full Moon) or Amavasya (for the New Moon).

Now, to complicate things a little further, we must take the waning and waxing periods of the Moon into consideration. There are thus a total of 30 kalas or tithis to make a complete lunar cycle. In Indian astrology these are divided into the Shukla Paksha (the waxing Moon) and the Krishna Paksha (the waning Moon). Thus, we can be more specific in our enumeration of the tithis, as follows:

1. Shukla Pratipada
2. Shukla Dwitiya
3. Shukla Tritiya
4. Shukla Chaturthi
5. Shukla Panchami
6. Shukla Shashthi
7. Shukla Saptami
8. Shukla Ashtami
9. Shukla Navami
10. Shukla Dashami
11. Shukla Ekadasi
12. Shukla Dwadashi
13. Shukla Trayodashi
14. Shukla Chaturdashi
15. Purnima (Full Moon)
16. Krishna Pratipada
17. Krishna Dwitiya
18. Krishna Tritiya
19. Krishna Chaturthi
20. Krishna Panchami
21. Krishna Shashthi
22. Krishna Saptami
23. Krishna Ashtami
24. Krishna Navami
25. Krishna Dashami
26. Krishna Ekadasi
27. Krishna Dwadashi
28. Krishna Trayodashi
29. Krishna Chaturdashi
30. Amavasya (New Moon)

The first tithi—Shukla Pratipat—is 12 degrees of the Moon away from union with the Sun. The second tithi—Shukla Dwitiya —is thus 24 degrees of separation from the Sun, etc. This concept is quite important because the relationship between the Moon and the Sun is central to Indian astrology which computes everything from the Moon rather than the Sun. As we mentioned before, Indian astrology is not solar-based. The positions of the planets are computed from the Moon, and the houses of the astrological chart are similarly constructed. In addition, the actual positions of the planets against the sidereal zodiac are employed, and the conventional dates of the zodiacal signs are not used. One's birthday, therefore, is calculated every year by reference to the original positions of both the Sun and the Moon on the day of birth. Thus, if one were born with the Sun in Libra and the Moon in the fifth tithi, one's birthday is not celebrated until both of those positions repeat themselves. So a birthday in Indian astrology is both solar return and lunar return. The exact degrees will not be repeated each year, of course, but to some Vedic astrologers the emphasis will be on the lunar phase (the tithi) being the same with the solar degree remaining the variable. When a Vedic astrologer computes an annual transit horoscope, for instance, it is calculated from the tithi (the same one that occurred on the day of birth) rather than from the solar return position. Both are taken into consideration, of course, because the angle between the Sun and the Moon—the two luminaries, but also representing the two essences that gave life to the individual, the kala and the bindu, the "blood" and the semen, the red and the white—is of utmost importance. It has been a defect of Western astrology that the emphasis is on the solar aspects of the cosmos rather than the mingling of the essences of Shiva and Shakti, of the Moon and the Sun.

Each of the phases of the moon—the tithis—have yantras (magic diagrams) and mantras associated with them. Each of the Nityas has her own yantra, mantra, and shakti as well. They also represent the sixteen vowels of the Sanskrit alphabet. According to several of the Tantras, the fifteen Nityas are to be visualized as occupying spaces around the central, downward-pointing, triangle of the Sri Cakra. This inner triangle represents the yoni of the Goddess. In the very center of this triangle is the bindu, the dot, that represents the Sixteenth Kala and therefore the Goddess Sixteen herself.

Recourse to a book on Indian astrology would be helpful to the reader who wishes to understand this concept better, especially with regard to the kalas, the tithis and their ruling Nityas. Inclusion of the appropriate mantras and yantras as part of the Ritual of the Fire Snake as offered by Grant may be helpful as well, at least in the beginning, in order to orient oneself with regard to the chakras, the kalas, the phases of the Moon, etc.

While this information concerns the vaginal secretions, the male secretion is not ignored entirely. It is believed by yogins, Ayurvedic physicians, and Indian alchemists that it takes fourteen days to replenish the semen after an ejaculation; this is roughly equivalent to one *paksha*—i.e., either the waning or the waxing period of the Moon—so it may be safe to say that they are connected. Remember that as the Moon waxes, amrita is being poured into it (according to the Tantras); i.e., it is being stored in the lunar vessel. The day after the Full Moon, the amrita begins pouring back to the Sun until the Moon is completely empty. It is the Tantrika who interrupts this process by drawing the amrita down into his or her own body. A relevant image would be the Tarot Trump known as Temperance in the old decks, which depicts a blonde Angel in robes and wings pouring liquid from one cup to another. The Tarot trump known as the Star depicts a naked woman pouring the liquid onto the earth; above her head are seven stars, surrounding a larger star in the central axis.

Thus, a word to the Wise is sufficient.

GLOSSARY

(E) indicates an Egyptian word

(G) indicates a word from Greek

(H) indicates a Hebrew word

(Ha) indicates a word from Haitian Creole

(J) indicates a Javanese word

(L) indicates a Lovecraftian term

(P) indicates a Pali term

(S) indicates a word from Sanskrit

(Su) indicates Sumerian

(T) indicates a word peculiarly Thelemic

(Ti) indicates a Tibetan word

Advaita (S) Non-duality; a mystical state in which Subject and Object are one.

Aeon (G) Gnosticism: an emanation from God, personified or identified as a particular Being or Characteristic. Thelema: a length of time identified with an Egyptian deity and partaking of its characteristics.

Agama (S) A word with many and various definitions depending on the cultural context. It can mean tradition or culture. A collection of scriptures peculiar to Tantra. Religion.

Agharta (S) A legendary underworld civilization of advanced spiritual beings.

Aiwass (T) The Being that dictated the Book of the Law; Aleister Crowley's Holy Guardian Angel; a Sumerian priest or god; Shaitan; Set; all of these.

Aiwaz (T) Variant spelling of Aiwass, q.v.

Ajna chakra (S) The chakra located in the center of the forehead between the eyes and above the nose, often referred to as the "third eye."

Amrita (S) Literally "no death"; the elixir of immortality.

Amun (E) The Hidden God of Egypt.

Anatta (P) Literally "Not-self" in the sense that phenomena are transitory and impermanent. They do not "belong" to one's self, but are instead a source of disappointment and sorrow.

Ankh (E) Egyptian symbol of life, also known as the crux ansata, the cross with a handle.

Antardasha (S) In Vedic astrology, a period of time in which a particular planet (or the Moon's North Node) rules.

Anuttara Amnaya (S) The "highest tradition." One of the six "subsidiary" vidyas of the Sri Vidya practice. To Grant, the Anuttara Amnaya is a cultus itself, and the sole repository of the deepest secrets of Sri Vidya.

Apana (S) One of the five principal vayus, or "airs" in Indian yogic theory and praxis. Apana refers to the elimination of waste products in the body.

Apophis (E) A serpent-god, often equated with the Greek Typhon.

Asana (S) In yoga, a physical position involving the whole body, used in meditation.

Atlantis A legendary lost civilization, buried under the sea.

Bala (S) One of the names for Lalita Tripurasundari (q.v.) meaning simply "the Girl."

Bizango (Ha) An occult organization or society in Haiti, linked to works of magic.

Bodhisattva (S) One who has attained the penultimate spiritual goal but who has resisted ultimate attainment in order to assist all other sentient beings.

Bön The pre-Buddhist religion of Tibet, often associated with shamanism.

Borobudur (J) The largest open-air Buddhist shrine in the world, located in Java, and considered by the Dalai Lama to be representative of Vajrayana Buddhism.

Chakra (S) Literally "wheel" or "circle"; in Tantra, a sensitive location in the etheric component of the human body analogous to a nerve nexus.

Chandra (S) The God of the Moon in Indian religion.

Cthulhu (L) The high priest of the Great Old Ones who lies "dead but dreaming" in his underwater or underground sunken city.

Cutha (He) An ancient city in Mesopotamia, known also as Gudua, associated with the entrance to the Underworld.

Dakshinachara (S) A form of the Sri Vidya practice in which an external form of the Goddess is required for the ritual. This can be a human female, but in this practice there is no physical contact with her.

Damaru (S) A ceremonial drum made from a human skull.

Dambhala (Ha) A serpent god in the Haitian vodun pantheon.

Daoism Also known as "Taoism," the indigenous, pre-Buddhist religion of China.

Diksha (S) Initiation.

Drukpa (Ti) A lineage in Tibetan Buddhism popularly referred to as "Red Hat" Lamaism, founded in the twelfth century CE. It is considerably more "magical" in some respects than the better-known "Yellow Hat" school represented by the Dalai Lama.

Durga (S) "The Invincible." A fierce goddess in the Indian pantheon.

Dvapara yuga (S) Literally the "second" of the yugas, or Indian aeons.

Fire Snake Kenneth Grant's term for Kundalini, the psycho-biological force at the base of the spine.

Geb (E) An Egyptian god of the Earth. Husband of Nut, the sky goddess, and son of Tefnut and Shu. He is the father of Osiris, Isis, Nephthys and Set.

Gematria (H) A method of assigning numerical values to letters and using those values to determine the numerical equivalents of words and phrases.

Gnosticism A religio-magical tradition contemporary with early Christianity which borrowed elements from Christianity, Judaism, and Greco-Egyptian sources.

Goran Sahr The name of a legendary sunken city in the Yezidi tradition.

Gudua (H) See "Cutha."

Hadit (E) In Thelema, the God of the Point within the Circle that is Nuit. A star within the Empyrean.

Hegemon (G) A leader. An officer in Golden Dawn ceremonies.

Hiereus (G) Priest. An officer in Golden Dawn ceremonies.

Hekhalot (H) "Palace," a term used to describe a specific form of Jewish mysticism.

Heru-Behedeti (E) A name of Hadit, q.v.

Horos (G) Literally "the Limit"; in Gnostic literature the boundary between the Pleroma (q.v.) and the visible, created world.

Horus (E) An Egyptian god, the son of Isis and Osiris.

Hounfort (Ha) The temple in Haitian vodun.

Inanna (Su) The ancient Sumerian goddess who descended into the Underworld. Ishtar is the ancient Syrian goddess identified with Inanna.

Isis (E) The ancient Egyptian goddess often associated with Inanna and Ishtar. She is the mother of Horus and the sister/wife of Osiris.

Isopsophy (G) The technical term for the type of gematria used in the Greek alphabet.

Kailasha Prasatara (S) In Grant's usage, the position of the woman over the man in an act of sexual intercourse that mimics that found on the Stele of Revealing and in some Indian iconography.

Kala (S) Depending on how it is written, kala can mean "digit"—as in digit of the Moon, or lunar phase—as well as "black," as in the Black Goddess Kali. It also refers to the etheric component of the female vaginal secretions that take place throughout the lunar and menstrual cycle.

Kala Chakra (S) Literally "Wheel of Time," a famous Indo-Tibetan diagram or mandala.

Kalachakra Tantra (S) A text and a method of Tantra that incorporates sexual elements as well as millenial predictions.

Kali (demon) The sword-wielding demon of the Kali Yuga, our present age, and sworn enemy of the Kalki avatar: the tenth and last avatar according to some Indian and Tibetan traditions who will come out of Shambhala to cleanse the world.

Kali (goddess) The Black Goddess of the Indian pantheon and symbol par excellence of Shakti, the divine power. Not to be confused with the demon Kali.

Kali yuga (S) According to Indian tradition, the yuga—or aeon—in which we now find ourselves, the last of the four yugas and the precursor to a Golden Age.

Kalpa (S) Aeon.

Kamite An old designation for "Egyptian," referencing Egypt as "the black earth." It is one possible root for the English word "alchemy," as in al-khemia.

Kapala (S) Literally "head," the term used in Tibetan Buddhist practice for a human skull used as a ceremonial cup.

Karezza A sexual technique that involves heightened stages of sexual arousal but avoiding orgasm, especially in the male.

Kaula (S) A word that may mean "clan" or "family." It refers in this context to a sect of Tantrikas that are closely allied in practice to the Nath Siddhis.

Kaulachara (S) The Sri Vidya practice in which physical contact between the male and female practitioners takes place.

Khonsu (E) An Egyptian god of the Moon, often depicted as a small child.

Kundalini (S) In Indian yoga, Tantra and alchemy, the coiled power at the base of the human spine usually depicted as a serpent goddess. The raising of Kundalini from its dormant position to the top of the skull is the goal of Kundalini yoga.

Kurmanji The dialect of Kurdish language most commonly found among the Yezidi.

Kutu (Su) A Sumerian word meaning "Underworld."

Lalish A town in Mesopotamia, now Iraq, that is the pilgrimmage center for the Yezidi.

Lalita Tripurasundari (S) Literally "Lalita of the Three Cities," a Goddess most identified with the Sri Cakra and with the schools of Tantra centered on that symbol.

Lara Kidul (J) The Goddess of the Southern Sea, a famous deity in pre-Islamic Java.

THE DARK LORD

Lemuria A legendary civilization buried under the Pacific Ocean.

Lingam (S) A term for the phallus in Indian literature.

Loa (Ha) A word meaning "god" in Haitian Creole, often also spelled "lwa" in academic literature.

Lukumi A form of Afro-Caribbean religion, identified with Santeria.

Lwa See "loa."

Maat (E) The Egyptian Goddess of Justice.

Madhyamika A school of Buddhism that states all phenomena are empty, and have no essence, no substance.

Mahakalpa (S) A "great kalpa," i.e., an enormous length of time. In Buddhism, an aeon comprising the four lesser kalpas and lasting more than one trillion years.

Mahasamadhi (S) The "Great" Samadhi, the ultimate samadhi experienced upon dying.

Maithuna (S) A term for the sexual embrace; intercourse.

Mantra (S) A syllable or series of syllables recited as a chant; often specific to certain deities or characteristics, enabling the chanter to attain experience of the deity. A kind of magic spell.

Marma (S) An intersection point on the Sri Chakra, analogous to points on the human body and to points in space.

Marma adi (S) A method of killing someone by applying pressure to one of twelve "death marmas" on the human body.

Mauve Zone A term unique to Grant, referring to the Abyss, or Daath on the Kabbalistic Tree of Life, or to a band of dark matter surrounding the Abyss. It is a destination for the occult practitioners of the Typhonian Order.

Melek Ta'us The Peacock Angel, the high god of the Yezidi.

Merkavah (H) Literally "chariot," referring to a specific form of Jewish mysticism.

Mosul A city in northern Iraq largely populated by Kurds and the Yezidi.

Mudra (S) A stylized gesture; a mesmeric pass; a magical arrangement of the hands and fingers—and also sometimes the entire body—representing specific powers or other spiritual or supernatural characteristics.

Muladhara chakra (S) The chakra (q.v.) at the base of the spine, where Kundalini is said to reside until awakened by the practitioner.

Mut (E) The mother of Khonsu, the Moon God. Self-created.

Nadi (S) A channel of energy in the etheric counterpart to the human body. There may be thousands of nadis, of which three are the most important: the Ida, the Pingala, and the Sushumna (q.v.).

Naga (S) A serpent or dragon god or demon.

Nakshatras (S) The lunar mansions in Indian astrology, either 27 or 28 in number.

Nath Siddhas A form of Hindu Tantrism and Kashmiri Shaivism devoted to attaining liberation in this life-time. It involves many of the Tantric practices normally associated with the Kaula circles, for instance.

Nefertum (E) The son of Ptah and Sekhmet (according to one tradition). The Blue Lotus that appeared at the beginning of the world. According to some texts, Nefertum was the adolescent form of Ra, the Sun God.

Nephthys (E) The sister of Set, Isis, and Osiris. Daughter of Geb and Nut. Nephthys is barren and therefore has no progeny, despite an apparent rape attempt by Set.

Nergal The God of Cutha and lord of the Underworld, whose symbol was a rooster (and sometimes identified with the god of the Yezidis, Melek Ta'us, q.v.).

Nineveh A city in northern Iraq, near present-day Mosul.

Nu-Isis The name of one of Grant's Typhonian lodges (sometimes spelled New-Isis) and identified with an extra-mundane source of occult knowledge and power, a "Double-Wanded One" and dweller on a distant planet.

Nuit (E) The Goddess of the Sky; the first Speaker of the Book of the Law. She represents the vastness of space, whereas Hadit represents a point or star within that space. In Egyptian religion, one of the oldest of the gods, often depicted with Shu holding her up to support the sky, while Geb—the God of the Earth—is below, supporting the whole assemblage.

Nut (E) See Nuit.

Nyarlathotep (L) An evil deity who appears as an Egyptian pharaoh but who behaves as a black magician. A dweller in the innermost chambers of the earth.

Nyingmapa (Ti) Another of the "Red Hat" sects of Tibetan Buddhism.

Obeah Originating in Jamaica, a form of Afro-Caribbean magic sometimes referred to as "hoodoo."

Ojas (S) Vigor, strength, power, light. A word indicating occult energy or power.

Osiris (E) The dead and resurrected God of Ancient Egypt. Husband and brother of Isis, father of Horus.

Palo Mayombe An Afro-Caribbean religion with roots in the Congo and manifesting in Cuba.

Panchamakara (S) "Five M's." One term for the central ritual of Tantra involving the breaking of tabus (represented by five words beginning with the letter M) and at times sexual intercourse.

Panchatattva (S) "Five elements," another term for panchamakara (q.v.).

Parah adumah (H) A red heifer, required for the purification ceremonies at Solomon's Temple.

Peristyle (Ha) The ritual space in which ceremonies of vodun are performed. In the center is usually found a poteau mitan, or central pole, up which the lwa of the Haitian pantheon ascend and descend.

Pleroma (G) The fullness of God and his emanations, where the emanations dwell on the other side of the Limit (Horos) that divides the divine state from the human state.

Points chauds A term unique to Michael Bertiaux, and used by Grant, to refer to "hot points" in the world—areas of particular occult energy or power—and also to analogous places on the human body as well as in deep space.

Pranayama (S) Breath control: a method of consciously controlling one's breathing as a precursor to attaining altered mental states.

Ptah (E) An Egyptian creator-god.

Puja (S) A term meaning "ritual."

Qlippoth (H) "Shell" or "shard": one of the broken pieces of Creation according to one school of Kabbalistic tradition; an evil spirit represented by one of these shards.

Ra-Herakhty (G) Greek form of Ra-Hoor-Khuit.

Ra-Hoor-Khuit (E) A form of Horus with Ra components, and the Third Speaker of the Book of the Law.

R'lyeh (L) A sunken city wherein Cthulhu sleeps, "dead but dreaming."

Rohini (S) "The Red One," referencing variously a Goddess or the star Aldebaran.

Samadhi (S) The highest state of consciousness, analogous to advaita or the experience of non-duality.

Samana (S) The vayu or "air" that aids in digestion. One of the five vayus, of which prana is the first.

Samayachara (S) The mental performance of the Sri Vidya ritual.

Samvartakalpa (S) One of the Buddhist Aeons, the Aeon of Dissolution.

Samvartathayikalpa (S) The Aeon of the Continuation of Dissolution, one of the Buddhist kalpas or Aeons.

Sandhi (S) The point where two lines intersect on the Sri Chakra.

Santeria A form of Afro-Caribbean magic.

Satya yuga (S) The first yuga or Indian Aeon.

Sefirot (H) (singular: sefirah) "Sphere," one of the emanations from God in Jewish mysticism, introduced by the Sefer Yetzirah and eventually the subject of much speculation concerning Creation. The Tree of Life is composed of ten sefirot in various arrangements, one of which was the template of Golden Dawn initiation and, later of initiation into Aleister Crowley's A∴A∴

Sekhmet (E) An Egyptian Goddess, usually depicted as having a lion's head.

Set (E) An Egyptian God of Chaos and Destruction, of the Other, of Foreign Lands, and often associated with Shaitan or Satan.

Shaitan (H) The Hebrew spelling of the English word "Satan": the Adversary. A name for the Lord of the Underworld, the King of demons, etc.

Shakti (S) "Power." The consort of the Indian gods is often referred to as their "shakti."

Shekinah (H) In Jewish mysticism, the Bride of God who is in the world, yearning for union with the Lord.

Shemitta (H) (plural shemittot) A cosmic cycle, according to the Sefer ha-Temunah, a Kabbalistic work. A shemitta is calculated as either 49 or 50 years in length.

Shiva (S) The Indian God most closely associated with Tantra. However, the Eye of Shiva is believed to be so powerful that once opened it would destroy the cosmos.

Shodashi (S) "the Sixteen," a reference to the goddess Lalita Tripurasundari and also a reference to the number of kalas, or etheric vaginal secretions of some forms of Tantra and of Typhonian magic.

Shu (E) The Egyptian God of the Air.

Siddhi (S) A power, usually a magical or occult power, obtained by the pracitioner.

Sitra Ahra (H) The "Other Side" of the Tree of Life, what Grant refers to as the Nightside: the realm of the qlippoth (q.v.) and of the Tunnels of Set (q.v.).

Soma (S) Analogous to the amrita (q.v.). Soma is lunar and a full moon is considered to be full of Soma.

Sophia Literally "Wisdom," a name of one of the Gnostic Aeons.

Sri Meru Cakra (S) The only three-dimensional cakra in Indian tradition, representing Mount Meru—the sacred mountain of Indian religion and analogous to the human body.

Sri Vidya (S) "Holy Knowledge." It is an important Tantric sect whose main feature is the three-dimensional Sri Meru Chakra (a form of the Sri Yantra), and the worship of the youthful goddess Lalita Tripurasundari.

Sri Yantra (S) A two-dimensional magical drawing of nine interlocking triangles representing the union of Shiva and Shakti.

Stele of Revealing (T) An Egyptian stele discovered in Egypt in the nineteenth century and identified by Rose Crowley—Aleister Crowley's first wife—as relevant in some way to Crowley; its identification was a precursor to Crowley's receiving the Book of the Law.

Sunyatavada (S) A form of Madhyamika, q.v.

Sushumna (S) In Indian yoga and Tantra, the central channel or nadi that runs from the muladhara chakra at the base of the spine to the sahasrara chakra at the top of the head.

Suvasini (S) A word used to describe one of the female participants in a rite of Tantra.

Svadisthana chakra (S) The chakra immediately above the muladhara chakra.

Sylph In European mythology and magic, one of the four elemental spirits, in this case of the Air. The others are Gnomes (for earth), Undines (for water), and Salamanders (for fire).

Syzygy (G) A term from Valentinian Gnosticism that refers to pairs of emanations. In this context, each emanation has its double; these may be conceived as male-female pairs. Sophia did not have a male emanation and attempted to give birth to a creation by herself, which resulted in the creation of the world as we know it (considered by the Gnostics to have been a mistake).

Tangential tantrums (Grant) A term used by Grant to refer to unexpected or unplanned side effects of magical operations.

Tantra (S) A magico-mystical tradition of India and Tibet which involves sexual metaphors and analogies which may or may not manifest as sexual ritual and magic. Ceremonial magic has been referred to as the "Tantra of the West."

Tantrika (S) A practitioner of Tantra.

Tattwas (S) One of the five basic elements of Indian cosmology: fire, earth, air, water and spirit.

Tefnut (E) One of the ancient Egyptian goddesses, representing water (specifically rain, dew, etc.). Sister of Shu, and mother of Geb.

Teratoma (L) Literally a "monster." In Grant's system, something that may have been created via intercourse between humans and extra-mundane beings through acts of magic.

Thelema (G) Literally "Will." The name usually given to the magico-religious movement instituted by Aleister Crowley and based upon his received scripture, the Book of the Law.

Themaist Another name for Maat.

Thoth (E) The ancient Egyptian God of Writing and Magic.

Tithi (S) A measurement of time—based on the moon's phases—in Indian astrology.

Transplutonic Isis (Grant) A hypothetical planet with which the Typhonian Order was said to be in contact.

Tree of Life A schematic of the ten sefirot and the twenty-two connecting paths between them, used by the Golden Dawn and the A∴A∴, as well as by numerous Jewish mystics. The Tree of Life represents all of creation and as such is a kind of mandala. Grant's interest lay in the "darkside" of this Tree and in the placement of the qlippoth.

Treta Yuga (S) "Third" yuga in the Indian system of yugas or Aeons.

Tulpa (Ti) A Tibetan version of the golem, or homonculus: an artificially created being with a (usually) limited lifespan, made for certain specific tasks.

Tunnels of Set In Grant's system, these are pathways to and through the darkside of the Tree of Life and represent gateways to other realms.

Tutulu A mysterious word found in Crowley's writings with analogues in Lovecraft's works.

Typhon (G) A Greek god of Chaos and destruction.

Udana (S) The vayu of exhalation and speech.

Vajrayana (S) The "thunderbolt" path; a form of Buddhism associated with Tibet.

Vajroli mudra (S) A method of contracting the penis during sex and retaining—or collecting the spent—seminal fluid (or its etheric counterpart).

Vama Marg (S) The "left hand" path of Tantric practice in which the female partner sits on the male's left side. The implication is that actual sexual intercourse will take place. This characterization of Vama Marg has been challenged, but it is the one most common among Western occultists.

Veve (Ha) A mystical diagram used in Haitian vodun, representing either one of the Haitian pantheon or a specific purpose.

Vidya (S) A word meaning "knowledge," and used in this context as the root of Sri Vidya.

Visuddha chakra (S) The chakra associated with the throat region.

Vivartakalpa (S) The kalpa—or Aeon—of Evolution, in which Creation occurs.

Vivartasthayikalpa (S) The Aeon of Duration of Evolution.

Vodun One of the more politically-correct ways of spelling the more common "Voodoo," to differentiate it from popular misconceptions and Hollywood interpretations of this Afro-Caribbean religion.

Voltigeurs (Ha) A term used by Michael Bertiaux and later by Kenneth Grant to refer to "leapers": those who can jump from one of the points chauds (q.v.) to another.

Voodoo The popular term for the Afro-Caribbean religion of Haiti, which is referred to more appropriately as vodun.

Vyana (S) The vayu or breath that moves internally in the body and which contributes to its motion through space.

Wanga In Afro-Caribbean magic, a small bag used to hold charms or spells; often used as a term to refer to acts of black magic.

Wayang kulit (Ja) The famous shadow plays of Java using puppets cut from leather strips.

Weran Sahr Another designation of Goran Sahr, q.v.

Yaksha (S) Guardian spirits, often protecting buried treasure.

Yantra (S) A mystical diagram in the Indian tradition, believed to contain power in its very design.

Yezidis A Kurdish sect that is said to worship the Devil. Found mainly in Iraq but also scattered throughout Central Asia and now in Europe and America. They were a focus of both Crowley and Grant.

Yog-Sothoth (L) The "Lurker at the Threshhold" and the "Opener of the Way." A cosmic being from the Lovecraftian pantheon who impregnated Lavinia Whateley in the story "The Dunwich Horror." A target of the rituals of Grant's Typhonian Order.

Yoni (S) A term for the female genitalia.

Yuga (S) An Indian term for Aeon.

Yuggoth (L) Lovecraft's word for the planet Pluto.

ALSO FROM IBIS PRESS

The Necronomicon
31st Anniversary Edition of the Schlangekraft Recension

EDITED AND INTRODUCED BY SIMON

- Gods that were ancient when Moses was a child.
- Temples that were gateways when Abraham came out of the desert.
- Rites that summoned forces Solomon never knew.

In the past decades, much ink—actual and virtual—has been spilled on the subject of the *Necronomicon* (also called the "Simonomicon"). Some have derided it as a hoax; others have praised it as a powerful grimoire. Despite the controversy, it has never been out of print for one day since 1977.

As the decades passed, more information came to light, both on the book's origins and discovery, and on the information contained within its pages. The *Necronomicon* has been found to contain formulae for spiritual transformation that are consistent with some of the most ancient mystical processes in the world—processes that involve communion with the stars.

The hardcover editions of the 1970s are exceedingly difficult to find, and can cost six hundred dollars or more for a first edition. However, in 2008, the original designer of the 1977 edition and the original editor joined forces to present a new, deluxe hardcover edition of the most feared, most reviled, and most desired book on the planet.

With a new preface by Simon, this 31st Anniversary edition from Ibis Press is available in two versions. The first is a high quality hardcover bound in fine cloth with a ribbon marker. The second is a strictly limited, leatherbound edition, personally signed and numbered by Simon. There are a small number of leatherbound copies still available.

POPULAR HARDCOVER, BOUND IN HIGH QUALITY CLOTH

$125.00 • ISBN: 978-0-89254-146-1 • 288 pages • Printed on acid-free art paper • 7¼ x 10¼ • Ribbon marker • Sold everywhere

NUMBERED & SIGNED, DELUXE LEATHERBOUND EDITION
Strictly limited to 220 numbered books, signed by Simon.

$275.00 • ISBN: 978-0-89254-147-8 • Three sided silver-gilding • Special binding boards • Deluxe endpapers

Signed edition available exclusively from www.studio31.com

ALSO FROM IBIS PRESS

Tantric Temples
Eros and Magic in Java

PETER LEVENDA

• A brilliant analysis on the erotic magic of the Javanese Tantrics.
• A lavishly illustrated full-color photographic survey of the most important esoteric centers of Tantric Magic, some never before seen.
• A scholarly presentation of Indonesian magic and its interaction with Tibetan Tantra, Hindu mysticism, and Sufi Islam.
• Offers a photographic record of recently uncovered temples that were damaged again by the 2010 volcanic eruption that buried the excavations.
• Provides extensive data of parallels with Western sexual magical practices.

Tantra is one of the most misunderstood of the esoteric disciplines. In order to get a clear idea as to the nature of Tantric ritual and belief, it is necessary to go where Tantra is still practiced and from where important Tantric teachings originated a thousand years ago: the island of Java in present-day Indonesia.

This book illustrates the history of Tantrism in Java with more than a hundred photographs of temples, statues and iconography dedicated to the system—some rarely seen before, including the recently-excavated "white temple" of Yogyakarta—and accounts of contemporary practices in the shrines, cemeteries and secret schools of Java. In the process, we will learn how this esoteric philosophy has affected the everyday lives of the most populous Muslim country in the world.

It was this Tantra—the real Tantra—that has influenced secret societies, mystics, alchemists, Kabbalists and magicians for hundreds if not thousands of years. This book tells the story of how human sexuality became a metaphor and a template for both spiritual transformation and the manipulation of reality; and how various sexual acts and psycho-biological states became the basis for a comprehensive cosmology that incorporates every aspect of human experience.

$69.00 • Hardcover • ISBN: 978-089254-169-0 • 352 pp. • 7½ x 10½ • Full color throughout

ALSO FROM IBIS PRESS

Ratline
Soviet Spies, Nazi Priests,
and the Disappearance of Adolph Hitler

PETER LEVENDA

• An exposé of Church and State involvement in the escape of Nazi war criminals around the world.
• A step-by-step refutation of the evidence that Hitler died in the bunker in April, 1945.

While searching through the jungles of Java in 2008, gathering material for his book *Tantric Temples: Eros and Magic in Java*, author Peter Levenda came upon evidence of a Nazi escape route that led from Europe to Argentina, Tibet, and eventually Indonesia. The rumors were persistent; the evidence suggestive.

Was it possible that the world's greatest symbol of evil had actually escaped Berlin in 1945? As the author began his research, more information came to light. In December of 2009, it was revealed that the skull the Russians claimed was Hitler's—salvaged from the bunker in 1945—was not that of Hitler at all. The news made headlines around the world. Then in 2010, files from the Office of Special Investigations of the Justice Department were declassified, revealing a history of American intelligence providing cover for Nazi war criminals.

How did the Soviet KGB, the Catholic Church, and governments around the world collaborate in the escape of this mysterious and most-wanted fugitive? *Ratline* is the documented history of this escape, and the mechanisms by which thousands of war criminals fled to the remotest parts of the globe. It is the story of how the Soviets lied about Hitler's death and continued to lie and change their story for decades to come. It's the story of a man who died quietly in Indonesia in January of 1970 ... and how a body was dug up from a German military base four months later and cremated. *Ratline* raises questions ... but more than anything else—in a time of citizen distrust of its own institutions in Europe, America, and Asia—it demands answers.

$26.95 • Hardcover • ISBN: 978-0-89254-170-6 • 256 pp. • 6 x 9 • includes 8 pages of glossy photographs

ALSO FROM IBIS PRESS

In the Center of the Fire
A Memoir of the Occult 1966–1989

JAMES WASSERMAN

• Offers an intimate history of the early development of the modern O.T.O.
• Provides an inside look at the spiritual practices of Aleister Crowley's magical system.
• Chronicles the magical battle between two legendary Thelemic magicians that continues to reverberate today.
• Presents a counter-cultural history of the New York City Underground through the 1970s and 1980s.

In this daring exposé by a survivor of a unique era in the New York occult scene, James Wasserman—a longtime proponent of the teachings of Aleister Crowley—brings us into a world of candlelit temples, burning incense, and sonorous invocations.

When he joined the O.T.O. in 1976, there were fewer than a dozen members. Today the Order numbers over 4,000 members in 50 countries. The founder of New York City's TAHUTI Lodge in 1979, Wasserman chronicles its early history and provides a window into the heyday of the occult community in Manhattan.

He also breaks his decades of silence concerning one of the most seminal events in the development of the modern Thelemic movement—detailing his role in the 1976 magical battle between Marcelo Motta and Grady McMurtry. Long slandered for his effort to heal the temporary breach between the Orders of A∴A∴ and O.T.O., he sets the record straight.

Finally, we share an intimate look at the New York Underground of the 1970s and 1980s in the company of such avant-garde luminaries as Alejandro Jodorowsky, Harry Smith, and Angus MacLise. This is a saga with a very human tableau, filled with romance, friendship, an abiding spiritual hunger, danger, passion, and ecstasy.

$35.00 • Hardcover • ISBN: 978-089254-201-7 • 336 pp. • 6 x 9 • Illustrated with magical diagrams and 24 pages of glossy photographs